University of Cambridge Department of Applied Economics

OCCASIONAL PAPER 41

EXPORTING WORKERS: THE TURKISH CASE

EXPORTING WORKERS:
the Turkish case

SUZANNE PAINE

Faculty of Economics, Cambridge University
Fellow of Clare College, Cambridge

CAMBRIDGE UNIVERSITY PRESS

Published by the Syndics of the Cambridge University Press
Bentley House, 200 Euston Road, London NW1 2DB
American Branch: 32 East 57th Street, New York, N.Y. 10022

© Department of Applied Economics 1974

ISBN: 0 521 09879 3

First published 1974

Typeset by EWC Wilkins Ltd, London N12 0EH and printed in Great Britain
by Alden & Mowbray Ltd at the Alden Press, Oxford

Contents

Tables and Charts

CHARTS

MAP

APPENDIX TABLES

Preface

I first became interested in the Turkish economy in 1966, when a member of the Turkish State Planning Organization with whom I had been working on manpower and educational planning invited me to visit the country. I have returned to Turkey virtually every year since then, and have had the opportunity both to travel extensively to all regions of the country and to work in cooperation with Turkish economists in universities and government.

Most of the fieldwork for this study was undertaken with the assistance of a travelling fellowship from Somerville College, Oxford, when I was a research fellow at Girton College, Cambridge. The results were written up during a year which I spent at the Oxford University Institute of Economics and Statistics, and the manuscript was revised substantially after my return to Cambridge in the autumn of 1973. I am very much indebted to all the members of these various institutions who gave me invaluable assistance and encouragement.

However, the project would have been impossible without the helpful cooperation of the Turkish authorities. It is a pleasure to acknowledge my debt to all those economists at the Turkish State Planning Organization (D.P.T), the Turkish Employment Service (İİBK), the State Institute of Statistics (D.İ.E), the Ministries of Labour, Finance and Industry, and various other public and private sector organizations who assisted me in my work. I should particularly like to thank Dr. Şadi Cindoruk, Mr. Ünal Ege, Mr. S. Saver, Mr. Nabi Dinçer and Mr. Yusuf Hamurdan from the D.P.T., Dr. Hakkı Aydinoğlu, Mr. Cevdet Kozinoğlu, Dr. İsmail Arıkan and Mr. Süha Döğruyol from the I.I.B.K., Mr. Yaşar Yaşer and Mr. Yilmaz Çinetci, from the D.İ.E., Mr. Mustafa Yuluğ from the Ministry of Labour, Mr. Haldun Akin from the Ministry of Finance, Mr. Arslan Sanır from the Ministry of Industry, Mr. Bedri Günel from the Central Bank, Mr. Rahmi Önen from the Halk Bank, Mr. Ferit Azkara from Türk İş, Mr. Ahmet Yoluç and Mr. Kubilay Atasayar from the Turkish Employers' Confederation, and Dr. Yalçin Küçük, formerly of the Middle Eastern Technical University. I should also like to thank all my non-Turkish friends and colleagues in Turkey, in particular, Monroe Burk, Duncan Miller, Ralph Holben and Betty Yaşer from U.S.A.I.D. In addition, I received considerable assistance from members of international agencies engaged on research into European migration movements (notably O.E.C.D., I.L.O., and I.B.R.D.) and from the W. German Bundesanstalt für Arbeit and the French I.N.S.E.E.

It is impossible to acknowledge all those in England who gave me help and encouragement while I was working on this study. But I should like to express my particular thanks to all of the following who commented on all or parts of the manuscript in one or more of its various revisions: Mahmoud Abdel-Fadil, E.F. Jackson, John Llewellyn, Myles Mackie, Alfredo Medio, Roger Owen, Prabhat Patnaik, Professor Brian Reddaway, Ajit Singh and Ron Smith. I should also like to thank Myles Mackie, who checked the statistics, and both Judy Chance at O.U.I.E.S. and the members of the Faculty and D.A.E. offices in Cambridge who typed the various drafts of the manuscript. The usual disclaimer should of course be added absolving all these from any responsibility for errors and opinions expressed herein.

Suzanne Paine
February 1974

Introductory note
To obtain a very brief summary of the nature and results of this study the reader should look at the Introduction, and the chapter summaries, especially those to chapters 3 and 4.

Introduction

One of the most important features of Western European post-war economic growth has been its dependence on the use of immigrant labour. Before the energy crisis of late 1973 and the policy changes which accompanied it, there were about eleven and a half million foreign workers in Western Europe.[1] Indeed, this number was expected to rise by half as much again by 1980 if economic growth were to continue at the same rate and no major policy changes were to be introduced. The main labour importing countries have been W. Germany, France, the Netherlands, Belgium, Switzerland, the U.K., Austria and Sweden. Moreover, most of the foreign workers in these countries have been imported on a temporary basis without any promise of permanent settlement. Selected workers could be creamed off, trained, and integrated into the permanent labour force, while the remainder could be used, sent home and replaced by their compatriots, depending on the state of demand in the host country concerned.

However, as dependence on temporarily recruited labour from countries on the European periphery increased, so did opposition to its use. Anti-immigration organizations began to force governments to consider policy changes such as reducing the demand for immigrant labour, settling those already there, and restricting new inflows, in order to alleviate some of the social problems which had arisen because of the way that the policy of labour import had been managed. Thus Switzerland attempted to "stabilize" its migrant labour force in spring 1971, and then introduced measures to reduce it in July 1973; in 1972 and 1973, France, Holland and W. Germany introduced restrictions on new entrants, culminating at the end of 1973 in a ban by the latter two countries on the entry of non-E.E.C. workers. Although both countries attributed their policy to the oil crisis, there is some evidence that this was merely a catalyst which made the change in migration policy politically feasible for governments which felt that this was the only way to cope with the social and political problems to which their management − or lack of management − of the system of temporarily recruited labour had led.[2] But even if similar policies are introduced by all host countries (some of which are of course not members of the E.E.C.) and are maintained on a permanent basis, the experience

---

1 The precise number depends on the definition of "migrant" which is used and on estimates of the extent of illegal migration.

2 See *The Economist*, December 1st and December 8th, 1973. Indeed W. Germany had tried to persuade the E.E.C. Commission to adopt a unified policy for all member countries to restrict inflows of non-E.E.C. migrants.

1

of the post-war decades still provides extremely important and interesting evidence about the impact of access to reserve supplies of labour on Western European economic growth, and about the effects of the consequent labour export on the emigration countries.

In this study we have concentrated on the latter, less well-researched question, though the former is discussed briefly in order to provide the reader with the background against which the particular events and policies with which we are concerned — the recruitment and export of labour from Turkey — took place. The paper is essentially a case study of Turkey's role in the supply of migrant workers to Western Europe and the effects to which this has led. Nonetheless, the results are of relevance not just to the particular Turkish situation but also to the more general question of what sort of effects the decision to export labour may have on a less developed country of emigration, a question which was becoming of increasing importance during the later 1960s as the field of recruitment expanded to encompass not just Southern Europe and the Mediterranean, but also Black Africa. Although a comparatively late starter in the labour export business, Turkey has become one of the leading countries of emigration and in 1973 had well over half a million workers in Western Germany alone. It is, of course, much less developed, and has much greater labour reserves than the earlier starters such as Italy, Spain, Portugal and Yugoslavia. On the other hand, it is more industrialized than some of the new emigration countries of Black Africa. Furthermore, unlike some of the countries of emigration, Turkey has had no direct colonial relationship with any of the host countries. These considerations should of course be taken into account when attempting any generalization of the results from the Turkish case.

This study arose out of my belief that the effects of Turkish migration to Western Europe have been more complicated than has popularly been supposed. Both in Turkey and in the host countries, this migration was normally presented as bringing great gains to both sides: the host countries would eliminate their labour shortages, while Turkey would get rid of some of her unemployment and at the same time obtain plentiful supplies of foreign exchange. For Turkey, migration would be a virtually costless way of reducing unemployment and acquiring foreign exchange. Indeed, some German publications had gone so far as to claim that German employment of Turkish workers was a form of foreign aid to Turkey.[1]

The aim of this study is to examine this picture, and in particular, to analyze just how the selection of a labour export policy has affected the basic course of Turkey's economic development and the lives of the migrant workers involved, rather than just looking at the gross outflow of workers and inflow of repatriated earnings. Although Turkish migration to Western Europe has now been taking place for almost a decade and a half, surprisingly little is known about it, and even less about the return flow. This study attempts to assemble all the available data on this migration so as to build up a detailed picture of the socio-economic characteristics of the workers who have left, what has happened to them while abroad, what their fate has been if they have returned, and what changes have taken place over the decade. The sources used include not only published studies but also a considerable amount of unpublished material supplied by the Turkish authorities. In particular,

---

1 For instance Neuloh 1970.

I was fortunate enough to be able to use the raw data from a survey of migrant workers who had returned to Turkey, carried out by the Turkish State Planning Organisation in February 1971. This contains the most detailed information as yet available on the experiences of ex-migrants and the use made of the domestic currency equivalent of their remittances. The main results of this survey have been incorporated into the text of this study, while the detailed data have been included for reference in an appendix. In addition, the Turkish Employment Service have supplied me with a considerable amount of unpublished material both on Turkish migration and on the Turkish labour market. But despite this assistance from the Turkish authorities, empirical information on a number of important questions was not available (as becomes clear in Chapter 4). Consequently one by-product of this study is to indicate to governmental and other agencies concerned with migration in which areas it would be useful to obtain empirical data so that a more complete description and assessment of the situation can be compiled. However, it was felt to be more useful to publish the existing results, imperfect as these are, rather than to await those of the further research required to compile a more comprehensive and statistically reliable picture.

The study is arranged as follows. Chapter 1 surveys the background in Europe and in Turkey to the emergence of the system of Turkish migration. Given space considerations and the immense scope of the ground covered in this chapter, it was not possible to analyze fully many of the issues raised. The themes discussed include the evolution of the system of temporarily recruited labour, the rationales for importing and for exporting such labour, and the magnitude of the migratory flows. The latter part of the chapter includes a brief summary of the recent development of the Turkish economy and of the changes in the Turkish labour market during the period over which migration has taken place.

Chapter 2 provides a framework for looking at the way in which exporting labour may affect the economy of a less developed labour exporting country of the Turkish type. The discussion is located firmly within an LDC pursuing a capitalist development strategy. Consequently, to avoid assuming that the interests of the various classes within such a country can be aggregated into a single whole which 'loses' or 'gains', we examine the impact of labour export on a selected list of economic variables. Two extreme cases — where labour export leads to an unequivocal improvement in these variables and where it leads to an unequivocal deterioration in them — are described, and the key determining factors identified. The distributional effects of migration are then discussed.

Chapter 3 surveys in detail the Turkish experience from 1960 to 1973. Initially it describes how the system of temporarily recruited migrant labour operates in Turkey, and her growth as a major supplier. It then surveys the socio-economic characteristics of the migrants, how these have changed over the decade and how they compare with the indigenous Turkish labour force and with other migrant labour flows from S. Europe. The story continues with what happens to the Turkish migrants while they are working abroad, and finally with the fate of those who return. It is in this chapter that the new material from the 1971 S.P.O. survey is to be found, though the description of the survey and presentation of most of the data have been relegated to appendices, as have the details of all the other data sources utilized in this chapter.

Chapter 4 attempts to evaluate Turkey's experience with labour export in the light of the factors discussed in Chapter 2. The evaluation concentrates on the effects which labour export actually had, rather than on these effects as compared with those of some hypothetical alternative policy package; the reason for this is that even if the strong assumption of no political change in the absence of labour export is made, of what such an alternative policy package would consist is a matter of speculation. Even so, the state of Turkish statistics is such that in many cases only fragmentary assessments of the effects are possible. But the impossibility of precise quantification is less of a problem than may be imagined, as usually the strength and direction of the impact is clear. To anticipate the conclusion, the impact of labour export on selected economic variables lies between the two extremes identified in Chapter 2. Against the substantial inflows of foreign exchange must be set the fact that many of the potentially favourable effects of migration did not happen while many of the potentially adverse ones did. Indeed, operation of the labour export system often brought great hardships to the migrants themselves, and did little to improve (indeed possibly worsened) the situation of the poorest amongst the Turkish population.

The final chapter initially discusses the problems, policy considerations and policy conflicts for countries of emigration which Turkey's experience with labour export suggests. Then the particular Turkish situation is considered more directly, including both some suggestions about obtaining the sort of statistical information required for effective policy formulation and a sketch of the possible effects on the Turkish economy of the 1973 moratorium on new labour export to W. Germany and the Netherlands.

The study comes up with no neat conclusions or policy packages. Much more extensive and reliable data are required before any conclusive verdict can be reached about the effect of migration on the Turkish economy. And appropriate detailed policy measures cannot be specified without making assumptions not only about the overall type of development strategy pursued but also about the government's ranking of policy aims. Instead, the study tries to build as comprehensive a picture as possible of Turkish migration abroad, the sort of effects which it has had and the sort of problems it has created up until the end of 1973. The significant gaps in and qualifications to the results are all too accurate an indication of our imperfect knowledge of this important subject.

Note

Part 1 of Appendix 1 contains an annotated bibliography of source material on Turkish migration, and of the main references on migrant workers in post-war Europe. Inter alia, the coverage and methodology of the main surveys of Turkish migrant workers are described. References to works cited in this bibliography have a capital letter (referring to the appropriate section of the bibliography) after the date of publication. References which do not have a capital letter after the date of publication are to be found in Part 2 of the bibliography.

1
The background

1.1 Migrant movements in postwar Europe

1.1.1 *The evolution of the system of temporarily recruited labour*

During the last two decades, fairly substantial flows of migrant labour have become
an increasingly important feature of most European countries. These flows have
occurred mainly from less to more developed countries, though there have been
much smaller flows between the more developed countries, particularly within the
E.E.C., (as well as *within* countries, as in Italy). The main underlying reasons for
these migratory movements have varied considerably − the migrants have, for
instance, included expatriates returning home from former colonies (e.g. French
from Algeria and Dutch from Indonesia), hopeful immigrants from newly independent ex-colonies (particularly to France, Britain and Holland), 'political' emigrants
(from E. Germany and Hungary), and workers from less industrialised neighbours
(or almost neighbours) who usually are initially recruited on the basis of a fixed
period employment contract abroad.

This study is confined to this last category, i.e. migrant workers from the less
industrialised parts of Europe and the Mediterranean where wages are much lower
and jobs much scarcer. From the standpoint of the individual worker, the normal
pattern of this migratory flow has been much like any other. The worker leaves for
a foreign country in order to build a better life for himself. If things work out well,
he may decide that he would like to stay for a few years and so send for his family,
if he has one, and if they did not accompany him initially. Indeed after experience
of life abroad, he may wish to settle there permanently. But this final decision to
stay or to return will normally be made while abroad, *not* in his home country
before his initial departure, unless the costs of migration are so high that return is
virtually impossible. In other words, the concept of the 'permanent' immigrant,
i.e. a worker who, together with his family, leaves his native land for ever, is rarely
met with in practice *unless* immigration restrictions or political factors make the
initial decision to go abroad into a once-and-for-all one. Such restrictions apart,
most migrants are semi-permanent migrants; they may wish to return home or they
may wish to settle abroad, depending on their experience in the host country.

The new feature of the postwar migratory movements from the Mediterranean
countries to Western Europe has been not the motivation of the migrant workers
but rather the policy pursued by most of the host countries. For previously it was
not customary for a country to import such large numbers of foreign workers on a

temporary but systematic basis to satisfy a long run excess demand for labour.[1] The temporary migrant worker is recruited for a specific time period on the understanding that he will, in the normal course of events, return to his country of origin after this time period has elapsed – when, if the host country still faces a labour shortage, he will be replaced by another foreign worker. He is recruited solely because of his ability to work, and is discouraged from bringing non-working dependants. In other words, the host countries are really importing man-hours, not families. In West Germany, the status of such a migrant worker is made quite clear – he is called a *'gastarbeiter'* or guestworker; in France, he might be called one of the 'new slaves'.[2] The duration of his work abroad would be expected to be two or three years – considerably longer than for a seasonal migrant – and would not be vocationally orientated as in the case of the trainee migrant. He might be able to stay longer than this original contract and might ultimately be able to settle permanently with his family,[3] but there is no guarantee that he will be able to do so, and it is the intention underlying his original recruitment arrangement that he should not. 'Temporary', in other words, means 'intended at the time of recruitment to be employed for a temporary period only'. Workers hired in this way will be called *temporarily recruited labour*. In addition to this category of migration, one can also define *permanently recruited* migration (e.g. from Europe to Australia), *spontaneous permanent* migration (e.g. from Europe to the United States during the nineteenth century) *spontaneous temporary* migration (e.g. some of the Commonwealth immigration to the U.K. before 1962), *recruited seasonal* migration (e.g. from Spain to France during the 1960s) and *spontaneous seasonal* migration (e.g. in West Africa at harvest time). Although this study is primarily concerned with temporarily recruited migration, part of the migration flows under consideration fall into some of the other categories.

The actual operation of a policy of temporarily recruited immigration depends on whether or not there are legal sanctions to enforce it and on whether or not these are actually used to exclude spontaneous flows.[4] In this respect there has been considerable variation between Western European host country governments. Switzerland, W. Germany and the Netherlands have had fairly strict regulations which can be used to enforce migrant repatriation and to prevent the entry of dependants, but which can also permit selected migrant workers to settle permanently

---

1 As compared with importing foreign labour for a particular 'large' project – e.g. building a new capital. The types of labour migration which took place within Western Europe before 1945 are summarized in Chapter 2 of Castles & Kosack, 1973E.

2 Böhning (1972bE) would call him a polyannual migrant.

3 For the German regulations concerning this, see § 3.3.2 below.

4 Most of the host countries in Western Europe have both recruited and spontaneous immigrant flows. Officially recruited migrants have been a particularly small proportion of the total in France, accounting for only 22% in 1967, 18% in 1968 and 33% in 1969. In W. Germany, 26% of the Greek immigrants had been recruited in 1967 (65% in 1968), 42% of the Spaniards (73% in 1968), 49% of the Turks (66% in 1968), and 46% of the Portuguese (70% in 1968) – van Houte and Melgert, Eds., 1972E, and Tables A3 and A4 below).

with their families.[1] France on the other hand had introduced fewer controls until the law was tightened up in 1968.[2] Before then the system of regularization meant that all illegal immigrants could register officially if they were healthy and had found a job. After 1968, regularization by non-Algerians was permitted only for selected occupations considered to be in excess demand (such as domestic servants and au pair girls), and for Portuguese citizens. Algerian workers were limited to a maximum entry of 35 000 per annum; if they found work within nine months they could stay for at least five years and also bring dependants if suitable housing were available. This policy has had only limited success — the proportion of new immigrants regularized fell from 82% in 1968 to 61% in 1970 — but the Algerian quota was still exceeded. The persistently high rate of clandestine immigration together with the increasing demands by migrant workers for more rights and better conditions (particularly during the Renault strike in Spring 1973),[3] and the increasing political pressure from anti-immigrant groups led the government to introduce new measures to improve their conditions and further regulate their entry.[4] However, the French regulations regarding settlement have meant that a higher proportion of temporarily recruited immigrant workers have been able to settle permanently with their families in France than in host countries such as Switzerland, W. Germany and the Netherlands, which has perhaps had the strictest policy towards family immigration. In contrast, many Finns have been able to settle down with the prospect of permanency in Sweden, and Irish and Commonwealth citizens in the U.K.[5]

1 Roughly speaking, the policy in these countries has been to maintain very strict control over the entry of new migrants, to limit severely their rights during the first few years abroad, but to permit those who last out some minimum period (ten years in Switzerland, five years in W. Germany) to settle permanently with their families. The German regulations are described in more detail in § 3.3.2. Italian migrants to W. Germany can of course settle permanently under the E.E.C. free movement of labour provisions.

2 In addition France has utilised a considerable number of seasonal workers from Spain and Portugal.

3 This strike was started by about three hundred unskilled men, almost all of whom were foreign. They were supported by 7,000 other Renault workers and the C.G.T. (Confédération Générale du Travail) and C.F.D.T. (Confédération Française Démocratique du Travail) union organisations. Although they returned to work before an agreement had been reached, they had been on strike for almost a month and were claimed to have caused a production loss of 50,000 vehicles. 21,000 of the 95,000 workers in Renault's French plants were immigrants. In addition, about 10,000 migrant workers had participated in the May Day parades in Paris to demand better pay and conditions. (See *The Guardian*, Friday, May 11th, 1973, *Daily Telegraph*, April 24th, 1973 and *The Times*, July 30th, 1973).

4 Illegal immigrants who arrived before June 1st 1973 had until September 30th to regularize their position. Those without a job would get a three-month residence permit to give them time to find one. Since June 1973 tourist passports have been date stamped to assist control of illegal immigration. Sanctions were proposed against employers who used foreign labour which did not come through the National Immigration Office, and against those who did not provide suitable housing.

5 The 1962 Immigration Act drastically altered the pattern of Commonwealth immigration to Britain. Before then there was a fairly high turnover of immigrant male workers. The introduction of the voucher system for all new workers together with the comparatively free admission of dependants led not only to a large immediate inflow of workers who wanted to get in before it was too late, but also to a shift towards permanent settlement since unskilled migrant workers who left the U.K. were not able to return (see Castles and Kosack, 1973E, Ch. 2, and Foot, 1965).

But the important point is that until now, it has been the host country governments which decide if and how many temporarily recruited workers can settle permanently with their families, though they may vary in their susceptibility to pressure on this issue, from the firm attitude of Germany to the more flexible attitude of France. The evolution of the system of temporarily recruited labour has meant that the host countries have been able both to utilize an extremely flexible supply of labour without incurring all the additional social costs which would arise if dependants were admitted, and to select a substratum out of these to fill vacancies which are expected to be permanent. In other words, the best of the temporarily recruited workers can be creamed off to satisfy long run excess demand while the remainder can be used to meet temporary fluctuations or to carry out occupations facing a long run labour shortage until a more suitable employee can be found. The gain in flexibility and savings in social-infrastructural costs obtained by rotating migrants can be combined with the gain in skills and experience obtained by absorbing some into the permanent labour force.[1] Consequently the implications of the use of temporarily recruited migrants in Western Europe should not be examined independently from the absorption of permanent immigrants into these countries.

Böhning has tried to take account of differences in migrants' length of residence in a host country by introducing the concept of 'maturity' in a migratory flow, and distinguishing four stages in it.[2] The first corresponds to temporarily recruited labour proper — the migrants are male, young target workers who are unaccompanied by their families. The second is essentially a transitional phase during which migrants' length of stay increases, as does their tendency to modify their consumption patterns towards those of their host country population. This tendency is accelerated during the third phase when vanguard migrants begin to bring their families, and when a growing, though still limited, proportion of foreign workers are employed to satisfy the needs of the immigrant population. In the fourth phase, the tendencies of the third phase are continued, and immigrant groups or 'colonies' with their own ethnic institutions such as schools, etc. are established. The overall impact of migration on a host country at any time would depend on the maturity composition of its migrant labour force. But although this typology is very useful for analyzing the potential impact of temporarily recruited migration on the host country, it is misleading to give the impression that this kind of migration has or will necessarily go through all Böhning's four phases in the order stated. Also, at times Böhning describes the phases as if the workers themselves choose whether or not to move to the next phase, when it is the host country government which plays the crucial rôle. However, the phase typology is a very useful way to summarize the way in which the characteristics of migrant workers in a host country may change over time.

1 There is an obvious analogy here with the use of various categories of labour in Japanese large firms (approximately during the period from 1920–1960). An élite were employed under the *nenkō joretsu* system which meant that they were paid according to seniority and employed for life, while the remainder were divided into various categories of temporary and subcontract labour, with low wages and little or no job security. (Paine 1971)

2 Böhning 1972bE and O.E.C.D. 1973aE.

1.1.2   *The rationale for the use of migrant labour in W. Europe*

1.1.2.1   *The growing labour shortages in the host countries and alternative policies
to counter them.*

The basic reasons underlying the growth of large migratory flows from Mediterranean
countries to W. Europe are well known.[1] Demographic factors in what are now the
host countries (in particular the changing age structure of the population[2]) were
reinforced by socio-economic factors (such as more higher education and earlier
retirement) to bring about a decline in the ratio of active population to total population. These factors, in a situation of rapid postwar growth with full employment,
led to the emergence of labour shortages, particularly in low level jobs with little or
no prestige attached to them. At the same time worsening unemployment and low
living standards produced the potential migrants in what are now the labour exporting countries. And colonial legacies or geographical proximity determined who went
where.

However, there remains the question of why the current host countries chose to
deal with their labour shortages through immigration, and also why the current
labour exporting countries chose to cooperate. Although such cooperation may
seem obvious because of the reduced unemployment and increased foreign exchange
earnings, other considerations may lead labour exporting countries to take measures
to stem the outflow of workers, as Yugoslavia has been doing (see below). In theory,
the policies available to the labour-short countries include (1) those which increase
the supply of labour (man-hours), (2) those which reduce the demand for labour,
and (3) those which operate on both the supply and demand. Policies to increase
the supply of labour include[3]

    1 (a) raising activity rates, particularly of women
      (b) lengthening working hours/working days/ working age, etc.

Policies to reduce demand include

    2 (a) utilising techniques which require less labour input to produce a given
         commodity mix
      (b) changing the commodity mix towards commodities whose production
         requires less labour input
      (c) encouraging research into labour saving technologies
      (d) establishing plants in labour surplus countries.

Policies to operate on both the supply of and the demand for labour include

    3 (a) increasing the remuneration for or improving working conditions in
         occupations where labour is scarce.

---

1 For a useful summary see Danieli 1972E; see also Marshall 1973E for the case of the
    Netherlands.

2 The ratio of working-age to total population fell from 67% in 1961 to 63% in 1970; that of
    working to total population fell from 48% in 1961 to 44% in 1970. If German nationals
    only had been counted, the ratio of working to total population would have been lower, as
    about 75% of foreigners are economically active.

3 Increasing the population permanently by raising the birth rate has not been included here,
    firstly because it is too long before it has any effect on the labour market, and secondly
    because it runs counter to the current environmentalist wisdom.

However, listing policies in this way obscures the fact that some require governmental implementation and are not policy alternatives for the individual employer who faces a labour shortage, and also the fact that it is particular occupations only which are in excess demand, that is those where working conditions are poor, or wages low, or both.[1] The problem is not to increase the supply of labour but to increase the supply of labour willing to be employed in certain (usually low grade) occupations. Consequently 1(a) and 1(b) can be ruled out as solutions, as can 3(a) if migrant labour prepared to accept employment at the existing wage rate is available. Furthermore, migrant labour has many positive features from the point of view of the prospective employer. It tends to be young, strong, single and cheap, with few dependants and without a psychological aversion to performing menial jobs; it tends to be unorganized and, before 1973, was usually comparatively free from industrial and political unrest.[2] Only if the government operated a tax-cum-subsidy policy to compensate employers for raising wages to attract indigenous labour could the individual employer be expected voluntarily to forgo the use of lower-wage foreign labour.

The extent to which the second group of policies can or will be used depends on the economic activity concerned. For instance 2(a), i.e. using less labour, could only apply where such a substitution possibility exists. But since although such a possibility is known, it is not (by definition) being used at the present time, it may be presumed to be the case that at the existing wage rate the current technique in use is most profitable in the existing economic environment. Thus if immigrant labour is available at the existing wage rate to fill labour shortages the employer will choose to utilise it rather than to move to a less labour-intensive technique, given the existing economic environment. The empirical evidence suggests that this has actually been the case in Germany and Switzerland, where many firms are known to have plans for utilising less labour-intensive techniques which they have chosen not to use because of the availability of immigrant labour.[3]

2(b), i.e. changing the commodity mix away from very labour-intensive commodities or services is a policy which requires government implementation. It is of no relevance for the individual firm, faced with a full order book and a labour shortage. In any case, the labour shortages have tended to occur either in low-wage and/or low-status activities particularly in the service sector, or in assembly-line

---

1 All studies on the nature of the employment of migrant workers in Western Europe bring this point out — see for example Castles and Kosack 1973E, Böhning 1972bE, and Livi Bacci 1972E. Swiss studies reported in a 1967 O.E.C.D. report indicate that the jobs filled by migrant workers tend to be those which (1) require long working hours (e.g. domestic jobs), (2) are disagreeable (e.g. mining), (3) have low stability (e.g. construction) or (4) have low wage levels (e.g. unskilled manufacturing occupations).

2 This situation was changed by the Renault strike in France in April 1973, the Ford strike at Cologne at the end of August, and the strike by North African workers in France during the racial trouble which also erupted at the end of August (as a result of which the Algerian government attempted to stop the outflow of migrant labour.)

3 For instance, a Swiss survey found that many firms had failed to utilize plans for changes in methods of production because they had been able to extend existing techniques by using foreign labour (*Bericht der Studienkommission für das Problem der ausländischen Arbeitskräfte*, 1964).

jobs in the fastest growing branches of manufacturing industry.[1] Since many of the former jobs occur in essential public services, governments have tended to take the option of filling them with readily available migrants, while attempts to reduce the growth of the latter would amount to slowing down national economic growth.

2(c), i.e. trying to develop labour saving technologies for labour-short branches of the economy, is a long run policy which does not circumvent the immediate labour shortage problem. But if immigrant labour is used to deal with the immediate shortage and this keeps down the wage rate, this will affect the type of innovations to which research is directed if we assume a Kennedy-type innovation frontier.[2] More specifically, the type of innovation to which research will be directed will be more labour intensive than would be the case in the absence of immigrant labour.

2(d), i.e. establishing plants in labour surplus countries abroad is a policy alternative which would only affect part of the demand for migrant workers and which would have to be implemented by the individual firm. However the evidence to date suggests that for those branches of the economy where this was a feasible solution, it has not been an attractive policy alternative as compared with importing migrant labour to work in the home country. It is not difficult to see why this has been so. Setting up a new factory abroad entails not just new investment but the transfer of management and skilled labour which cannot be recruited locally, together with the provision of necessary infrastructural facilities (unless the host country government can be induced to provide them) — quite apart from any political risks etc. which may be involved. Consequently since the workers were prepared to come to the work, this was preferred to taking the work to the workers in those situations where this was feasible.

So far it has been argued that given a reserve pool of migrant labour upon which to draw, it was rational for employers to prefer to use this rather than to adopt alternative policies. From the employer's point of view, utilisation of migrant labour enabled him to keep his labour force at a figure close to its desired size at any time, without directly incurring any of the extra social infrastructural costs which use of foreign labour might entail.[3] Not surprisingly therefore, employers have usually been in favour of continuing utilisation of migrant labour after governments have decided to impose restrictions. However, the arguments presented so far have been essentially static and micro in content, and so have ignored what is perhaps the most powerful argument for the utilization of migrant labour from the point of view of employers and government alike: that is, that a dynamically expanding economy requires an increasing supply of labour, and that the most important impact of the use of immigrant labour has been to promote sustained growth in the host countries.

1 Nikolinakos 1973E, Ch. 4.

2 Kennedy 1962.

3 Though in 1973, proposals to make German employers contribute directly towards this were mooted, and in September the fee which they paid the government for the recruitment of a migrant worker was raised from DM300—DM1000.

1.1.2.2 *The impact of importing labour on the host countries*[1]

The ability to import labour as required means that a country has, in effect, a reserve supply of labour. If we assume away market imperfections, then access to such a supply by an economy currently at full employment means that the labour requirements of planned investment can be satisfied without any increase in money wages or prices (assuming that there is no rise in raw material costs). But in a closed economy operating at full employment, total output will rise only if the use of migrant labour leads to either a higher level of aggregate investment, a better direction of investment, or a better utilization of investment. In the case where an economy with access to surplus labour has lower money wages and prices, but the same real wage and employment as one without such access, such an increase in investment may occur because of the reduced risk and uncertainty in the labour surplus economy.

But if we now assume open economies under a régime of comparatively fixed exchange rates, a country in which access to reserve supplies of labour keeps down money wages and prices will have a potential competitive advantage against ones not similarly endowed. Whether or not such an advantage is realized depends mainly on whether the country can expand its export markets; if it can, new investment will be undertaken to satisfy the new export demand. Essentially this potential advantage obtained from the availability of surplus labour is similar to that from devaluation, without the disadvantage which the latter entails through higher import prices.

The best known advocate of the advantages which can be realized from access to reserve supplies of labour is C.P. Kindleberger (1967E). He approaches the question in a completely different way, by assuming that for one reason or another, a dynamic growth process has started in an economy. He then goes on to argue that an abundant labour supply has a crucial rôle to play in sustaining such a process by keeping down wages and prices and keeping up profits and investment:

> "In the country of immigration, short-run elasticity of the labour supply has a favourable impact on wages (holding them down), on profits (holding them up), on investment and growth, and on price stability." (p. 200)

As initially presented, his model of the impact of immigration on economic growth is essentially supply dominated, being derived basically from the Lewis dual economy model. Thus, because he assumes away the demand side, access to reserve supplies of labour is even of great advantage to a closed economy.

However, his analysis of the rôle of labour supply in postwar Western European economic growth is more realistic. Here he concentrates on the importance of a sufficient supply of labour in sustaining 'the virtuous circle of exports leading to higher incomes, profits, and investment, which in turn lower prices and stimulate exports once again' (p. 3). But without access to reserve supplies of labour, there is a tendency for a country to suffer the 'negative-feedback mechanism in which increased exports are followed by higher prices, which cut off exports and attract additional imports' (p. 3). In other words, immigration has kept down wage and

---

1 An extremely valuable (though not entirely uncontroversial) survey of the impact of immigration on the main Western European host countries is made by Böhning (O.E.C.D. 1973aE).

12

price increases, particularly in the crucial export sector, and so has sustained the growth process.

The particular chain of causation suggested by Kindleberger will be discussed further below, with other hypotheses about the impact of immigration on economic growth in the host countries. Firstly, however, the evidence relevant for one crucial postulate in all analyses of the impact of immigration will be reviewed, that is, that it has been counter-inflationary.

There is a considerable amount of evidence to support the alleged counter-inflationary impact of immigration. For instance, G.C. Schmid (1970–71E) found that German utilization of migrant labour not only reduced wage pressure when the German economy was operating at overfull employment because firms could obtain migrant labour for full capacity utilization at the peak of the cycle without competitive bidding up of wage rates, but also led to strong productivity gains during recessions, when employers were able to cut their labour forces instead of hoarding them until the upswing.[1]

> "While this increase in labor productivity can be fully understood only in light of many other factors, such as capital investment patterns and lags in labor market response, the evidence is strong that in Germany hoarding of the marginal worker during slack production periods has been low (or rather that turnover at the margin has been high) while expansion of employment when demand first picks up has been rapid. This has meant either larger profits for the German firm and, thus, relatively higher levels of savings and investment, or lower prices for German goods vis-à-vis foreign goods." (pp. 251–2)

Certainly there is substantial evidence about the dampening effect which utilisation of migrant workers in Germany has had on money wages. Bain and Pauga (1972E) tested the relationship between money wages, prices, employment of foreign workers and unemployment for eighteen industries over the period 1961–9.[2] They found that an increase in the level of prices caused intra-industry money wages to rise, while an increase in the employment of foreign workers and the number of unemployed workers in an industry retarded money wages. Garbers and Blankart (1973E) found that Switzerland had had rather a similar experience: while there were comparatively few controls on the entrance of foreign migrant workers, their competition with Swiss nationals in the labour market kept down money wages, but when stricter immigration controls were introduced, the consequent decrease in potential foreign competition led to much sharper wage increases than had previously been the case.[3] On the other hand, Barentsz (1972E)

1 This contrasts with the situation in the U.K., where employers have tended to hoard workers during recessions, and to adjust the size of their labour forces primarily by cutting down on new hiring (see a forthcoming paper by T.F. Cripps and R.J. Tarling of the Cambridge University Department of Applied Economics).

2 They used a linear model according to which money wages in the ith industry in year t were taken to be a function of (i) the number of foreign workers employed in the ith industry during the year $t - 2$, (ii) the consumer price index during the year $t - 1$, and (iii) the number of workers unemployed in the ith industry during the year $t - 1$.

3 For a rather different interpretation of the Swiss case, see Rossi and Schiltknecht 1972E. However Maillat (OECD 1973bE) also points out the more rapid wage increases which occurred after migration was reduced.

has argued that it costs a Dutch enterprise roughly 25 per cent more to employ a foreign migrant than to employ the equivalent Dutch worker. This is because the employer pays for part of the foreign worker's housing and food costs, and for his annual trip home, while he also incurs higher recruitment costs than for an indigenous worker. However, this analysis is faulty because it assumes that an indigenous worker would have been forthcoming at the same wage as the foreign worker receives, and ignores the effect of the utilisation of foreign labour in keeping down money wage levels.

The dampening impact of use of migrant labour does not, however, just arise from its direct effect on wages. As Böhning argues (O.E.C.D. 1973aE p. 50), migrant workers' high average propensity to save and repatriate earnings and their comparatively low dependency ratio may combine to exert a strong deflationary impact on consumer goods prices and, indirectly, on capital goods prices as well. However, this will be partially offset it repatriated earnings are subsequently spent on host country products. Also, if immigration increases profitability because of its dampening effect on wages, and if investment is positively related to the profit rate, then use of immigrant labour may stimulate investment demand until the profit rate has been reduced to its initial value, and so may contribute to the creation of excess demand. Because of these possibilities, any deflationary impact from migrants' high propensities to save and repatriate earnings may be weak, particularly in comparison with any direct impact on money wages, and so through the cost side, on prices.

But although there is considerable agreement about such direct dampening effects of the utilisation of foreign labour in most of the countries of immigration,[1] by no means all commentators would agree that the overall impact has been stabilising and disinflationary. Two arguments have been advanced against this view. According to the first, although immigrant workers raise total output, this is more than offset by the corresponding increase in expenditure (particularly on the capital goods which, it is assumed, are required to employ them), so that a situation of excess demand develops. The leading advocates of this view are Rüstow (1966E), who was writing about W. Germany,[2] and Mishan and Needleman (1966 (a and b) E) who were writing about the U.K. The analysis proceeds by calculating the expenditure on social and industrial capital which, it is argued, will have to be made for each new immigrant worker, and then estimating how long it will take for the worker to produce a surplus equal to the initial investment expenditure. Rüstow argues that this period will be longer for the economy as a whole if immigration continues than it will be for the individual worker, and estimates the latter to be six years, but the former twelve years.

However, this view ignores the temporarily recruited character of most West

1 Jones and Smith (1970) did not find that immigration had led to lower increases than would have otherwise been the case in the U.K. Böhning (OECD 1973aE) argues that any dampening effect is confined to slow growing low wage industries and does not apply to trend setting high wage industries, though he does not provide any detailed evidence for this view.

2 See also Föhl (1967E), for, although his analysis would perhaps more appropriately be classified as an exposition of the second type of approach to the inflationary impact of immigration, since he concentrates more on its longer run inflationary consequences, he also suggests that the initial impact may be inflationary as well.

European immigration. For industrial investment is not made so as to employ an immigrant worker. Rather it is undertaken so as to enable production of the estimated level of output which will be demanded, and immigrant workers are then *recruited* to fill the associated job vacancies. Expenditure from the incomes paid to immigrant workers will of course subsequently lead to induced investment, but this may well be lower than the expenditure which would have taken place had the jobs been filled by indigenous workers.

It is equally important to distinguish between the social capital expenditure which would have been required if a vacancy were filled by an indigenous worker, and that required if it were filled by an immigrant. Only the *extra* expenditure (if any) that an immigrant requires is relevant when assessing the impact of *immigration* on social capital requirements. It is important to stress this point as it is often implied in discussions of the effects of immigration that, if a job vacancy is filled by an indigenous member of the economically active population, this does not involve any net increase in social capital requirements. Yet if the recruitment of an indigenous worker involves his family moving to a new town, this will normally involve some net increment in social capital requirements. The amount involved is quite likely to exceed that for a foreign worker in the short run, so that use of foreign labour permits short-term saving in social infrastructural savings. Furthermore, whether or not the extra increment in social capital requirements which immigrant labour may entail actually has an inflationary impact is a view whose accuracy can be tested empirically, since it depends on such capital investment being (i) made on or very soon after workers' arrival and (ii) so high that it takes a number of years before it is offset by the output which they contribute. But Castles and Kosack demonstrate, convincingly in my view, that neither of these requirements has in practice been fully satisfied,[1] so that immigration into Western Europe – in the initial years at least – has not tended to have an inflationary impact.

But might it not have an inflationary impact subsequently? This is the view which is held by advocates of the second type of approach to the inflationary impact of immigration. Proponents of this view suggest that although initially immigration has a dampening effect on wages and prices, subsequently it leads to the creation of excess demand.[2] This happens because (i) as they settle down immigrants consume more, particularly if they send for their dependants; and (ii) as more immigrants arrive to satisfy the labour requirements of an expanding economy, their social infrastructural investment requirements can no longer be postponed. In other words, it is argued that in the longer run, the extra increment in demand which immigration generates is high and exceeds immigrants' contribution to production. Furthermore, if utilisation of immigrant labour has kept down commodity prices, one would expect to find considerable foreign demand for exports at the prevailing exchange

1 'Since the social and industrial investment postulated by Rüstow and Mishan and Needleman does not take place at the time and to the extent they suppose, their arguments lack foundation', (Castles and Kosack 1973E, p.39). Anyone in doubt of the delays which have occured in the provision of social infrastructural facilities should read the masterly survey of migrant workers' social conditions which was compiled by Castles and Kosack. The comparatively low social infrastructural costs are of course an important reason why governments permitted the use of temporarily recruited labour.

2 Böhning, for instance, argues that by the time the third phase of maturity has been reached, the wage-dampening effect of immigration is more than outweighed by immigrant-induced demand pressure.

15

rate. But to satisfy the excess demand created in these ways, additional labour is required, and so more immigrants are admitted, thus reinforcing the whole process. In Böhning's terminology the migration process becomes self-feeding; migrant workers are increasingly imported to provide the goods and services demanded by the existing migrant population, as well as to satisfy the demand which results mainly from the success of existing migrant workers in keeping down export prices. Again, however, it is important to specify the argument precisely. Multiplier effects on employment and income would arise even if the indigenous non-employed population filled the jobs carried out by immigrants (unless they saved all their incomes). It is only the extent to which use of immigrant labour leads to higher multiplier effects that can be attributed to employing foreign rather than indigenous workers. Böhning has suggested that immigrant-induced demand may be for very labour intensive commodities such as infrastructural services (OECD 1973aE). But apart from effects such as this, induced increases in employment arise from the initial employment expansion, and not from the use of foreign rather than indigenous workers. On the other hand, if immigrant workers are not available, the initial employment expansion would have been smaller because of increased utilisation of more capital intensive techniques, where feasible.

Consequently evidence of association between sustained immigration and increasing inflation[1] must be interpreted cautiously; the rising prices may be caused by the *maturing* of the migratory flow — as migrants' characteristics approach more closely those of the host country population, the dampening effect on wages and prices becomes weaker so that the rate of inflation approximates to that which would have occurred in the absence of inflation.

The theory that, although immigration has a disinflationary effect to start off with, at some time there may be a turning point after which its impact becomes inflationary, has also been put forward on a cyclical basis, i.e. that the lagged effect of rising immigration on total demand during the upswing of the cycle has a destabilising effect.[2] Whether or not this would be a problem depends on the time lag between initial immigration and the subsequent associated investment expenditure. For if this is more than two or three years, while cycles last four to five years from peak to peak, the investment expenditure will not have been made before the peak of the cycle has been reached. In any case, the social infrastructural investment for an immigrant is normally not made until it is certain that his labour will be required for some years, for in this way the labour importing country can economize on the capital costs of immigration. There is no doubt that the German authorities recognize this — according to figures calculated by the economics ministry, the full investment charge for the job of a permanent worker, and in social infrastructure for him and his family, is five to seven times the amount required for the temporarily

1   For the Swiss experience, see Gnehm 1966E.

2   See for example, Föhl, 1967, who writes:
    "The hoped-for stabilising effect of the employment of foreign workers has proved to be . . . illusive. Experience up to date (1967) and theoretical assumptions, which are well-grounded, both lead to the probability that the effect is, on the contrary, unsettling, so that we may assume that higher employment of foreign workers overheats the boom and leads to price inflation." (Translation by Kade and Schiller 1972E).

16

recruited migrant worker who stays for only a few years – his associated investment would have hardly begun before he departed.[1]

Altogether therefore this brief review of the relationship between immigration and inflation tends to support Böhning's view that the impact of immigration has for the most part tended to be deflationary, though the strength of this depends on the size[2] and maturity composition of the migrant population, and government policy on the provision of social infrastructural capital. A strong deflationary influence in the early years of migration brought about partly by postponing migrants' social capital requirements may, however, be obtained at the expense of subsequent inflationary tendencies when requirements accumulated over a number of years can be postponed no longer.

However, the above argument has primarily been concerned with the impact of immigration on inflation, and so is only indirectly concerned with its impact on economic growth. The impact on growth may arise in a number of closely inter-related ways, for instance (1) by preventing production bottlenecks from emerging because of labour shortages, (2) by contributing to export-led growth through helping to keep down export prices, (3) by permitting the realization of economies of scale, (4) by increasing capital accumulation and (5) by raising overall productivity by sending home instead of hoarding labour during depressions in the cycle.

The role of immigration in preventing the emergence of production bottlenecks because of labour shortages is its most obvious effect on growth, and has of course been presupposed in the previous discussion of the counter-inflationary impact of immigration.

Kindleberger's argument about the role of immigration in sustaining export-led growth has already been described above. In view of the evidence about the dampening effect of immigration on industrial wages and prices, the core of his argument is clearly substantiated. However, as has already been pointed out, Kindleberger concentrates on the supply side, and, in particular, on the role of immigration in preventing the emergence of the inflationary pressure which would destroy an already existing process of export-led growth. He is much less concerned with the role of immigration in creating opportunities for such export-led growth by giving the host country a competitive advantage in export markets, to which other commentators such as Nikolinakos (1973E) attach equal importance. Nikolinakos shows the importance of immigrant labour in maintaining the competitiveness of German exports, and goes on to argue that by contributing to the expansion of export demand in this way, the use of migrant workers stimulated investment and

---

1 *The Economist*, May 5th 1973, pp. 70–71. According to these estimates, the investment cost of a temporarily recruited worker is about £4000 as compared with £20 000–£30 000 for a permanent immigrant. However, it should be recognized firstly that the immigrant contributes as much as the indigenous worker in social security payments for infrastructural investment, whereas because of the age structure of the immigrant population, his demands on social services are likely to be less, and secondly that any associated industrial investment will only be made if his employer finds that it is profitable to do so. Indeed immigration may even help to provide additional investment capital (see pp. 19–21 below).

2 Thus in Switzerland, where immigrant workers constitute over one-quarter of the labour force, the impact of immigration on prices would be much stronger than in the other Western European countries of immigration where the proportion of immigrant workers did not yet exceed 10 per cent in 1973.

growth. It did not just sustain increases in demand determined by other factors, but contributed to those increases itself through its effect on exports (other ways in which use of immigrant labour may affect demand are discussed below (pp. 18–20)).

Although taking into account both the demand and the supply effects of immigration gives a more complete explanation of its impact on growth, two qualifications to the argument as presented need to be made. Firstly, it assumes that immigration has, overall, a counterinflationary impact and that any possible inflationary effects such as those described above never arise to offset this. Secondly, it does not draw attention to the fact that it is not so much the absolute effect which immigration has on prices (particularly export prices) as the relative effect compared with other countries which is relevant. For, just as countries can undertake competitive devaluations, they could also compete in their use of temporarily recruited labour by adopting an aggressive immigration policy. Whether or not they can do so will depend primarily on the resistance of the indigenous labour force to such an attempt to keep down their wages, and on the extent of social and political pressure against such an 'aggressive' policy. The situation in post-war Western Europe seems to have been one in which immigration policy has been restricted to satisfying unfilled vacancies — in other words it has been used primarily for supply-orientated reasons, but has, as a by-product, had an important influence on demand. And given the currently increasing public resistance to the system of temporarily recruited migration in the host countries, the possibility of an 'aggressive' immigration policy seems remote.

Access to immigrant labour may make a different though interrelated contribution to growth by permitting the realization of economies of scale. This is the essence of the theory which has been put forward by Kaldor (1966), though it should be noted that this is a theory of structural change, as compared with the previous theories, which were concerned more with the short-term import of immigration. According to the Kaldorian model, the rate of growth of manufacturing productivity depends on the rate of growth of manufacturing output, which itself is closely related to the rate of growth of the manufacturing labour force. The idea underlying it is that when output is rising quickly, significant economies of scale can be realized so that productivity also rises fast. This model performs extremely well in explaining the growth of Western European economies up until the mid-1960s, for there is a surprisingly high correlation between growth in the manufacturing labour force and growth in manufacturing labour productivity.[1] Indeed variations in the growth of manufacturing output show a more than proportionate response to variations in the growth of manufacturing employment.

However, the model cannot be used without modification to explain subsequent Western European manufacturing growth experience after 1965, when productivity and employment growth in manufacturing are no longer correlated.[2] In most countries the manufacturing labour force grew only very slightly, while in some (for instance, the Netherlands and Austria) it actually declined. This means that sustained increase in the manufacturing labour force cannot be regarded as a necessary condition for sustained manufacturing productivity growth.

1 Cripps and Tarling 1973, Chapter 3.

2 *Ibid.*

However, this does not mean that the expansion of the manufacturing labour force did not make an important contribution to increasing productivity in the earlier period. Productivity in manufacturing may rise for a number of reasons: it may rise primarily through a move to the use of more efficient machinery; on the other hand, in conditions of labour surplus, it may rise primarily through realization of potential economies of scale and improved use of capacity. Since the rate of recruitment of migrants has continued to rise sharply in most of the countries under discussion, after the temporary recession in 1967, yet the size of the manufacturing labour force has remained constant or even fallen, then it is clear that there would either have been serious labour shortages in the absence of immigration, or an even greater shift towards capital intensive investment and rationalization of industry. The availability of migrant labour which could either be used only temporarily while the economic situation required it, or which could be trained and used on a permanent basis to operate new investment, meant that, depending on the precise circumstances facing any particular industry, a balance of different types of productivity gains could be realized.

Indeed, it has been argued that the use of immigrant labour may itself have promoted capital accumulation.[1] This argument hinges on whether or not its use leads to a lower rate of growth of real wages than would otherwise have been the case during periods of economic expansion, and on whether or not it reduces the wage bill during recessions. If so it must keep up profit rates. The argument continues:

> "The redistributive effect of immigration therefore increases the supply of capital in two ways: firstly, it increases profits as a proportion of turnover, allowing increased reinvestment by industrialists; secondly, it raises the rate of return on investments, encouraging people to save and invest a higher proportion of their incomes. Low wages and high profits are also likely to pull in money from abroad, providing further capital."[2]

As stated, this argument seems to imply that given the postulate about wages, profits will rise with immigration, in periods of expansion at least. But this may not be the case. The point is that given the postulate about wages, *profits will be higher than they would otherwise have been*,[3] so that more investment than would otherwise have been the case is possible. There will be a positive influence on the capital-labour ratio which may or may not offset the negative influence which the initial immigratory flow may cause, though if such a fall in the capital-labour ratio is caused by improved use of existing capacity, then the output-capital ratio will rise.

However the above argument is a supply orientated argument, saying essentially that the impact of immigration on profitability *may permit* higher investment than would otherwise have been the case. It lacks any theory as to why such increased investment should be made. To answer this, it is necessary to look at the impact of immigration from the demand side. Access to a reserve supply of labour can be

1 Castles and Kosack 1973E, pp. 402–3.

2 *Ibid.*, p. 403.

3 Though up to 1972 the share of gross profits in national income seems to have been falling in most of the host countries under discussion.

expected to give a country's entrepreneurs a potential competitive advantage, both directly through the impact of lower wages on prices, and more indirectly through the realization of scale economies to which immigration may contribute. As a result, if demand conditions are favourable, entrepreneurs can expect expanding markets, stimulated particularly by expanding export markets, because of which ('animal spirits' being high) they invest more (which in turn keeps up profitability). In other words, in these circumstances an economy with access to a reserve supply of labour would accumulate faster than one without.

However, if the economy's immigrants represent a net addition to the labour force, the investment which takes place will not normally be of the same kind as that which would have been made in the absence of immigration. It is likely to be of the capital widening variety as compared with the capital deepening which would otherwise have occurred. But if the indigenous labour force is declining so fast that there is hardly any net increment after importing immigrant labour (as has recently been the case for the manufacturing sector in many Western European economies) then immigration will normally be accompanied both by capital widening and by capital deepening investment. In theory of course expansion could always be effected by capital widening if the required amount of immigrant labour could be imported. However, for political and social reasons this is not possible, and an upper limit is effectively placed on the volume of new immigrants in any year and on the total stock resident in the host country.[1] Given such a limit, the most rapidly expanding industries will normally be unable to meet their expansion plans by capital widening alone, so that in these industries utilization of immigrant labour may be accompanied by capital deepening investment. And insofar as capital widening and capital deepening have different levels of skilled labour requirements, then the current system of immigration, whereby employers can select and train chosen migrants to be permanent additions to the skilled labour force and hire others on a temporary basis, is particularly suited to employers' needs.

Immigration may also lead to an increase in the amount of machines in use at any given time. This will happen if by providing supplies of labour at the existing wage rate it permits the survival of old techniques which would have been forced out of production when wages rose. This in turn may (i) retard the structural shift in manufacturing from declining to expanding industries and (ii) retard the speed of industrial concentration if small enterprises using inferior techniques are able to remain in production. However, it is important to bear in mind that this does not restrict the expansion of expanding industries or the growth of bigger firms.

1 For Germany, see, for example, *The Economist, op. cit.*, May 5th 1973. Before the ban on non-EEC immigration in 1973, the maximum acceptable threshold for immigrant workers was regarded as 10 per cent of the labour force, and measures were introduced to prevent this limit from being exceeded.
For France, see *The Guardian*, May 11th 1973.
For the Netherlands, see *The Times*, November 1st 1972 and *Financial Times*, February 21st 1973. After the anti-Turkish riots in August 1972, Rotterdam put a limit of 5 per cent on the number of foreigners who might settle in any district (*The Economist*, March 31st 1973). In December 1973, the government banned all immigration from non-EEC countries. For a summary of the proposals which were under consideration to limit and control immigrant labour in Germany, France, Switzerland and the Netherlands in August 1973, see *The Economist*, August 25th 1973.

Indeed in Germany, immigrant workers have been concentrated in larger firms (§3.5.2).

Not all economists agree that immigration can have a positive effect on capital accumulation. For instance, Mishan and Needleman argue that if the required social capital expenditure per immigrant is carried out soon after arrival, this will actually reduce the capital available for industrial investment and so may cause a decline in the absolute industrial capital stock. However, as reported above, there is no evidence that social capital investment for new immigrants has been all carried out at the time of their arrival. As Castles and Kosack put it, 'social requirements are met, if at all, with a long delay'.[1] For this reason any effect of the sort which Mishan and Needleman envisage would be most unlikely.[2] And in any case, they ignore the dynamic effects of immigration which raise the total available for both social and industrial investment.

The positive effects of access to a reserve supply of labour on the rate of growth described above are medium-term arguments. However access to a reserve supply of labour of the temporarily recruited variety brings certain advantages to the host country during the trade cycle.[3] During recessions, excess workers can be sent back to their home country instead of hoarded by their firm of employment or paid unemployment benefit by the state. Consequently productivity in recessions tends to be higher than it would otherwise be,[4] and demands on unemployment insurance funds lower. On the other hand, sending workers home instead of paying them unemployment insurance may exaggerate the trough of the cycle as demand falls more than it would otherwise have done.

A slightly different approach which integrates many of the positive effects of access to a reserve supply of labour which have been discussed above is provided by Marxist analysts, such as Nikolinakos (1973E).[5] In his view, the use of migrant labour by Western European countries is 'a structural characteristic of the later phases of capitalism.' Most countries cannot cut their intake without adversely affecting their economic growth. Foreign workers constitute the modern reserve army of labour whose presence is essential for sustained accumulation: their availability has rescued the capitalist system from crisis. Indeed, the import of the last foreign worker would 'mark the gravestone of capitalism.'

However, Nikolinakos holds over his theoretical analysis of the use of immigrant labour as a stage in capitalist development for a future publication, so that in

1 Castles and Kosack 1973, p. 402. See also evidence which they cite. In any case, employers would be unlikely to encourage increasing use of migrant labour if this led to such high taxation to provide social capital that it necessitated a reduction in their planned investment.

2 There is a contradiction in Mishan and Needleman's views that Castles and Kosack bring out clearly. This is that in one place they argue that immigration will be inflationary because of both the industrial and the social capital investment which must be carried out immediately on immigrants' arrival, whereas in another place they argue that because no new investment is carried out, the capital-labour ratio will fall.

3 For more detailed information on the cyclical use of migrant labour, see § 3.2.3 below.

4 See passage from G.C. Schmid (1970–71E) quoted above (p.13) on the German case.

5. And Marshall 1973E, which is not discussed here as it became available while this book was in press.

fact he concentrates on the demand and supply effects which have occurred in the German case, particularly on the role of immigrants in the export sector, and on their rôle in permitting the realisation of scale economies and in keeping up rates of accumulation. He argues that they perform a buffer function, not just giving flexibility to the economies of their host countries, but also syphoning off potential social and political discontent from their homelands, which he divides into first grade (e.g. Italy and Spain), second grade (e.g. Turkey and Yugoslavia), third grade (the Arab countries of North Africa) and fourth grade (the countries of black Africa). He envisages a sort of satellite-metropolis relationship with the countries surrounding the metropolis slowly being absorbed into it so that it is necessary to seek new satellites further out.[1]

However, though Nikolinakos' analysis is illuminating in certain respects, it only gives a rather crude picture of the Western European experience with migrant labour. How big need the reserve army be? Why did accumulation take place as quickly when the manufacturing labour force ceased to rise? And why did European capitalists import labour while the Japanese started to export capital when they were faced with a situation of labour shortage? These are all questions which the crude reserve army theorists must face. They can be avoided if we settle for a lower level generalization: importing workers was one of a number of responses to the growing labour shortages in what we now call the host countries.

The ability to recruit both temporary and permanent immigrant labour certainly seems to have contributed towards sustained growth with less inflation than would otherwise have been the case, particularly in Germany. But while the economic demand by industry for immigrant labour continued unchecked until mid-1973,[2] opposition to the continuation of this policy increased. This partly arose from the distributional impact of immigration. For although this probably works to the advantage of most of the indigenous population because (1) nationals move to better jobs, (2) receipts from immigrants tend to reduce the tax and social security payments required from nationals,[3] and (3) per capita growth in the real wages *of the indigenous population* will probably be somewhat higher because of the faster growth in output which labour import permits, this does not preclude the possibility that certain subsections of the indigenous population become worse off.

1 This process was becoming more noticeable in the early 1970s. For instance, in 1973, 20 000 North African workers were employed in Greece to fill the labour shortages created by the employment of 300 000 Greek workers in W. Europe. In addition, there were 40 000 foreign workers in Italy and 100 000 in Spain, of whom about one half were illegal North African immigrants.

2 See *Financial Times*, April 6th, 1973.

3 The argument is spelt out in full in Böhning (O.E.C.D. 1973aE, pp. 44–5), though he provides no detailed evidence of how strong this effect has been in any of the host countries.

4 For instance, in Germany it was suggested that employers of foreign workers should pay a payroll tax to finance their social infrastructural investment, and in July 1973, quotas on foreign workers were introduced for the cities in which they were most heavily concentrated. Then in late November 1973, all recruitment of non-E.E.C. workers was terminated, officially because of the oil crisis (see also § 3.3.2.). Also, anti-immigration organisations began to appear in the host countries, such as the Swiss National Movement Against Undue Foreign Influence (founded in November 1972), and the Committee for the Defence of the People of Marseilles (founded at the end of August 1973).

Added to this economic source of opposition are the social problems raised by immigrants' presence. These led increasingly to demands that the inflow should be strictly controlled.[4] Use of immigrant labour had reached such a scale that the previously postponed social infra-structural investment which immigrants required could be delayed no longer without increasing social tension. Also migrant labour supplies from neighbouring countries were becoming increasingly exhausted so that it was necessary to open up new sources of supply in lands which were geographically, ethnically and culturally more distant. Accordingly in some host countries the policy of using temporarily recruited and permanent migrant labour is being or has been adjusted; new cohorts of the former are being discouraged or prohibited, some already abroad are being encouraged to return home, while others are being encouraged to settle.[1] And in Germany at least, there has been considerable discussion about the possibility of establishing plants in the recruitment countries.[2]

If all these proposed policy changes materialize and actual policy changes are sustained, they will have a major impact on all the estimates of migratory flows during the remainder of the 1970s, as these have been based on the assumption that no new institutional barriers to migration would be created.[3] Any significant reduction in the export of migrant workers would have a serious impact on those exporting countries which, like Turkey, are relying on migrant remittances to satisfy their foreign exchange requirements.[4]

1.1.3   *The rationale for the export of migrant labour from S. Europe, N. Africa, etc.*

The popular rationale for the export of migrant labour from the immigration countries (a rationale which has been given on innumerable occasions both in the literature and in policy discussions) is that this reduces the level of unemployment and makes available substantial amounts of scarce foreign exchange. The extent to which this has been true is discussed for the Turkish case in the subsequent chapters of this study. Of course, if this has been so, the reason why emigration country governments have cooperated with host country agencies in migrant selection is obvious. But what if it has not? If the host countries still require migrant labour,

1 See p. 20 footnote 1, above. In 1973, Germany considered the enforced return of Turkish workers in Germany after 5–7 years (reported in *Cumhurriyet*, May 12th, 1973, p. 7); in January 1974, the German Labour Ministry considered offering foreign workers a departure gratuity of between £165 and £230 a head (*The Times*, January 11th, 1974 and *The Guardian*, January 11th, 1974), and the Netherlands subsequently introduced one of £750 per head.

2 Information about the German-Turkish negotiations was supplied by the Turkish Employment Service in September 1972.

3 See, for example, Danieli, 1972E.

4 For instance, in the 1973 annual programme, Turkey planned to finance over $715m out of a planned trade deficit of $750m by workers' repatriated earnings (State Planning Organization 1973). At any rate, Turkish departures only started to fall off in mid-1973. From January to March 1973, 22 548 workers were officially despatched (making a cumulative total of 677 015 official departures since the system was negotiated in 1961). Repatriated earnings received during the same three months amounted to $199m. (*Milliyet*, 16th May, 1973).

the emigration country government can either try to prevent workers from leaving or try to cooperate with the host countries in an attempt to minimize their losses. Since in most of the countries under consideration any attempt to stop the outflow of migrant labour would merely generate organized illegal channels of migration,[1] as long as expected income abroad greatly exceeds that which can be obtained at home,[2] the emigration country governments are in effect forced to cooperate with the host countries so long as the latter want to employ foreign migrant labour. Non-cooperation in the export of labour only becomes a practical proposition if the country can really control the outflow of its citizens and it is politically possible to do so. The difficulties which certain emigration country governments (e.g. Yugoslavia) have faced in preventing the export of skilled migrants, and which host countries have faced in preventing illegal inflows suggest that this is unlikely. Cooperation with the host country government may at least mean that the emigration country government has some influence on the selection of migrant workers and possibly on their working conditions abroad. However, in the absence of monopsony or collusive oligopoly in the supply of migrant workers, the host countries can usually impose their terms by threatening to use alternative sources of supply, to the extent that they are able to prevent the entry of nationals from non-cooperative potential emigration countries.

Furthermore, migration abroad plays an important political function, providing as it does a sort of safety valve whereby discontented nationals can leave to seek abroad the fortune which eludes them in what they feel to be their unsatisfactory life and work situation at home. Any attempt to close this outlet can be expected to have serious political consequences.[3]

---

1 Indeed, the longer official channels of migration have been established, the more difficult it will probably be to suppress further outflows, as more information about the contacts to support migration will be available.

2 Of course, the existence of international income differentials is a completely inadequate explanation of the postwar migrant labour flows in Western Europe. The existence of such differentials merely implies that there is likely to be a demand by nationals of poorer countries for jobs in richer ones. It says nothing about the conditions under which such labour will be demanded by the richer countries nor about the political, social and cultural factors which determine from which countries migrant labour will be recruited.

3 In 1973, the Yugoslav parliament considered measures to stem the outflow of migrant labour, including exit fees or even a ban on recruitment by foreign firms or their local representatives. All migrant departures would be handled through the federal employment bureau, who would not consider anyone with a job or a job offer in Yugoslavia, a skilled worker, engineer or qualified specialist; see *The Economist*, January 27th 1973, and *Newsweek*, April 9th 1973.

1.1.4   *The magnitude of the migrant flows*[1]

There are many problems in the utilisation of the available data on migrant workers in Western Europe. First of all, different countries use different definitions of 'migrant'; some base this on length of stay, some on registration and some on residence. Only some countries record seasonal migrants or highly qualified migrants (such as doctors) separately. Indeed there is very little information about the various different types of migrant worker flow: information about those who have managed to settle permanently is normally available only from sample surveys. Furthermore official migration statistics usually underestimate the actual number of immigrants since some aspirant workers enter on tourist passports and so avoid registration as migrant entrants.[2]

The precise number of foreign migrants in Western Europe is not known. Hume (1973C) estimated that there were about 9 million such immigrants in 1971, of whom about 8 million were workers. According to Castles and Kosack (1973E) the total of immigrants into Western Europe amounted to 10.8 million, although most of the national data on which this estimate was based were for years before 1970. In January 1974, the European Commissioner for Social Affairs estimated the number of migrant workers at 11.5 million. A more detailed breakdown showing the countries of origin of foreign worker stocks in the main host countries, excluding the United Kingdom, is given in Table 1.[3] It should be noted that these data cover *all* foreign workers of the nationalities listed, irrespective of their duration of stay. The main countries of immigration are France and W. Germany;[4]

1 The problems concerned with utilising data about immigrants in France, W. Germany, Switzerland and Britain are summarised in Castles and Kosack 1973E, Appendix. Source material for the countries to which there is a significant amount of Turkish migration is given in Appendix 1 below. Some idea of the statistical problems involved is given in a mid-sixties O.E.C.D. report: 'The statistical categories used for immigrant workers or the foreign population vary considerably from one European country to the other. The timing and scope of surveys of this type of population also differ widely. In one country, a thorough census is made, four times a year, of the "controlled" foreign workers, while the number of foreigners classified as "permanently established" is only estimated, at irregular intervals, over periods which cannot be compared with the period chosen for the first category (Switzerland). In another country, the number of frontier and seasonal workers is included with that of permanent workers (German F.R.), whereas in a neighbouring country (Switzerland), they are deducted . . .' (Descloîtres 1966). The passage dealing with the statistical problems at that time is quoted in full in Rose 1968E.

2 For instance, in 1973 the German authorities estimated that in addition to 2.4 million workers and 1 million dependants resident in the Federal Republic, there were an additional 150 000 illegal worker immigrants, (*Sunday Times*, April 22nd 1973.)

3 Although the United Kingdom has not been included in this study since it does not participate in any formal system of recruited migration from Mediterranean countries, there are signs that United Kingdom employers have not failed to notice the advantages that their Western European counterparts have gained by utilising temporarily recruited labour – see, for instance, the recruitment of Filipino girls for the Lancashire textile industry. In fact, there were 56 500 immigrant workers from Southern European countries in the United Kingdom in 1968 (see Nikolinakos, 1973E, Table III-1, p. 26).

4 And the United Kingdom, which had 2.6 million immigrants according to the sample survey of 1966. However, from 1964–1969, emigration from the United Kingdom exceeded immigration to it, so that there was a net outflow of migrants (Nikolinakos 1973E Table III-3, p. 29, based on statistics from the supplement to *Migration News*, November–December, 1970).

Table 1: *Stocks of foreign workers by main host and emigration countries (1000s)*

	W. Germany	France	Austria	Switzerland	Belgium	Netherlands	Sweden
Turkey	449.7 Jan 1972; 528.2 Jan 1973	3.7 1968; 22.0 Oct 1972	22.5 Aug 1972	9.5 Dec 1971; 6.2 1969	8.5 Dec 1971; 8.0 1968	16.5 1969; 21.0 Jul 1972	2.8 Aug 1970
Yugoslavia	434.9 Jan 1972	32.1 1968; 65.2 Jan 1972	154.2 Aug 1972	17.2 1969	1.0 1968	3.4 1969; 8.8 Jul 1972	
Greece	264.4 Jan 1972	6.1 1968; 10.1 Jan 1972	0.6 Aug 1972	5.3 1969	6.5 1968	1.3 1969; 1.2 Jul 1972	
Italy	384.3 Jan 1972	247.5 1968; 590.0 Oct 1972	1.6 Aug 1972	385.9 1969	70.0 1968	10.0 1969; 10.0 Jul 1972	
Portugal	57.2 Jan 1972	171.8 1968; 600.0 Oct 1972	n.a.	n.a.	3.0 1968	12.0 1969; n.a. Jul 1972	
Spain	174.0 Jan 1972	270.4 1968; 650.0 Oct 1972	0.3 Aug 1972	89.4 1969	27.0 1968	11.8 1969; 15.0 Jul 1972	
N. Africa		333.3 1968; 1 000.0 Oct 1972					
Other	394.2 Jan 1972	195.4 1968	18.0 Aug 1972	131.9 1969	66.5 1968	25.3 1969	
Total	2 158.7 Jan 1972; 2 345.0 Jan 1973	1 260.3 1968; 3 500.0 Oct 1972	197.1 Aug 1972	635.8 1969	182.0 1968	80.3 1969; 75.0 Jul 1972	

Sources: Germany: Data supplied to Turkish Employment Service (T.E.S.) by Bundesanstalt für Arbeit, Nürnberg.
France: Institut National de la Statistique et des Etudes Economiques; Oct. 1972 estimates: *Milliyet*, 21 Ekim 1972, p.3
Jan. 1972 estimates: *The Guardian*, May 11th 1973.

Austria: Data supplies to T.E.S. by Labour Directorate in Vienna.
Switzerland: '*La vie économique*', 1970 for 1969 data; 1971 data supplied by T.E.S.
Belgium: 1968: I. Hume, *Migrant Workers in Western Europe*, I.B.R.D. Staff Working Paper No. 102, Oct. 1970; 1971 estimate: T.E.S. data
Netherlands: 1969: I. Hume, *op. cit.*; 1972 estimates: *The Times*, Nov. I. 1972, 'Made in Holland'. Workers resident for over 5 years are excluded.
Sweden: T.E.S. data.

Note: Totals may not add precisely because of rounding.
The figures give the number of foreign workers in the host countries listed, irrespective of their date of arrival.

these two countries have over three-quarters of Western Europe's foreign workers, who originated from the Mediterranean recruitment countries, followed by Switzerland, Austria, Belgium and the Netherlands. However, the nature of this immigration has varied substantially between host countries, as was described above (pp. 6–7). Switzerland has the highest proportion of foreign workers in its labour force (25%), followed by W. Germany (10%), France (8%), Belgium (7%) and the Netherlands (3%).

There are also considerable differences between the supplying countries. During the last two decades, the eight main European supplying countries of migrant workers have been Italy, Spain, Portugal, Greece, Yugoslavia, Turkey, Ireland and Finland,[1] to which should be added the three North African countries of Algeria, Tunisia and Morocco. Italy, Spain, Portugal and Greece were early starters; but Yugoslavia, Turkey and the North African countries soon caught up in terms of the despatch of new entrants. The rising share of Turkey and Yugoslavia in new migration can be seen clearly in Table 2, though the early starting countries are still very important in stock terms (Table 1).

However, despite all these differences between host and between exporting countries, utilization of migrant labour come increasingly to be regarded as a 'European problem'. During 1970–3 four countries – Germany, France, Switzerland and the Netherlands – made statements to the effect that the current proportion of migrant workers in the labour force should be regarded as a maximum,[2] and by the end of 1973 all had restricted or banned new recruitment of workers from non-E.E.C. countries, (or in the case of Switzerland, from all foreign countries). It remains to be seen whether this was just a temporary expedient or a permanent change of strategy.

1.2 The Turkish background to labour migration

1.2.1 *The Turkish economy*

According to the national population census of October 1970, Turkey had a population of 35.7 million, which made it the sixth largest country in Europe and the seventh largest in Asia.[3] However, since per capita GNP was only about $350 in 1969 and $360 in 1970, this means that Turkey has the lowest p.c. GNP in Europe though she is comparatively well-off by Asian standards where, for instance, India, Pakistan and Afghanistan[4] all had a p.c. GNP of $110 or below in 1969, while only

---

1 Since Irish migration was to the United Kingdom and Finnish was to Sweden, they are not discussed further in this paper.

2 See above, p. 20, footnote 1.

3 According to the World Bank Population Atlas, in mid-1969 Turkey had the seventeenth largest population in the world (*Finance and Development*, No. 1, 1972). Turkey's population in 1973 is estimated at 38.3m. (State Planning Organization 1973).

4 The World Bank estimated Chinese per capita GNP in 1970 at $160 (*Finance and Development*, Vol. 10, No. 1, March 1973), though this gives a misleading picture because it understates the purchasing power of the yuan.

Table 2: *Intra-European flows of migrants by country of emigration and year (1000s)*

		Turkey			Countries of emigration				
		T.E.S. des-patch	Total departures (1)	(2)	Port-ugal	Spain	Italy	Yugo-slavia	Greece
1960	W	–	–	–		30.5			
	T				3.8		309.9	5.7	27.0
1961	W	1.5	7.1	7.1		43.0			
	T				6.0		329.6	13.0	41.5
1962	W	11.2	16.0	15.5		64.8			
	T				9.2		315.8	33.2	62.1
1963	W	30.3	35.3	36.1		83.7			
	T				17.1		235.1	27.7	75.6
1964	W	66.1	75.9	76.6		102.0		11.8	
	T				38.4		216.5	27.7	80.2
1965	W	51.5	67.4	67.6		74.5		35.9	
	T				71.5		232.4	48.9	88.1
1966	W	34.4	46.5	45.9		56.8		55.0	
	T				87.0		219.4	78.9	53.8
1967	W	8.5	17.0	17.5		25.9		28.6	
	T				63.9		164.0	32.5	16.4
1968	W	43.1	67.3	64.9		66.7		70.3	
	T				53.4		158.4	109.9	25.0
1969	W	102.9	128.9	127.4		80.0*			
	T				41.6		176.3	243.5	63.1
1970	W	127.5	153.9	185.2	n.a.	n.a.	n.a.	n.a.	n.a.
	T								
1971	W	86.3	137.9	147.3	n.a.	n.a.	n.a.	n.a.	n.a.
	T								
1972	W	85.2	n.a.	n.a.	n.a.	n.a.	n.a.	n.a.	n.a.
Turkish Total (W) 1961–71		605.8	753.2	791.1					

Notes: 1. Unofficial departures are estimated on the assumption that 9 out of 10 unofficial departures go to Germany.
2. Unofficial departures are estimated on the assumption that the proportion of unofficial departures going to Germany is the same as that of official ones.
* Provisional.   W Workers.   T Total migrants (including dependants).

Sources: Turkey: Turkish Employment Service, *Annual Labour Reports*, 1962–71, Ankara, 1963–72; 1972 data supplied by T.E.S.
Portugal, Spain, Italy, Greece: M. Livi-Bacci & H.M. Hagmann, *Report on the demographic & social pattern of migrants in Europe, especially with regard to international migrations*, 2nd European Population Conference, Strasbourg, 31 August–7 September 1971.
Yugoslavia: Workers 1964–8: *O.E.C.D. Kayser Report*, Paris, February 1972.
Total: Livi-Bacci & Hagmann, *op. cit.*

a few rather exceptional countries had a per capita GNP above the Turkish level.[1] Such per capita GNP comparisons calculated using par value exchange rates should obviously be treated with extreme caution but do give a rough idea of Turkey's situation vis-à-vis other countries in Europe and S. Asia.[2]

1 Such as Japan, Saudi Arabia, Hong Kong, Singapore, Israel, Iran (just) and various oil sheikhdoms.

2 Turkey's rank in fact tends to fall when the purchasing power of currencies is taken into account (see Maddison 1970, Table A11).

The modern Republic of Turkey emerged in 1923 as a one-party state under the rule of Mustafa Kemal Ataturk. He embarked on an extensive programme of reforms, aiming to transform Turkey from a poor economy, weakened by half a century of foreign control and smashed by a decade of war, into a prosperous, western-orientated and secular state. Initially the government tried to foster economic growth by introducing incentives for private enterprise, but when the failure of this policy was compounded by the effects of the Great Depression, a new type of strategy based on direct government intervention (*devletçilik*) was introduced. At the time this was seen by some intellectuals as a middle way between socialism and capitalism: the state was the pioneer and director of industrial activity in a country where private enterprises and capital were too weak to do anything effective.[1] In fact, however, the government saw this policy as a prerequisite for the ultimate success of a capitalist development strategy. A national plan of sorts was introduced and the first fully-fledged state economic enterprises were formed, with the task of mobilising resources for and controlling production of various branches of economic activity (particularly industry and mining).

This policy of *devletçilik* has more or less survived Turkey's post-war transition to a multi-party state,[2] a decade of anti-Kemalist policies under Menderes,[3] and a decade of so-called planned development since 1963. State economic enterprises produce about half the industrial output and operate with varying importance in most of the main sectors of economic activity, including public utilities (e.g. railways) and various financial institutions such as social security organisations and banks, (Torun 1969).

1.2.2 Planned development 1963–73[4]

Planned development was started again in Turkey as a result of the 1960 military coup. Before they returned power to the civil authorities (which in fact turned out to be a coalition government under İnönü) the generals made sure that national planning was written into the new constitution. The first five year development plan was drawn up and its implementation begun in 1963.

1 For a useful study on the emergence and growth of capitalist economic development in Turkey, see Şnurov and Rozaliyev, 1972.

2 In 1946 İnönü, who succeeded Ataturk as President on the latter's death in 1938, legalized a new party to oppose the ruling Republican (Halk) Party. This new (Democrat) party won the election in 1950 and set up a new government under Menderes, based on the support of the newly emergent entrepreneurial class and on the rural peasantry.

3 The Menderes régime revoked many of Ataturk's social reforms and abandoned many state controls so as to open the economy more to the free market. But the failure to coordinate different economic policies had disastrous effects, and in most respects the Menderes decade provides a classic example of economic mismanagement. By 1958 rampant inflation and a huge balance of payments deficit brought things to a halt, and forced devaluation plus a stabilization programme. But to counter the criticism against them, the Democrats had increasingly resorted to unconstitutional tactics to silence or eliminate the opposition. This led directly to the revolution of 1960 when the army seized power.

4 The first part of this section is based on Paine 1972.

At that time Turkey was a predominantly agricultural country.[1] Agriculture produced about 41% of national income and over 80% of exports, and it employed about 77% of the civilian active population. The main agricultural exports were cotton, tobacco, dried fruit and hazelnuts. Industry produced about 17% of national income and employed about 10% of the active population. Industrial production was concentrated mainly in textiles and food, although there was a national iron and steel industry. Despite the low level of industrialisation, imports consisted primarily of machinery and raw materials.[2] But as imports were rising while exports were stagnant, Turkey was faced with a growing current account deficit.[3] Furthermore, savings amounted to only 12.2% of GNP in 1963. Regional income inequalities were severe, with most industry concentrated around Istanbul, Ankara or Izmir (Tekeli 1967). Similarly personal incomes were very unequally distributed (Griffin and Enos 1970, pp. 204—9).

The First Five Year Plan aimed to transform this rather depressing picture. But although it was reasonably successful insofar as the planned overall growth rate of 7% was almost achieved, it basically failed to reach most of the sectoral targets — the most significant deviations being underfulfillment in agriculture and overfulfillment in services.[4] But since growth in service sector output chiefly reflects the increase in people reporting service sector employment, this was more of a statistical myth than a real achievement. The overall investment target was almost reached because above-target private investment compensated for the public shortfall, but the qualitative transfer of resources to the productive sectors was not. Private investment was still channelled into building, light industry and services.[5]

The First Plan trade balance and current account targets were achieved but (1) the planned shift towards manufactured exports was not (these actually fell *absolutely* in 1965, 1966 and 1967),[6] and (2) only 76% of the planned external aid was forthcoming, a situation which would have caused serious difficulties had it not been for fortuitous receipt of repatriated earnings from Turkish workers abroad. Three quarters of the aid shortfall was made up by remittances, though in July 1964 a 27% premium on the official exchange rate had to be introduced to attract these. Here was clear indication of troubles to come: at the beginning of the Second Plan, Turkey failed completely to effect the essential target growth in manufactured exports, aid forthcoming fell way below target but repatriated earnings could not be used to rescue the country from foreign exchange difficulties as substantial receipts from these were already required by this Plan.

1 State Planning Organization 1963 and O.E.C.D. 1963.

2 The share of machinery and raw materials in total imports amounted to 44% each, while consumer goods amounted to only 12%.

3 In 1961 the trade deficit amounted to $163m, and in 1962 to $235m.

4 For a more detailed assessment of this plan, see Paine 1972. From 1962/3—1967/8, the average annual growth rate for agriculture was 3.3% instead of the target 4.2%, and for services 8.4% instead of 6.2%.

5 From 1963—7, only 8% rather than the planned 25% of private manufacturing investment went into machinery industries (O.E.C.D. 1967).

6 The share of agricultural exports rose from 88% in 1963 to 89% in 1967, while that of manufactures fell from 8% to 4%, their value falling absolutely in 1965, 1966 and 1967.

Again, superficially Turkey seemed to have been reasonably successful in maintaining price stability during the First Plan, during which the average annual increases in the various wholesale and consumer price indices were all in the order of 5%. However, nothing had been done to stem any of the basic sources of inflation: for instance, the Demirel government continued to run huge budget deficits to finance the investment plans of state economic enterprises, and to secure its rural political base by periodically increasing cereal support prices, although this had a direct impact on industrial wages owing to the cost of living element in most union agreements. Not surprisingly therefore price increases began to accelerate in mid-1968 and increased still further after the 1970 devaluation.

The fate of other Plan targets ranges from disappointing to positively bad. The unemployment situation deteriorated over the Plan period. Regional development policy consisted only of a few incentives, completely inadequate to bring about the required result. Even after a conservative government abolished most of the planners' tax reforms, it still failed to collect the extremely moderate planned revenues. Actual tax revenues fell below targets by an annual average of 17%: by 1966 revenues amounted to only 24% instead of 27% of GNP. The State Economic Enterprises failed to raise substantially the own-financed proportion of their investment programmes — a serious problem given the government's budgetary failure. An unduly modest birth control programme was introduced in 1965 (given a population growth rate of about 2.7%) and then insufficient resources were allocated to permit it to achieve even the moderate target. Nothing whatsoever was done about the planned land reform (until a modified bill was passed by the Turkish parliament in June 1973). And the distribution of income actually became more unequal during the plan period.[1] Thus the optimistic picture of plan success which is given from looking at growth rate realization turns out to be completely misleading when the fate of the other targets is taken into consideration.

The Second Five Year Development Plan for the years 1968–72 was basically a grander and more ambitious version of the First. Both the target overall and target sectoral growth rates were very similar to those of the First Plan (but not, as we shall see, to those actually realized). The share of investment in GNP was to be raised to 24% (from 18% in 1967) by the end of the plan period (1972). Substantial foreign aid was required to finance the import substitution programme.

However, the problems which had become apparent during the First Plan period became more serious: notably, the trade deficit continued to widen and the rate of inflation to increase. Donors became increasingly reluctant to produce promised foreign aid and so the consequent check on the progress of the development programme in addition to the deteriorating economic situation forced the government to devalue the lira and to inaugurate a much more export-orientated planning strategy.[2] These events had a sharp impact on the growth rate of industrial output, which fell from 10.0% in 1968 and 9.4% in 1969 to 2.5% in 1970, the year of the devaluation. Although it improved, reaching 8.7% in 1971, and 10.7% in 1972, it

1 See the data reported in Griffin and Enos 1970, and in Kryzaniak and Özmucur 1972.

2 During the 1960s Turkey had operated a multiple exchange rate system. In August 1970 it had to devalue its 'official' rate from T.L.9 to T.L.15 to the $ and to liberalize controls over foreign trade.

still fell below the target of an annual average increase of 12%. This comparative failure to achieve the industrial targets of the plan tends to be obscured when GNP growth only is considered, for during the Second Plan, as during the First, this was strongly influenced by overfulfillment in the service sector. In addition Turkey was fortunate enough to enjoy a bumper harvest in 1971 (when output increased by 10% as against the planned 4%) and another good one in 1972. Thus the average annual growth rate of GNP over the Second Plan equalled the target of 7%, as compared with 6.5% if 1971 is excluded. But the annual average industrial growth rate was only 8.3% as compared with a target of 12%. And, as one would expect, this was associated with a substantial shortfall in the extent of industrial employment creation (§1.2.3).

Many of the problems which had arisen during the First Plan were repeated. Planned public sector investment was slowed down, in some cases because of delays in project preparation or in availability of external finance, in some cases (particularly during the devaluation year) because of budget difficulties – though one favourable consequence of post-devaluation tax reforms was that revenue in 1971 was virtually on target. Private sector investment continued to exceed its target (except during the 1970 recession) but this was again channelled predominantly into housing and light industry. The rate of inflation continued to rise until stabilisation measures succeeded in reducing it from 17% in 1971 to about 8% in 1972. The deficit on commodity trade continued to widen substantially though this was chiefly because imports continued to exceed their targets – exports exceeded plan targets in both 1971 and 1972, and furthermore, the share of manufactures in the total rose from 5% in 1968 to 14% in 1971. However, the current account deficit on the balance of payments has improved annually owing to sharply rising receipts of workers' remittances from $107m in 1968 to about $740m in 1972. Increasingly Turkey has been using workers' repatriated earnings instead of foreign aid to finance her current account deficits, and proposed to continue this policy throughout the Third Five Year Plan.[1]

The Third Five Year Development Plan for 1973–1977 was even more ambitious than the Second, aspiring to an average annual GNP growth rate of 7.9%. Per capita GNP was planned to rise from T.L. 4901 (£144) to T.L. 6640 (£192). New investment in the public sector was to be confined mainly to more risky or 'large' ventures, particularly in the intermediate and capital goods industries, and to projects in the least developed regions. Nonetheless, planned public sector investment amounted to 56% of the planned total. Within manufacturing, production of investment goods was planned to rise by 16–17% over the plan period, of intermediate goods by 14–15%, and of consumer goods by 6.5–7.5%. But as in previous plans, the main contribution to output growth was to come from services, with planned growth of 52% over 5 years, as compared with 36% from industry and 12% from agriculture. Foreign exchange shortages were not expected since it was assumed that the current high level of remittances would persist, and since three-quarters of the required foreign aid credits were already in the pipe-line.

The achievements of the economy during the first year of the plan (1973) were again patchy. Whereas industrial output grew at an estimated 15.2%, agricultural

1 See, for instance, p. 23 above.

output fell by 8.2% compared with 1972 (which was a good year as concerns the weather). Manufactured exports doubled, but the rate of inflation continued to rise — for instance, the wholesale price index rose by about 25%, repatriated earnings reached a record level of around $1200 and this strengthened the reserve situation. But hardly any of the basic problems which manifested themselves during the first two plans were actually tackled.

This development plan was part of a longer-term strategy designed to prepare Turkey for full membership of the E.E.C. in 1995. For although Turkey has trading connections with Iran and Pakistan through the R.C.D. (Organisation for Regional Co-operation and Development), and with neighbouring Arab countries, the old E.E.C. countries are her main trading partners,[1] followed by the U.S.A. and the former E.F.T.A. countries. Prospective membership of the E.E.C. has a dominant influence on all Turkish economic planning. The original Association Agreement came into force in December 1964; an Additional Protocol concerning the transitional phase was signed in 1970 — of this, the commercial provisions were implemented in 1971. Turkish tariff barriers to E.E.C. imports are to be abolished in two phases — most non-manufactures by 1985 and most manufactures by 1995, when Turkey will also be expected to apply the Common External Tariff in full. By this time, the Turkish planners hope that the structure of the Turkish economy will have reached the stage which Italy occupies today.

1.2.3   *The Turkish labour market*

According to the Third Five Year Development Plan the Turkish economically active population (e.a.p.) in 1972 amounted to 15 512 000 of which 13 262 000 were employed in Turkey, 650 000 were employed abroad, and 1 600 000 were unemployed,[2] (Table 3). The e.a.p. has been growing at around 4% per annum which has meant about 400 000 new job seekers every year.

Agriculture still has the dominant though declining share of employment — about 77% in 1962, 73% in 1965 and 65% in 1972 (Table 3). Employment in industry and construction has expanded steadily during the 1960s but at a rate well below both plan targets and the rate necessary to absorb the growth of the e.a.p. For example, in the First Plan it was envisaged that industrial employment would expand by 7%, total non-agricultural (industry, construction and services) employment by 8%, and total employment by 3% annually. However, the realised figures were 3% for industrial, 5% for total non-agricultural, and 2% for total employment — this last figure being about half the annual growth rate of the e.a.p., so that unemployment increased substantially. The actual increase in employment amounted to only 58% of the target of 1 215 000.[3]

During the Second Plan yearly industrial employment was planned to increase annually by 9%, total non-agricultural employment by 7% and total employment

1 In 1970, 40% of Turkish exports went to and 34% of imports originated from E.E.C. countries, in 1971, the percentages were both 39%, and in 1972, they were 39% and 42% respectively. Nearly half of this trade was with W. Germany (Table 19).

2 The evidence on unemployment in Turkey is reviewed on p. 35 below.

3 State Planning Organization, 1967, and Yalçintas 1971.

Table 3: *Employment and unemployment in Turkey 1962–77*

	1962 No. (1000)	1962 %Dom. civil employt.	1967 No. (1000)	1967 % Dom. civil employt.	1971 No. (1000)	1971 % Dom. civil employt.	1972[3] No. (1000)	1972[3] % Dom. civil employt.	1967 Index 1962=100	1972 Index 1967=100	Mean annual increase 1963–1967	Mean annual increase 1st Plan 2nd Plan 1968–1973	1977 No. (1000)	1977 % Dom. civil employt.
Agriculture	9 216	77	9 073	71	8 763	66	8 763	65					8 600	58
Industry	995	8	1 175	9	1 450	11	1 519	11	118	129	3.4	5.3	2 102	14
Construction	305	3	369	3	419	3	433	3	121	117	3.9	3.2	682	5
Trade	328	3	395	3	581	4	605	5	120	153	3.8	8.9	726	5
Communications	258	2	325	3	424	3	450	3	126	139	4.7	6.7	615	4
Services	768	6	1 058	8	1 490	11	1 579	12	138	149	6.6	8.3	2 072	14
Unknown	81	1	338	3	133	1	133	1					133	1
Total non-agricultural employment	2 654	22	3 322	26	4 364	33	4 586	34	125	138	4.6	6.6	6 197	42
Total domestic employment	11 951	100	12 733	100	13 260	100	13 482	100					14 930	100
Employment abroad	–		204		570		650						50[1]	
Total employment (excl. military)	11 951		12 937		13 830		14 132						14 980	
(i) Manpower in 15–64 age group	15 967		17 919		19 948		20 350						23 371	
(ii) Economically active population[4]	12 755		13 798		14 576		14 862						16 080[2]	
(iii) Total employed (civil & military)[4]	12 520		13 268		13 875		14 112						14 980[2]	
(iv) Non-agricultural unemployment	235		530		701		750						1 100	
(v) Agricultural unemployment in peak season	750		910		860		850						700	
(vi) Total unemployment	985		1 440		1 561		1 600						1 800	
(i) Manpower in 15–64 age group index	100		112		125		128						146	
(ii) E.a.p. index	100		108		114		117						126[2]	
(iii) Employment index	100		106		111		113						120[2]	
(iv) Non-agricultural unemployment index	100		226		298		319						468	
(v) Total unemployment index	100		146		159		162						183	

Source: Republic of Turkey, State Planning Organization, *Yeni strateji ve kalkınma planı, üçüncü beş yıl 1973–1977*, Ankara 1973, Tables 508, 510, 511, 512, 515, 516, 517, 518, 519.

1. Includes workers sent abroad in 1977 only.
2. Excluding military.
3. 1972 programme.
4. Excluding employment abroad.

Note: The 1977 estimates were made before the ban on recruitment of non-E.E.C. labour in the main European host countries for Turkish migrant workers.

34

by 3%. Thus even if this had been achieved, unemployment would still have increased because of the higher growth rate of the e.a.p. But it was not. Over the period 1968–72 industrial employment increased by an annual average of 5% and employment in construction by 3% p.a. As during the First Plan, the situation was nominally saved by substantial overfulfillment of the planned increase in service sector employment: employment in distribution grew by an annual average of 9%, in transport and communications by 7% and in other services by 8%. This raises again the question of the extent to which growth in the service sector labour force represents a real expansion of job opportunities or just growth in the numbers awaiting modern sector jobs. In the absence of any detailed information about the precise content of these 'new' jobs, it is impossible to estimate any precise division between these two categories; however, the particularly large expansion in the retail and distributive trades (plus casual observation while travelling) suggest that the proportion 'waiting' is by no means small.

The deviation between actual and planned employment during the Second Five Year Plan can largely be attributed to the mistaken basis of the original estimates – insufficient attention was paid to the importance of labour productivity increases in off-setting employment increases when output rises. A similar sort of mistake had been made when calculating the employment estimates of the First Plan, for there employment was treated simply as a linear function of output without any allowance at all for productivity increases.

However, various other factors have contributed to the lower growth of employment opportunities. Firstly agricultural mechanization tended to reduce labour requirements and to displace the rural proletariat. Secondly, certain policies seem to have led to attempts to substitute capital for labour. These include all those which tended to cheapen the relative price of capital (e.g. maintaining an overvalued exchange rate to keep down the price of capital imports, subsidizing loans used to purchase machinery, etc.) together with all those policies which tended to raise wages (such as increasing prices – e.g. foodstuffs, public utilities, etc. – which directly raise the cost of living, and so all wage rates which have a cost of living element in their determination (i.e. most union-negotiated wage agreements). In addition, the prospect of losing newly trained skilled workers to foreign firms seems to have made firms more reluctant to train them, and to have encouraged use of techniques less sensitive to skilled labour loss (see ch. 4).

Not surprisingly therefore, the domestic employment situation seems depressing. Indeed in 1973, the *official* planned unemployment rate was 11.2%, of whom almost half were in the non-agricultural labour force.[1] Yet this implied an extremely optimistic interpretation of the agricultural employment situation, where there are very large seasonal fluctuations. For instance, an S.P.O. survey in 1967 estimated rural seasonal unemployment at 77% and 9% for December and July respectively, a much more careful estimate by Hamurdan (1971) put as conservative estimates the peak period surplus at 13% and the slack period at 61% in 1967. Yet the 11.2% estimate quoted above was based on an estimate for agricultural unemployment not exceeding 10%. When a more realistic picture of agricultural employment was taken into account, the situation indeed looked bleak. In the light of this, it is not

1 See *Milliyet,* February 23rd, 1973.

surprising that certain Turkish planners saw migration as the only solution (e.g. Alpat 1970 and Yaşer 1972).

1.3   Summary

During the postwar years a more or less organized system of recruitment of labour from Mediterranean countries for temporary employment in W. Europe emerged. The main host countries for migrant workers have been France, W. Germany, Switzerland, and the Netherlands, and the main countries of emigration have been Italy, Spain, Portugal, Greece, Yugoslavia, Turkey, Algeria and Tunisia. The administration of the system has varied considerably between host countries, with countries like the Netherlands and W. Germany being particularly strict about the admission of dependants. However, overall the host countries' access to reserve supplies of labour seems to have had both a counter-inflationary effect and a positive impact on the rate of economic growth, (pp. 12—23). But governments' collective failure to undertake the social infrastructural investment requirements of their immigration policies led to increasing social tension. Although for economic reasons employers wished to retain uncontrolled acess to supplies of cheap labour, for political and social reasons governments began to turn away from their immigration policies. Most of the main host countries' governments had introduced strong controls on new migration from the Mediterranean countries before some introduced a total ban because of the energy crisis at the end of 1973.

Turkey was a late starter among the emigration countries. Her emergence as a significant exporter of labour coincided with the beginning of a new attempt at planned development in 1963. At that time, Turkey was a predominantly agricultural country, with agriculture producing about 41% of national income and over 80% of exports, and employing over three-quarters of the civilian active population which then amounted to almost 12 million. Although the first two five year development plans were reasonably successful in achieving their aggregate targets (in particular, an average annual growth rate of 7%), they were less successful in bringing about basic structural transformation in the economy, or in spreading the gains from development to those most in need (pp. 29—33). Furthermore, the near achievement of the planned G.N.P. growth rate covered up important failures both at the sectoral level and in the achievement of subsidiary objectives such as price stability and improvement in the employment situation. The latter has steadily deteriorated — the *official* total unemployment index rose from 100 in 1962 to 162 in 1972, and the non-agricultural unemployment index from 100 to 319 during the same period (Table 3); in 1973, the official total unemployment estimate approached two million, out of an e.a.p. of nearly 16 million (including military employment and employment abroad). In the face of this, exporting workers on a temporarily recruited basis became an increasingly attractive policy to the government, especially when it discovered the inflow of savings and remittances to which labour export led. The outflow of migrant workers was primarily determined by host country demand and so was subject to large fluctuations (3.2.3 below). But despite the high risk attached to the adoption of a mass labour export policy, the achievement of Turkey's development plans was made increasingly dependant on labour export.

36

2
The impact of exporting labour on the country of emigration

2.1   Introduction

The aim of this chapter is to analyse the effects on a less developed country's (L.D.C.'s) economy if its government decided to go ahead with a policy of labour export on a temporarily recruited basis. Such a policy is of course only feasible if there are suitable host countries to admit the labour inflow. The type of L.D.C.s to which the following analysis applies are those mixed economy L.D.C.s which (i) have manpower resources which are not being fully utilized (i.e. there is unemployment and underemployment), and which (ii) face a foreign exchange constraint, in the sense that the foreign exchange required to sustain some minimum target growth rate exceeds the supply. The framework outlined in this chapter is then used in chapter 4 to examine the actual effects of labour export on the Turkish economy.

Various types of models have been proposed to analyse the impact of emigration on an economy. These have, however, tended to concentrate on the cases of 'permanent' flows (e.g. from Britain to the former colonies and the U.S.A.) and on seasonal flows (e.g. in much of Africa today). Neither of these is appropriate for analysing the impact of labour emigration on a temporarily recruited basis from a less developed country. The former is unsuitable because a large number of temporarily recruited migrant workers eventually return to their home country,[1] the latter, because temporarily recruited migrants normally have to give up all the economic activities carried on before departure (rather than just taking on an additional job during the slack season).[2] Rather, a combination of elements from both these types of analysis is required, adjusted where necessary to take account of the fact that the type of migration under consideration is largely recruited not spontaneous.[3]

However, much of the literature on the impact of exporting labour on a

1 Thus not only are analyses such as Thomas' examination of emigration from the U.K. to the U.S. (1840–1940) unsuitable (Thomas 1954), but also those concerned with emigration from L.D.C.s but which assume that the outflow is predominantly permanent (e.g. Freidlander 1965).

2 For a useful analysis of seasonal labour migration, see Berg 1965.

3 There is a close analogy between the use of temporarily recruited labour in Western Europe and that of black labour in the South African gold mines. However, the latter is recruited on an annual basis, after which workers must return to their home village, though subsequent periods of one year employment are possible. But since there is no possibility of settling permanently with the family and since the rural base of the migrant worker plays an important role, the system is more like one of seasonally recruited migration (Wilson 1972).

temporarily recruited basis treats the subject from a partial equilibrium point of view: with emigration, unemployment is what it would have been without emigration minus the number of emigrants;[1] with emigration, foreign exchange reserves are what they would have been without emigration plus the total of remittances received. This sort of approach may not lead to serious errors when the ratio of emigrants to the economically active population is very small, but as this ratio rises, it becomes increasingly important to assess how emigration affects economic indicators which were treated as parameters on the partial equilibrium approach. Ignoring for instance the feedback effects of the receipts of repatriated earnings on, say, the propensity to import, or that of the loss of skilled workers on the extent to which workers are trained and so on the types of techniques utilized, can no longer be excused.

For this reason Kindleberger's analysis cannot be regarded as adequate.[2] He analyses the impact of emigration on a number of variables — production forgone, consumption forgone, remittances, loss of skilled labour, gain in training, and the impact of rising wages on industrial investment. The main limitations of his analysis are that his list of effects is not long enough, and that the number of interactions considered are too few. In particular, he fails to consider both the distributional effects of emigration and the implications of dependence on repatriated earnings. Furthermore, much of his analysis is in certain respects inapplicable to the Turkish case since he normally assumes that migrants are the agricultural under- or unemployed rather than skilled industrial workers.

The following analysis begins by building on Kindleberger's approach in an attempt to produce a more complete analysis of the impact of exporting labour on a temporarily recruited basis on an L.D.C.'s economy. Rather than constructing a model which would inevitably be based on assumptions which ignore important features of reality, given the complex socio-economic determinants of emigration and its impact, the method used here has been to examine the impact of the migration system on numerous variables in the economy, to identify the most favourable and unfavourable effects on these variables, assuming that the country can maintain its labour outflow at a level such that the stock of workers abroad does not fall, and then to introduce the implications of recession in the host country. Next we consider two countries, A and B, which are identical in all respects at time t, after which B starts to export labour. An attempt can then be made to discover in what ways the values of the economic variables in country B differ from those in A after the migration system has been underway for some years.

The approach described so far is concerned only with the effects of labour export on economic variables such as growth, employment and the balance of payments, abstracting from all the human considerations which should be taken into account when evaluating a policy of this sort. Since this is the way in which flows of intra-European migrants seem to have been regarded both by most

1 See for instance Sengölge 1969A, Yaşer 1972A, Redding 1967C and Alpat 1970A.

2 Kindleberger 1967E, Ch. 8, and 1965E.

38

emigration and most host country governments,[1] this procedure enables the construction of a framework in which to assess whether labour export has brought about the results which the emigration country government hoped to achieve. Subsequently, however, an attempt is made to assess the actual socio-economic effects of migration on both the migrants and various groups of the Turkish population.[2]

2.2.   The effects on an L.D.C.'s economy caused by the introduction of a labour export system

2.2.1   *Population and labour force*

The size of the economically active population will obviously fall as a result of emigration, though this may be partly offset if emigration causes previously inactive persons (notably women) to seek work. This may be because they become the bread-winners during their spouses' absence, or because contact with western attitudes towards women's employment results in increased women's participation rates[3]. On the other hand, the labour force will fall if previously active wives give up work to live on remittances. However since most emigrants are in the prime of their working life, i.e. between the ages of 18 and 45, large scale emigration leads to a significant deterioration in the age structure of the labour force.

The rate of population growth may tend to fall if migrant workers leave their wives at home, or may show little change, because separated spouses make frequent visits home, or because migrants with their families abroad have more children (say because of reduced infant mortality) and when they return, this offsets any lower rate at home.

The rate of urbanization will tend to fall (i) if people who would have migrated to the towns go instead to work abroad, and if at least some of these do not settle in urban areas on their return; (ii) if expenditure from repatriated earnings creates new demand for labour in rural areas. On the other hand, the rate of urbanization will tend to rise (i) if people who would otherwise not have left their home villages move to the cities to use them as staging posts for migration abroad, (ii) if expenditure from repatriated earnings creates new demand for labour in urban areas; and (iii) if rural workers become more likely to settle in towns after they have worked abroad.

---

1 Neither tends to regard the migrants primarily as people. Host country governments and employers seem to look at them in terms of manhours imported; emigration country governments to look at them as a passport to foreign exchange which can be used to raise the growth rate.

2 Indeed looking at the effects of migration on economic indicators alone can lead to misleading conclusions, as Grubel and Scott (1966) have pointed out. For if a nation's per capita income falls because individuals with above-average income migrate this does not imply that those who remain are any worse off.

3 Since in Turkish rural areas most women work in agriculture, this possible effect would mainly be confined to women from urban areas.

39

2.2.2 *The agricultural sector*

The volume of agricultural output may rise or fall depending on (i) what organisational arrangements are made to compensate for any losses caused by departing migrants, (ii) what changes emigration causes in the terms of trade between agriculture and industry, and what supply responses peasants make to such relative price changes,[1] and (iii) the extent to which migrants bring back and utilize new skills and machines which raise productivity.

The effect of the resulting changes in the volume of output on the level of agricultural income depends on the prevailing price and income elasticities of demand. In addition, emigration will have a positive effect on the level of per capita money incomes because of receipt of savings and remittances. However, this may be offset by increases in industrial commodity prices if demand created by expenditure from repatriated earnings causes inflation in the industrial sector.[2] Also if the country finds it necessary to devalue in order to keep up the supply of repatriated earnings (see below) then if the price elasticity of demand for primary commodity exports is low, devaluation would tend to have a depressing effect on agricultural incomes.

Agricultural employment will fall[3] if (i) departing migrants are not replaced and do not subsequently return to rural areas, (ii) new demand for industrial goods created by expenditure from migrants' repatriated earnings leads to additional migration to urban areas, and (iii) new agricultural techniques introduced by returned workers displace labour. Although increases in the level of real income could help to offset the declining proportion of the labour force employed in agriculture, whether this will happen depends on distributional factors, (who get the increased incomes) and the system of land tenure. For instance if it is landlords' income that rises, then they might mechanize and reduce the size of their labour force, thus increasing the size of the unemployed agricultural proletariat. On the other hand, if the income of poor peasants rises, then they may be able to buy sufficient land to make an adequate living for themselves and their offspring, instead of perhaps being forced to try their luck in the towns. (See also § 2.4 below).

---

1 The various changes in output and employment which may accompany migration, if this leads to a money wage increase in the urban sector, are systematically analysed in Knight 1971. In his model, if migration raises the urban money wage, in a protected L.D.C. this leads to a rise in modern sector prices relative to agricultural prices, and so to a redistribution of income from the traditional to the modern sector, unless this is offset by a net increase in agricultural incomes caused by a sufficiently large rise in agricultural prices if the income elasticity of urban demand is high, but the price elasticities of supply and demand are low.

2 Inflation would tend to hit agricultural landlords least because they would be able to offset price increases by raising rents or by reducing the wage bill if they use hired labour. (Agricultural labourers are unlikely to be sufficiently organized to fight wage cuts). Thus poor and middle peasants may have their real incomes cut not just because of inflation in industrial commodity prices but also because of the policies pursued by landlords in reaction to this inflation.

3 Since the proportion of the population and of the labour force in agriculture is declining annually, it is extremely unlikely that agricultural employment would rise substantially, although the introduction of certain sorts of new techniques might lead to an increase in the number of man-hours worked.

2.2.3. *The industrial sector*

Industrial output may rise or fall depending on (i) what arrangements are made to compensate for any losses caused by departing migrants, e.g. whether substitute workers can be hired or whether new labour saving techniques are used, (ii) the extent to which expenditure from repatriated earnings creates demand for industrial goods which can be supplied by the domestic economy, (iii) the extent to which migrants bring back and utilize new skills and machines which raise productivity.

The net impact of migration on industrial employment depends on (i) the decrease caused by failure to fill the jobs of departing workers, (ii) the decrease which would arise if employers reacted to the loss of skilled workers who migrate by training fewer of them and shifting towards techniques which are skilled labour saving,[1] (iii) the increase resulting from an increase in operations caused by higher demand for industrial products because of expenditure from repatriated earnings (once all spare capacity has been utilised), and (iv) the increase caused by the establishment of new industrial enterprises by returned workers.

The effect of emigration on the industrial money wage depends on (i) the extent to which it generates demand for replacement and additional labour, and the extent to which this can easily be satisfied, and (ii) the extent to which the influence of returned workers raises unionization rates and encourages greater trade union demands over pay and conditions, etc.

However, the net effect of migration on the industrial real wage will depend on the amount and direction of the price changes which occur (a) because of migration abroad from rural areas (b) because of increased demand from expenditure out of repatriated earnings on industrial wage goods (c) because of increased demand from abroad for industrial commodities and the increased price of imported wage goods (or components thereof) if a devaluation becomes necessary to maintain the inflow of repatriated earnings.

2.2.4. *The service sector*

Service sector output will (i) fall in the unlikely event that migrants leaving this sector cannot be replaced, and (ii) rise to the extent that returned workers who move into this sector supply a net increment to existing services (rather than just replacing them by more modern methods). If such new entrants have a 'deepening' effect by adding to the value of output, then this will raise, not just redistribute, service sector incomes.

Service sector employment[2] will rise if (i) rural workers who hope to work abroad and who move to the city as a preliminary step cannot find industrial employment and so are forced to take up some service sector activity (e.g. working as a shoe-shine boy or a tea boy), (ii) returned migrants choose to set themselves up in

---

1 Although these may be either more capital intensive or more unskilled labour intensive, the former is more likely in LDCs like Turkey where during the 1960s an overvalued exchange rate was combined with a low interest rate policy.

2 Service sector employment is here regarded as a residual category whose membership consists of all those who claim that they are employed in it. It therefore may contain a vast amount of disguised unemployment.

a service sector business, e.g. running a shop or a dolmuş (shared taxi) business, and (iii) new demand for service sector products created by expenditure from savings and remittances leads not just to the fuller employment of existing workers but to the movement of new workers into this sector.

2.2.5. *The supply of skilled labour and production techniques*

Migration abroad reduces the supply of skilled labour insofar as (i) skilled workers leave and (ii) employers are less keen to train skilled workers in case they leave. It increases the supply of skilled labour to the extent that workers learn relevant skills abroad, return home and take jobs in which they make use of their new skills.

It has already been mentioned that migration may lead to labour saving investment if domestic firms keep losing their best workers. In addition it may encourage the utilization of more modern techniques because of information about or experience of working with them. Workers may even bring a new machine home on their return. Were workers' savings invested in industry on their return, this would tend to make capital less scarce and so less expensive, thus encouraging its increased use. On the other hand, if operating a migration system leads to the need for a devaluation, then this raises the price of imported machinery and so discourages the use of more capital intensive techniques which require the import of machines.

2.2.6. *Aggregate demand, savings, investment and inflation*

As long as repatriated earnings from abroad exceed the incomes forgone as a result of migration,[1] aggregate demand in monetary terms will rise,[2] unless government monetary and fiscal policies bring about a compensating reduction. The share of consumption in national income will fall if the propensity to spend out of repatriated earnings is lower than the national propensity to spend out of domestically earned income. This does not of course necessarily mean that the income not consumed has been productively invested. Nor can we assume that the increase in monetary demand will be accompanied by a proportionate increase in gross domestic product in real terms, partly because at least some of the extra

---

1 Assuming of course that the excess of repatriated earnings over income forgone is not all hoarded.

2 The rise will depend not just on the scale of migration but also on the magnitude of the income differentials between the host and the exporting country and on the propensity of migrants to spend out of savings and remittance income. *Ceteris paribus,* the larger the income differentials, the greater the potential rise in demand.

demand will normally spill over into imports,[1] and because the extra demand may have inflationary consequences if there is no spare capacity to produce the additional commodities in the short run. On the other hand, the extra demand may make possible full capacity utilization and the achievement of scale economies in production: for instance, increased rural income from repatriated earnings may have a very favourable effect on the development of the domestic agricultural machinery industry. Furthermore, in theory, governments can use the foreign exchange obtained from repatriated earnings to create the capacity to supply the demand resulting from expenditure from their domestic currency equivalent. Nonetheless, the danger of inflation in certain sub-sectors remains very real given the supply bottlenecks which L.D.C.s usually face, one particularly notorious example of such a sub-sector being the urban housing market. However, in the event of a Western European recession and the consequent fall in repatriated earnings, the Turkish economy might well suffer severe recession, which is a more serious danger in the long run.

Inflation may also arise if emigration leads to selected labour shortages and so increases wages, or if returned workers influence unions to pursue more militant policies. It is also very likely to arise if devaluation of the exchange rate to keep up the flow of repatriated earnings proves to be necessary.

One further point about the relationship between emigration and inflation requires mention. This is the argument that the forgone consumption of the migrant workers has a deflationary impact which contributes to capital formation. This will be true so long as there is some net reduction in consumption which is not accompanied by an equal reduction in output. However, this effect is not likely to be strong if, for instance, relatives take advantage of a family member's departure to raise their consumption. Furthermore, although technically all forgone consumption contributes to capital formation, its subsequent impact on growth depends on the type of investment which takes place. As Kindleberger (1965E, p. 242) says, 'On a static basis, forgone consumption by emigrants is likely to be matched almost entirely by increased consumption by those left behind, assuming that output has not declined, leaving but a small residue for capital formation, and this by and large in the sector where the income per capita increased'.

2.2.7. *Balance of payments*

Perhaps the most striking change in a country's economic circumstances as a result of participation in the labour migration system is the impact of repatriated earnings on its balance of payments. This is rather underrated by Castles and Kosack, who argue that 'they are not sufficient radically to change the balance of payments

---

1 However, as Kindleberger (1965E) points out, as foreign exchange earners, remittances are superior to ordinary exports because there is no precedent payment to factors which may spill over into imports. He goes on to argue (i) that the propensity to save out of remittances will exceed that out of ordinary income and so lead to an increase in capital formation, and (ii) that the propensity to import out of remittances will be low because consumption expenditure out of remittances goes to the subsistence of low income groups 'with limited taste for foreign articles of consumption'. But the propensity to import out of remittances may well be high, not low, because recipient families now have contact with foreign goods and living standards, particularly if the migrant worker member has returned home.

situation'. However, they use data from the early 1960s[1] before repatriated earnings had reached peak levels. In 1970 and 1971 for instance, the proportion of Turkish imports offset by repatriated earnings was 43%; the share of such earnings in national income in 1972 was about 5% (see §3.5.12).

However, participation in the migration system affects other items in the balance of payments. Firstly, the propensity to import out of repatriated earnings may well be higher than that out of indigenous income, thus raising the share of imports in G.N.P. This will also rise if repatriated earnings are spent on goods with above average import content, or if other nationals demand more imported goods because of a demonstration effect — though in all three cases such a rise in imports could in theory be prevented by quantitative controls. Thirdly, exports may rise if migrants abroad demand home country products (e.g. canned food). Fourthly, foreign exchange from tourism may rise if increased knowledge about the country of emigration stimulates host country nationals to take their holidays there. Fifthly, if the host country cannot obtain migrant labour elsewhere, sending workers abroad tends to keep down the prices of imports from the host country. This means (i) a steeper protective tariff or stricter controls will normally be required if any such goods are to be produced as import substitutes in the country of emigration;[2] migrant workers abroad produce for export to their own country with the results (i) that foreign rather than domestic enterepreneurs obtain all the profits and continue to expand production at home rather than in what is now the emigration country, and (ii) that instead of producing labour intensive goods at home and exporting them abroad, the emigration country exports labour directly.

In this case, migration abroad has important implications both for the development of export orientated and of import substitute industries in the emigration country. The infant export-orientated or import substitute industries which might have been established are instead established in the host country abroad. Although the emigration country obtains the foreign exchange requirements for establishing such infant industries through the receipt of repatriated earnings, by so doing it may have lost the potential market for their products. The situation is completely changed if the assumption that the host country cannot obtain *equally cheap* migrant labour elsewhere is abandoned. Then, whether or not a particular country exports labour will have no impact on the import prices which it faces or on the difficulties facing the establishment of export-orientated and import substitute industries.

However, whatever assumption is made about the availability of alternative supplies of migrant labour, migration may also affect imports, exports and infant industries through the exchange rate. For in order to persuade migrants to repatriate earnings officially, the exchange rate offered to them must not be substantially overvalued or earnings will be despatched clandestinely through a black market, or invested in bank accounts abroad. Because of this, the govenment of the emigration country either has to operate an exchange rate at a value which does not lead to substantial imbalance in foreign payments or to operate a system of multiple

1 Table IX.2, p. 417.

2 On the other hand, the prices of the import requirements of import substitute industries are kept low.

exchange rates, though the survival of such a system requires the cooperation of those repatriating earnings if such earnings constitute a major source of foreign exchange[1] – for they can always withold their money and so force a devaluation if their home country cannot obtain an alternative source of foreign currency?[2] Thus migrants must be offered a 'realistic' exchange rate. Yet if the official rate is lower, international pressure is likely to limit the maximum sustainable differential between the official rate and whatever premium rate is offered for remittances under a dual or multiple exchange rate system. In other words, a country dependent on workers' earnings as a major supply source of foreign exchange cannot let its exchange rate(s) remain substantially overvalued over a long period and may have difficulty sustaining it (them) in the short period. This means that if the labour exporting country does not already have a 'realistic' official exchange rate, it will probably be forced to change to one,[3] though once it has done so the sustained repatriation of earnings will itself help to maintain the exchange rate. However, should a deficit subsequently appear because of excessively high imports, or should workers abroad expect exchange rate depreciation for some other reason, they will again be able to force a devaluation. Furthermore, if demand for temporarily recruited labour and so repatriated earnings declines, this would lead to a large balance of payments deficit or substantial import cuts or both, and so probably to exchange rate devaluation (See Ch.5).

One conclusion from all this is that exporting labour cannot simply be used as a policy to fill the existing foreign exchange gap when an L.D.C. is short of the foreign exchange requirements for its planned development, *without affecting the size of the gap*. This is because (i) it affects the demand for imports because of expenditure from repatriated earnings (this is also likely to affect the composition of imports), (ii) it may have a small effect on exports because of demand from workers abroad (iii) it may increase foreign exchange from tourism and (iv) it may lead to a devaluation. Furthermore, if labour export from a particular emigration country keeps down host country prices, then in the absence of devaluation, it raises the ratio of the price of domestically produced commodities to that of both host country exports and imports – though no effect of this sort will arise if the host country could have obtained labour elsewhere at no extra cost. Because exporting labour affects the size of the emigration country's foreign exchange requirements, the change in foreign exchange reserves brought about because of emigration will not normally be equal to the amount of earnings repatriated.

A further point concerns the way in which dependence on repatriated earnings constrains policy. The smaller the contribution of such earnings, the less the

1 This can be assumed to be the case here since countries which have established a labour migration system on a large scale are the ones under discussion here.

2 Strictly, under a multiple exchange rate system, migrants should only be able to force a revaluation of the premium rate for repatriated earnings. However, any pressure by them on the premium rate is likely to be accompanied by international pressure on the non-premium rate if the latter is considered to be overvalued.

3 A further contributory factor which may help to necessitate a devaluation is the domestic inflation which, as was argued above, may accompany the large scale export of labour from a poor to a much richer country.

emigration country's policy is constrained by the need to acquire them; the larger the contribution, the more the government has to concentrate on obtaining expected repatriated earnings rather than earning or saving foreign exchange by other means. In addition, if migrant workers abroad cease to send earnings if they are able to bring their families after a few years, the emigration country will have to keep up the despatch of new workers in order to keep up the supply of repatriated earnings, though the permanent departure of families will tend to reduce foreign exchange requirements somewhat.

2.2.8. *The transfer of social capital*

One other effect of introducing a labour export policy should be mentioned here for the sake of completeness. This is the question of the cost incurred in the emigration country by the production of the labour which is exported, that is the amount that has been invested in the upbringing of the persons who migrate. There are two approaches to this issue. According to the first, since the persons are there anyway, previous costs incurred in their upbringing should be ignored when examining whether or not they should be exported. In Kindleberger's words (1965E, p.246) 'the young people exist, and we need to apply to them not the 'real cost', but 'opportunity-cost' analysis. What is the most effective use to make of existing labour, to employ it abroad, or leave it unemployed at home; or if there are job opportunities at home, to employ it at home with a small amount of capital, or abroad with more'.

Castles and Kosack (1973, pp. 409—410) take the opposite view, arguing that the total cost of raising a child until working age should be taken into consideration as it is a charge on the country's national income. They go on to quote widely ranging estimates of such costs — which have in common the fact that all are high.

One strong argument for this real cost approach is that it recognizes that surplus labour does not exist like a pool, but rather as a result of the type of policies which an economy pursues. However, if the great political and institutional changes which would permit productive employment of the so-called surplus population are unlikely to occur, then the question of the most effective use of the labour surplus, given the existing political and institutional framework, can legitimately be asked. Then if one adopts the real cost approach one is essentially assuming that the government in the country concerned can actually decide whether or not it is advantageous to bear and bring up children for the purpose of export and that if it decides against, it can avoid the costs which would be incurred from a surplus population by reducing the birthrate such that only the numbers required for the domestic economy are produced. Since it is impossible to plan with any accuracy manpower requirements twenty years hence, let alone to control the birthrate so precisely in an L.D.C., implementation of such a policy would be extremely difficult and would not eliminate the possibility of subsequent labour surpluses which could be exported. But just as the 'real cost' approach is appropriate when deciding whether or not to bring up children for labour export in the long term, the 'opportunity cost' approach is appropriate for deciding whether or not to send individuals now of working age to work abroad. This is not to say that the real cost of bringing up these workers should not be taken into account when negotiating the terms of export. However, governments in the emigration countries are unlikely to have any success in recouping such costs if they compete with each other in the labour export business, and so upbringing expenses (which typically are only borne in part by the government) will have to be written off. Finally it should be noted that the whole argument about the transfer of social capital is usually framed in terms of costs and benefits to the emigration country's economy in the abstract, and takes no account whatsoever of the welfare of the individuals concerned, nor of the distribution of costs and benefits within the economy.

2.3 The range of the alternative outcomes in a labour exporting country and a comparison with a non-exporting one

In order to clarify just how varied the changes brought about by introducing a labour export system can be, it is useful to identify the extreme cases. Consider initially the case favourable for economic growth. Here only the unskilled unemployed would be recruited so that there would be no problem of output forgone. The forgone consumption resulting from departures from the agricultural sector would result in savings channelled into productive investment.[1] Migration would cause no skilled labour shortages so there would be no feedback effect on choice of techniques in industry. In agriculture, the removal of surplus labour would lead to labour productivity increases. The migrant workers would have very high propensities to repatriate their earnings, which would be used mainly to finance new industrial projects which would create sufficient new jobs to employ the returned workers who would utilize new skills learned during their work abroad. The goods to satisfy consumption expenditure from repatriated earnings would be supplied either out of existing capacity or out of new capacity created by projects financed by repatriated earnings, with no inflationary consequences. The repatriated earnings not required to finance imports for new projects to employ returned workers would be available for the finance of imports required for other development projects, and so would lessen dependence on foreign aid. Migrant workers abroad would demand commodities produced in their native country so that exports from there would rise. And they would not work in industries competitive with new export orientated industries in their home country.[2] The absence of inflationary pressures would keep exports in a competitive position and prevent the need for a depreciation of the exchange rate caused by poor export performance. In other words, migration would alleviate unemployment, not just temporarily, but also permanently, by creating new job opportunities;[3] it would also provide savings, foreign exchange and trained manpower for economic growth. It might also lead to a reduction in the birthrate, thus permitting higher per capita incomes.

On the other hand, a completely different situation might arise as a result of the introduction of a labour export system. In this case it would not be the unskilled unemployed but rather the skilled industrial workers who migrated — and who could

1 Assuming that demand was such that there were profitable investment opportunities.

2 Though if the host country could obtain labour from elsewhere without incurring any additional costs, the above argument would not hold.

3 It would also alleviate unemployment to the extent that workers settled permanently abroad.

not easily be replaced so that there would be at least some loss in output, and quite possibly bottlenecks in key industries. Insofar as any migration came from the agricultural sector, this would be accompanied by a combination of output losses and increased consumption so that it generated no new saving. The loss of skilled industrial workers would raise wages and discourage training and utilization of skilled labour as compared with the introduction of more capital intensive techniques.[1] Repatriated earnings would be utilized not for productive investment but exclusively for consumption expenditures, which would lead to inflationary pressure at home and an increase in the propensity to import. A good deal of the repatriated earnings would be required to finance the consequent increase in imports. Any increase in employment would arise from the expansion of consumption goods industries to meet the increased demand from expenditure from repatriated earnings; there would be few examples of returned workers setting up their own productive enterprises to create new employment opportunities for themselves. Indeed, insofar as such workers did attempt to establish businesses, they would be small service sector enterprises. Few would have learnt new skills abroad and those who did would either find them irrelevant or choose not to use them on their return as they would despise going back to wage employment. While abroad they would prefer foreign goods so that there would be little expansion in their home country's exports. They would be working in industries competitive with new export orientated industries in their home country.[2] Also the incidence of inflationary pressure at home would make it even more difficult to increase export earnings, thus encouraging the need for a depreciation in the exchange rate caused by poor export performance. This would be perceived by the migrants abroad who would withold repatriating their earnings so as to force a devaluation. In other words, emigration would do little to alleviate the unemployment situation, provide few, if any, savings for capital formation or trained manpower for new industrial projects. Rather it would increase inflationary tendencies, tie the country to dependence on repatriated earnings to finance the new demand for imports by returned workers (and by other nationals if there is a demonstration effect), and so tie the country to adopting an exchange rate which reflected the uncompetitiveness of its exports, so increasing the cost of imports required for the establishment of new import substitute industries.[3] This is not to say that the country could not achieve some sustained growth in the accounting sense, but rather that the main source of new growth would be from income earned from exporting labour abroad rather than from production of goods and services at home. In effect the country would become a satellite of the industrial metropolis to which it exports its labour, sharing some of the metropolis' prosperity in good years but taking *most* of the burden of adjustment in bad years.

The incidence of any severe and sustained depression in the metropolis would of course have serious effects on the migration country whether or not it had previously

---

1 See p. 41, fn. 1.

2 Though again, this would be of no significance if the host country could obtain equally cheap migrant labour elsewhere.

3 In extremum, the country could suffer a net loss of output if skilled labour shortages led to serious production bottlenecks and a very strong demonstration effect led to deterioration in the balance of payments.

48

approximated more to the favourable than to the unfavourable outcome described above. Changes in economic activity abroad have been accompanied by more than proportionate changes in the employment of foreign workers (Chart D), so that recession would not only cause an immediate increase in unemployment because of returned workers, but would also reduce national income and lead to immediate balance of payments difficulties and industrial excess capacity because of the fall in repatriated earnings. Changes in the stock of workers abroad have been accompanied by more than proportionate changes in repatriated earnings (even allowing for inflation and exchange rate adjustments). For instance between 1966 and 1967 the stock of workers abroad fell by one-eighth while repatriated earnings fell by one-fifth, and between 1967 and 1972 the former rose by a factor of about 3½ while the latter rose by a factor of 8 (Tables 15 and A6). This happens because it is the more recently arrived workers who, after they have initially settled down, tend to repatriate most of their earnings (§ 3.5.11–3.5.12) and who (because they have not yet obtained residence rights, etc.) tend to have to bear the main burden of adjustment in a recession.

But although a major recession abroad would have very serious consequences for the emigration country, the situation would be less disastrous if labour export had had a favourable impact on economic growth. Consequently it is doubly important whether or not the introduction of a labour export policy lays the foundations for sustained economic growth and provides a comparatively costless solution to the problem of reducing unemployment and acquiring foreign exchange, or whether it condemns the country to a permanent existence as an underdeveloped satellite of a prosperous metropolitan area. To which extreme a country approximates depends on certain key factors:

1. the occupational composition of emigrants (in particular how many are unemployed and how many are skilled industrial workers) and, associated with this, the magnitude of output forgone,
2. the propensity to save and to remit earnings while abroad,
3. the acquisition of new skills while abroad and the extent of their subsequent utilization on return,
4. the proportion of repatriated earnings invested in producer goods on return,
5. the proportion of repatriated earnings spent on imported commodities on return,
6. the change which expenditure from repatriated earnings brings to the price level,
7. the impact which employment of migrant labour abroad has on actual and potential trade between the host and the exporting country,
8. the proportion of migrants who settle permanently abroad.

It is one aim of the remaining chapters of this study to examine what has happened to these factors in the case of Turkish migration and to identify towards which of the two extremes described above the Turkish experience approximates. It should, however, be remembered that the identification of an economy's position between these two extremes indicates little about who benefits or suffers from the effects of labour export. Indeed even if labour export facilitated attainment of sustained economic growth, this might well be accompanied by a worsening distribution of income. Such distributional considerations are discussed further in § 2.4 below.

Here, it remains to compare the two extremes defined above in an economy (B) whose government exports labour, with the situation in economy A, whose government chose not to export labour at all. Obviously the favourable effect on growth which can arise from labour export will mean that country B enjoys higher growth than country A because in B, savings, investment, foreign exchange reserves and the stock of skilled manpower will be higher, and unemployment lower.

But how does country A compare with the unfavourable effects (as characterized above) from labour export? At worst, the propensity to save and invest and the stock of skilled manpower in country B will fall, the propensity to import and to consume will rise, and output will fall by more than the total of repatriated earnings.[1] In these respects the situation in B will indeed compare unfavourably with than in A, though it is unlikely to persist in the long term as employers in B should learn about the problems caused by skilled labour loss and move to techniques which enable them to avoid high output losses and severe supply bottlenecks.[2] But one problem cannot be avoided in A by choosing not to export labour as long as other countries participate in the system. This is the way in which access to migrant labour keeps down host country commodity (especially export) prices, and so makes it more difficult for the L.D.C. to develop export markets and set up infant industries. For as long as some countries supply labour to industries abroad which are competitive with A's, then A's population will be affected even though they do not participate in labour export. Of course, if they did, the depressant effect of immigration on wages and prices abroad would probably be greater. But the point is that A's population cannot avoid the consequences of other labour exporting countries' action.

A could, however, avoid the other adverse effects characterised above (pp. 47–49) by non-participation in labour export. The decision about whether or not to act in this way should be made in the light of the government's expected ability to control the key determinants of the outcome of labour migration as listed above (p. 49),[3] and in the light of the prospects for the successful operation of alternative policies, such as commodity instead of labour export. The actual and potential effects of migration should be specifically taken into account and appropriate policies be undertaken (see Ch. 5). Otherwise the country may find that the export of labour is a vicious circle from which there is no easy escape.

2.4 The impact of exporting labour on the migrant workers and on the home country population

So far only the impact of emigration on economic variables such as growth in the home country has been considered. This is obviously an important indicator for the assessment of an emigration policy. But if fails to take account of the impact of emigration on the migrants themselves and on those whom they have left behind.

---

1 This is unlikely to happen unless the departure of labour from certain industries causes bottlenecks elsewhere in the economy.

2 Though any demonstration effect would still persist.

3 Assuming of course that a ban on emigration is a feasible strategy – as if not, the decision would not arise.

Whether or not the migrants themselves will be financially better off depends on (1) whether what they earn while abroad exceeds the costs of migration and residence abroad and (2) whether they obtain a higher income (in real terms) and better living conditions on return. (We are not concerned with migrants who settle permanently abroad since in this case they can be assumed to think that they have made a better life for themselves.) Added to this are all the social costs and benefits of migration – for instance, separation from family, poor housing, unfamiliar, arduous and monotonous work and loneliness, as compared with the 'bright lights' of foreign city life, status of having been abroad, etc. For the individual migrant worker, these non-quantifiable aspects of working abroad will affect his life as much as, if not more than the prospects for financial gain, and should be taken into account in any attempt to assess whether migration abroad on a temporarily recruited basis makes workers better off. Similarly migrants' experience abroad may change their entire political perspectives and transform their attitudes towards participating in political and in organized labour movements in their home country.

Emigration not only affects the incomes of migrants and their families, but those of the whole home country population. The way in which it may affect G.N.P. through the growth rate has already been discussed above. But an improvement in per capita income may not necessarily be accompanied by an improvement in personal income distribution and could make at least some of the non-migrant population worse off. The first order effect of migration on income distribution depends on who migrates. If it is the poorest from the agricultural and urban proletariat, then this will obviously lead to an improved income distribution, and if it is the upper levels of the peasantry and of the industrial working class, it will tend to worsen it. But the overall impact on personal income distribution is more complicated since it is necessary to take into account not only the change in the circumstances of migrants and their families but also the effect that this has on the incomes of others. For instance, although a poor peasant may return, buy land and set himself up as a farmer using mechanized techniques, this may force existing tenants and sharecroppers not only to join the ranks of the landless rural proletariat but also to become unemployed if only some are subsequently hired. Similarly even if rich peasants and farmers migrate, this may improve the distribution of income on return if they hire previously unemployed peasants. Within industry, migration will affect workers' income distribution if, for instance, by creating skilled labour shortages it increases skill differentials – or leads to the introduction of more capital intensive machinery so that workers are made unemployed.

Introduction of a system of temporarily recruited migration may also affect the distribution of income between (i) industry and agriculture, (ii) profits and wages, and (iii) regions. It will affect income distribution between agriculture and industry if it affects their terms of trade (§2.2.2). It will affect the distribution of factor incomes if it leads to a rise in the real wage sufficient to increase labour's share (§2.2.3 above) or to a substantial fall in profits occasioned, say, by the difficulties faced when replacing departing workers; it will increase the share of profits if these rise sufficiently because of inflation or devaluation. (Devaluation tends to raise the incomes of those employed in the foreign trade sector – e.g. landowners and businessmen – relative to those employed in the domestic sector.) The effect of

51

migration on regional income distribution will depend on all the income changes brought about in the provinces from which migrants depart and to which they return; just as in the case of personal income distribution, these will be fairly complicated.

Returned migrant workers will also affect the incomes of others by the way in which they use their savings and remittances, in particular the proportion which they spend and what they spend it on. Thus although returned workers improve their own living standards by spending their repatriated earnings on better housing, they would probably make a greater contribution to national income in the longer run by using their savings for investment instead (assuming that the L.D.C. concerned faces a savings constraint).

From the point of view of the emigration country population (including all ex-migrants), these distributional effects of temporarily recruited migration are as important as its impact on the growth rate and on such other macroeconomic indicators as the propensity to save and the balance of payments. In Chapter 4 an attempt will be made to assess whether the migrants themselves have gained from work abroad, and the distributional effect which this has had on their non-migrant compatriots.

2.5   Summary

In this chapter the main potential effects on an L.D.C's. economy caused by the introduction of a labour export system were described. It was shown how, under certain circumstances, labour export could facilitate the achievement of sustained economic growth, and how under other circumstances it could make this more difficult. The actual outcome would depend mainly on eight factors (listed on p. 49). But it was argued that it was insufficient (and possibly misleading) just to look at the impact of labour export on selected macroeconomic variables such as growth, inflation and employment; to obtain a more complete picture of the consequences of labour export, its distributional effects need also to be taken into account, as do less tangible political effects.

3
The Turkish experience, 1960–73

3.1   Introduction

The emergence of Turkey as a leading supplier of labour to Europe has already been
described in Chapter 1. The aim of this chapter is to describe Turkey's experience
in more detail, and in particular, (i) the changes which have taken place over the
decade in the nature of the migration, and (ii) the socio-economic characteristics of
the migrants as compared with the Turkish economically active population. The
way in which the socio-economic characteristics of Turkey's migrants compare with
those of other non-E.E.C. supplying countries such as Greece and Yugoslavia is also
discussed where this is of particular value for comparative purposes. A full comparative survey is, however, beyond the scope of this study.

The chapter draws on a wide variety of source material obtained in both Turkey
and the host countries for Turkish migrant workers. All the items used are listed in
Appendix 1, together, where this is important, with details of the coverage, method
of collection and reliability of the statistics concerned. Summary information about
the main surveys used is given for convenience in Table 4.

The chapter makes considerable use of previously unpublished data obtained by
the author in cooperation with the Turkish State Planning Organization as a result
of a survey carried out in February 1971. The S.P.O. retained all responsibility for
the detailed formulation of the questionnaire and for the actual conduct of the
survey (foreigners are not normally permitted to carry out field work in the social
sciences in Turkey), though they were willing to consider suggestions of questions
for inclusion — the precise wording of which, however, was determined by them.
After the survey had been carried out, there was a major administrative reorgan-
ization in the S.P.O. which delayed access to the results. However, when this was
ultimately granted, every facility was made available to the author to assist with
work on the raw data (the S.P.O. had themselves done little work on the results
because of the need to concentrate all resources on preparing the 3rd Five Year
Development Plan).

Although this survey contained many serious defects, it found out much more
'follow-up' information about the fate of ex-migrants after their return to Turkey
than had previous studies. A full description of the methodology, coverage and
limitations of this survey is given in Appendix 3; however, it will be useful to
mention the main points here. The S.P.O. first located the addresses of as many
ex-migrant workers as possible. Then it selected a list of what were considered to be
representative towns and villages, and then took a 50 per cent random sample of the

Table 4. *Summary information about the main surveys of Turkish migrant workers,* (for details see Appendix 1). (*Mimeographed report.)

Author of survey and publication date	Date of survey	Place of survey	Actual coverage	Comments
Abadan 1964A	1963	Germany — all the main centres of employment for Turkish workers.	494 workers including 67 women.	Very detailed and fairly reliable survey of atypical vanguard migrant workers.
*Tuna 1967A	1966	Turkey — Marmara region	280 returned migrants, 67 women.	Unrepresentative because it covers returnees to Turkey's richest most industrialized region, but valuable information about migrants after their return.
*Hentschel 1968D	1967	Cologne	400 foreign workers including 100 Turks. All males.	Unrepresentative of migrants in Germany. Results not very reliable.
German Bundesanstält für Arbeit 1970B	1968	Germany	9,087 foreign workers of whom 2,741 were women; of the 1,607 Turks in the sample, 379 were women.	Very reliable survey of socio-economic characteristics of foreign worker stock.
*Neuloh 1970D	1969	Germany and Turkey	163 in Germany of which 50 were women. 774 in Turkey.	Very sociologically orientated.
*Krahenbuhl 1969C Results published in Kayser 1971C	1969	Turkey — Izmir, Zonguldak and Kocaeli	Interviews with 34 firms in Izmir, 14 in Kocaeli and 2 in Zonguldak.	Concentrates mainly on sociological characteristics of migrants from these areas.
T.E.S. 1968–71A	1967 1968 1969 1971	Turkish border on return	20,897 15,573 13,393 27,730	Useful because carried out over a long period. Although it included only those who said they were returning permanently, many did not.
*Abadan 1971C Results published in Kayser 1972C and Abadan 1972C	1970	9 German towns; Turkey	89	Little new information obtained Mainly case histories concentrating on workers' attitudes.

54

Table 4. Continued.

Author of survey and publication date	Date of survey	Place of survey	Actual coverage	Comments
Aker 1972D	1970/ 71	Turkey, before departure	590 including 51 women.	Survey carried out very carefully – it contains a representative sample of migrant departure. But information is only about socioeconomic character-istics before departure and intentions on return.
*S.P.O. 1972A	1971	Turkey, after return	361 returned migrants including 20 women.	Detailed information about migrants on return, but biased sample (see Appendix 3).

replies from these. The actual interviews were carried out by qualified Turkish investigators and there is little reason to suspect that the respondents gave false replies.[1] On the other hand, certain important qualifications must be taken into account when utilizing the results.

Firstly, the survey only covers workers who had *returned* at the latest by 1970, and so includes many vanguard migrants who have tended to be better-off and more educated than those in subsequent flows. For the same reason, it includes a disproportionately small percentage of women. Secondly, the method used to obtain ex-migrants' names and addresses biased the sample against the inclusion of the fully or partially unemployed, and those employed in small or family concerns. Thirdly, the sample was not geographically representative of migrant worker departures over the period 1963–69. However, this largely follows from the inclusion of many vanguard migrants who have tended to come from the richer provinces of Marmara (around Istanbul), the Aegean (around Izmir), and to a lesser extent, North Central Anatolia (around Ankara). Fourthly, since nearly three-quarters reported that they wanted to work abroad again, there is obviously some doubt about classifying them as permanently returned workers, though they were clearly sufficiently much so as to have given up their jobs abroad. Fortunately many of these limitations can be taken into account without too much difficulty when interpreting the data, though it is obviously important at all times to bear in mind the possible unreliability of some of the figures. Altogether the data do provide a very detailed picture of the socio-economic characteristics of migrants before departure, while abroad and on return. In presenting this picture, text tables have been kept to a minimum, but the main results of the survey[2] together with import-ant results from other sources have been included for reference in Appendix 2.

The S.P.O. survey classified all respondents according to their sex and their

1 Except perhaps to the questions about their income in Turkey (if they feared being required to pay higher taxes).

2 The complete results of the S.P.O. survey are presented in Paine 1972D.

55

residence in town or country. Since only twenty women were included in the survey, the male-female breakdown of the results has not generally been presented. However since there were often significant differences between the urban and rural sub-groups, this breakdown of the data has frequently been included, though it is important to remember that *in this survey,* 'rural' and 'urban' refer to the size (greater or less than 10,000 people) of the place of residence *on return,* so that there are fewer 'rural' and more 'urban' migrants than would have been the case if they had been classified according to the size of their place of residence before departure.[1] If village or sub-district centres are used as a rough proxy for places with a population of 10,000 or less (see §3.4.3 below), 50 per cent of the sample would have lived in rural areas before departure as compared with the known 43 per cent on return.

3.2   Turkish migrant worker stocks and flows

3.2.1   *The countries of destination*

Turkey only began exporting labour to Western Europe on a significant scale after the negotiation of an official agreement with the Federal Republic of Germany in 1961. Germany has been the dominant host country since then, taking 512,252 out of 605,786 officially recruited migrants from Turkey from 1961 up to August 12th, 1972[2] (i.e. 85%), and having about 497,000 out of an estimated 600,000 Turkish workers in Europe employed there in June 1972, (see Tables 1 and 5). Of Turks who have been officially recruited, the proportion despatched to Germany has varied from a minimum of 76% in 1970 to a maximum of 100% in 1961[3] when Germany was the only possible official destination[4] (see Table 6). Subsequently agreements were made with Austria (1964), Belgium (1964), Holland (1964), France (1965), Switzerland (1967) and Australia (1967). However, migration to Australia is of the permanent rather than the temporarily recruited kind and so hardly falls within the scope of this survey.[5] Also migration to Denmark has taken place under a bilateral agricultural training scheme whereby Turks learn various agricultural techniques, marketing and distribution methods in Danish cooperatives.

3.2.2   *Turkey's increasing importance as a supplier*

Despite her later start and greater distance from the host countries, by 1970 Turkey

---

1 It was not possible from the original survey replies to reclassify accurately all the respondents according to the size of their place of residence before departure.

2 These are *gross* figures which do not take account of workers who returned from employment abroad and subsequently successfully reapplied through the T.E.S.

3 With some cyclical variation: for instance, the share of neighbouring countries rose during the German 1967 recession.

4 Excluding, for instance, departures of high level manpower to the U.S.A. etc. For a discussion of such migration, see P.G. Franck's chapter on Turkey (Franck 1970).

5 Nevertheless, quantitatively it has been increasing in importance: at the end of 1972 there were about 11,000 Turks (including 3,000 workers) in Australia.

Table 5: *Stocks of Turkish workers abroad by host country*

	1970 (or most recent estimate before that)[1]		1972 (or most recent estimate before that)			Total official T.E.S. despatch by host country 1961–Aug 12 1972 (1000)
	Number (1000)	% European total[2]	Number (1000)	Date of estimate	% European total[2]	
W. Germany	373.0	86	497.0	June 1972	84	512.3
Austria	12.3	3	23.2	August 1972	4	25.7
Netherlands	16.5	4	27.2	June 1971	5	21.0
Belgium & Luxemburg	8.5	2	8.5	November 1971	2	15.0
Switzerland	6.5	2	9.5	December 1971	2	4.6
France	10.0	3	18.8	January 1972	3	21.9
Denmark	2.4	1	2.4	August 1970	–	
U.K.	1.4	–	2.7	December 1971	1	1.9
Sweden	2.8	1	2.8	August 1970	1	
Norway	0.2	–				
Other			1.1	December 1971	–	
Total European	433.6		593.1			
Libya	0.1					
Somali	–					
S. Arabia	0.4		n.a.			
U.S.A.	0.1					
Canada	0.5					
Australia	2.3		3.0			3.5
Total non-European	3.4					
Country unspecified	–					6.9
Total world	437.0					612.6

Sources: Column 1: Türkiye Ticaret Odaları, Sanayi Odaları ve Ticaret Borsaları Birliği, *İktisadı Rapor 1971*, based on data supplied by the T.E.S.
Column 3 & 6: Data supplied by T.E.S.

Notes: 1. Precise dates to which data refer not given.
2. Percentages may not add to 100 because of rounding.

57

Table 6: *Annual flows of Turkish workers officially despatched by T.E.S., by host country, 1961–73.(1000s)*

	1961	1962	1963	1964	1965	1966	1967	1968	1969	1970	1971	1972 1.1.1972– 12.8.1972	1973
F.R. Germany	1.5	11.0	23.4	54.9	45.6	32.6	7.2	41.4	98.1	96.9	65.7	33.9	103.8
% European total	100	99	77	83	89	95	85	96	95	76	76	80	n.a
Austria	–	0.2	0.9	1.4	2.0	0.5	1.0	0.7	1.0	10.6	4.6	2.8	n.a
% European total	–	1	3	2	4	1	12	2	1	8	5	7	n.a.
Netherlands	–	–	0.3	3.0	2.2	1.2	0.1	0.9	3.4	4.8	4.9	0.3	n.a.
% European total	–	–	1	5	4	4	1	2	3	4	6	1	n.a.
Belgium	–	–	5.6	6.7	1.7	–	–	–	–	0.4	0.6	0.1	n.a.
% European total	–	–	19	10	3	–	–	–	–	0	1	0	n.a.
Switzerland	–	–	0	0.2	0.1	0.1	0.2	0.1	0.2	1.6	1.3	0.7	n.a.
% European total	–	–	0	0	0	0	3	0	0	1	2	2	n.a.
France	–	–	0.1	0	–	–	–	–	0.2	9.0	7.9	4.7	n.a.
% European total	–	–	0	0	–	–	–	–	0	7	9	11	n.a.
Denmark	–	–	–	–	–	–	–	–	–	0.4	n.a.	n.a.	n.a.
% European total	–	–	–	–	–	–	–	–	–	3	n.a.	n.a.	n.a.
U.K.	–	–	–	–	–	0	–	–	0	0.6	1.3	0	n.a.
% European total	–	–	–	–	–	0	–	–	0	0	2	0	n.a.
Total Europe	1.5	11.2	30.3	66.0	51.5	34.4	8.5[1]	43.1	102.9[1]	127.5[1]	86.3	42.5	n.a.
Australia	–	–	–	–	–	–	–	0.1	1.0	1.2	0.9	0.3	n.a.
Country unspecified	–	–	–	–	0	–	0.4	0	0.1	0.9	1.3	0.6	n.a.
Total world	1.5	11.2	30.3	66.2	51.5	34.4	9.0	43.2	104.0	129.6	88.4	43.4 85.3[2]	135.8

Source: İş ve İşçi Bulma Kurumu, Genel Müdürlüğu (Turkish Employment Service), *Yıllı Çalışma Raporu* (Annual Labour Reports) 1962–71, Ankara 1963–72; 1972–3 data supplied by T.E.S.
1 Excluding any migrants to European countries included under 'country unspecified'.
2 Jan–Dec. 1972.

Note: Zero represents positive number rounded downwards; percentages may not add to 100 because of rounding.

had become the second largest supplier after Yugoslavia of new worker arrivals in Western Europe. This rising share in new migrant flows was of course to be expected in view of the size of Turkey's economically active population (about 15 million in 1973 (Table 3)) as compared with that of Yugoslavia (8.8 million in 1971), Greece (3.8 million in 1970), Spain (12.7 million in 1970), Portugal (3.2 million in 1970) and Italy (19.8 million in 1970). In Turkey, the ratio of migrant workers to the economically active population (e.a.p.) is still substantially lower than that for Yugoslavia and that for Greece,[1] being only around one in fifteen, or 6.5 per 1,000 e.a.p. (for the period 1960—73).[2]

Turkey's share in the total *stock* of migrant workers in W. Europe is still relatively low, though at the beginning of 1972 she had the highest share in Germany

Chart A. *The changing ethnic composition of the stock of foreign workers in W. Germany, 1959—72.*

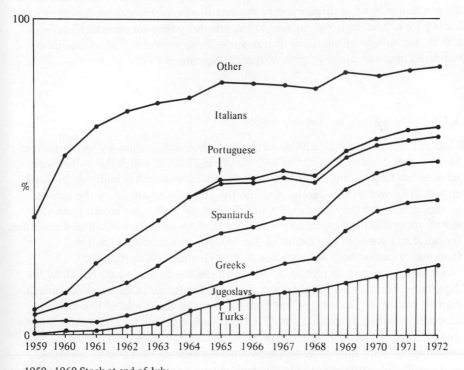

1959—1960 Stock at end of July
1961—1971 Stock at end of June

Sources: Germany, Bundesanstalt für Arbeit, *Ausländische Arbeitnehmer.*

1 Over the period 1960—9 the number of emigrant workers per 1,000 active individuals in the country of origin was 3.6 for Turkey as compared with 6.9 for Yugoslavia and 13.6 for Greece (Livi-Bacci 1971E p. 13). Both Greece and Yugoslavia have to varying extents been facing domestic labour shortages and have been considering restrictions on labour export (see p. 24 fn. 3). By 1973, Greece had *imported* 20,000 foreign workers (mainly from N. Africa) because of the acute labour shortage.

2 Taking an economically active population of 15.8 million, a stock of migrant workers abroad (at the end of 1973) of 850,000, and of returned migrants of 180,000.

(21%)[1] and in the Netherlands (almost 50% of migrants from S. Europe), offset by her relatively minor importance in France (2%), Belgium (4%) and Switzerland (1%) (Tables 1 and A1). The rising share of Turks in the stock of foreign workers in Germany is shown in Chart A.

Estimates of the total stock of Turkish migrants are normally provided by the host country and so include those who have left Turkey unofficially. As can be seen from Chart B, the volume of unofficial migration has been subject to sharp cyclical fluctuations (§3.2.3), being high in 'good' years when Western European demand for labour was high (e.g. 1964, 1969) and low in 'bad' years when such demand was low (notably 1967). The S.P.O. survey found that roughly one in five of *all* migrant workers had not been officially recruited (Table A2). Rural migrants were slightly more likely to have left officially; also, surprisingly few migrants used different channels in later years (even if they had left on tourist passports in the first place). However, since an official agreement was signed with Germany in 1972 to regularise the position of existing illegal migrant workers there (conditional on their return to Turkey for official registration), and to toughen the policy on new unofficial arrivals, the volume of unofficial migration declined somewhat,[2] at least until the ban on all immigration of Turkish workers in November 1973.

3.2.3   Fluctuations in Turkey's supply

Fluctuations in Turkey's supply have obviously been determined by fluctuations in host country demand. This can be seen clearly in Chart B, which shows the close relationship between the Turkish supply of migrant workers (as indicated by total arrivals in Germany) and German demand for Turks (as measured by the number of vacancies which they have sought to fill). Turkish arrivals in Germany are also closely related to total vacancies for migrant workers from the recruitment countries, though they have both changed much less sharply than unfilled vacancies (nationality unspecified) and even less so than German G.N.P. (Chart C).

However, new arrivals represent Turkey's gross supply as they do not allow for departures. Turkey's *net* supply is measured by the change in the stock of Turkish migrant workers in Germany; Chart B shows that this too is related to German demand (measured by vacancies for Turks) though less closely so than the relationship between arrivals and vacancies (since vacancies represent gross demand, including both additions to and replacements for existing members of the stock).

The role of German demand in determining the magnitude of the inflow of foreign workers has been analyzed by Böhning (1970b E). He regressed annual totals of foreign worker entrants on annual averages of demand and wage indicators. New

---

1 Just overtaking Yugoslavia with 20%. At the end of September 1971 Yugoslavia however had been in the lead with a share of 21% as compared with 20% for Turkey.

2 Though in September 1973 it was reported that organized routes for Turkish unofficial immigration via Bulgaria and East Berlin were in widespread use (*The Times*, September 10th, 1973).

Chart B. *Changes in Turkish migration to W. Germany, 1961–72.*

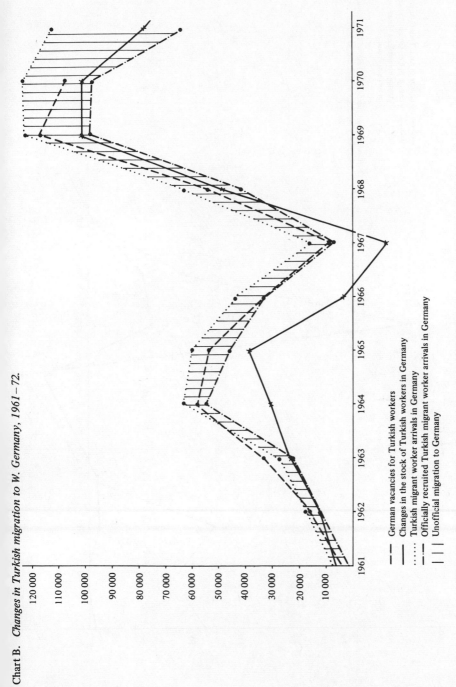

- – – German vacancies for Turkish workers
- —— Changes in the stock of Turkish workers in Germany
- ······ Turkish migrant worker arrivals in Germany
- – · – Officially recruited Turkish migrant worker arrivals in Germany
- ‖‖‖ Unofficial migration to Germany

Source: Germany, Bundesanstalt für Arbeit, *Ausländische Arbeitnehmer.*

61

Chart C. *Changes in total Turkish arrivals, unfilled vacancies, and vacancies for workers from the recruitment countries, W. Germany, 1962–72.*

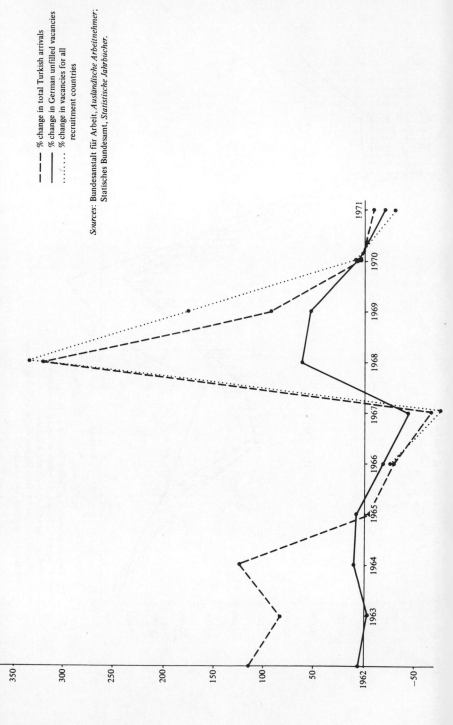

- – – – % change in total Turkish arrivals
- ——— % change in German unfilled vacancies
- ·········· % change in vacancies for all
recruitment countries

Sources: Bundesanstalt für Arbeit, *Ausländische Arbeitnehmer;*
Statistisches Bundesamt, *Statistische Jahrbücher.*

62

Chart D. *Changes in foreign workers, Turkish workers and G.N.P. in W. Germany, 1963–72.*

Legend:
—— % change in G.N.P.
– – – % change in stock of foreign workers
...... % change in stock of Turkish workers

Sources: Germany, Bundesanstalt für Arbeit, *Ausländische Arbeitnehmer*;
Statistisches Bundesamt, *Statistische Jahrbücher*

entrants were used instead of employed foreign workers because of the very high autocorrelation obtained when the latter was used.[1] He found that for the nine emigration countries considered (which included developed countries such as France, the Netherlands and Great Britain) demand factors were more important than wage factors in determining international labour mobility. Furthermore, for the less developed emigration countries with large labour surpluses 'the *demand* pressure in the labour *receiving* country is the *sole* determinant' (Böhning 1970bE, p. 196).

The way in which the stock of foreign workers in Germany has fluctuated more sharply than G.N.P. can be seen clearly in Chart D. The stock of Turkish workers has fluctuated considerably, rising more sharply than that of all foreign workers as the level of economic activity rose, and falling less sharply during the 1967 recession. Then Turkish workers in Germany certainly fared rather better than those of some other nationalities: the percentage drop in Turkish workers between September 1966 and March 1967 was only 16.6% as compared with 29.5% for Italian, 23.2% for Spanish and 17.4% for Greek workers (Bundesanstalt für Arbeit). Furthermore, the fall in Turkish employment in Germany was almost entirely accounted for by male workers – the number of Turkish women remaining almost constant (see §3.4.1).

Various explanations have been advanced for the fact that Turks in Germany were less affected during the 1967 recession than other migrant worker nationalities. Nermin Abadan (in Kayser 1972c) has suggested that employers preferred Turkish workers as they were less likely to join unions, less demanding, more work-disciplined and content with cheap housing, citing evidence from interviews with personnel managers, etc. But it may also have been the case that Turks were more determined not to return home because the gap between Turkish-German living standards was higher than that between, say, Greece and Germany or Italy and Germany. Certainly a considerable number of 'unofficial' Turks received work permits during the recession, and many of these may have been existing migrants whose contracts had been terminated, rather than new arrivals. Turkey again faced quite a substantial fall in migrant worker demand after the peak of 1970 – indeed by 1972 the rate of new departures had fallen by 25%.[2] But this time there was no fall in the actual stock of workers abroad.

Cyclical conditions have not only affected the total supply of Turkish workers but also the countries of destination. Of official departures the proportion to countries other than Germany has been highest in 'good' years, though there was a small but significant movement as a result of the German recession, when migrants who could not find work in Germany left to seek work in neighbouring countries.[3]

3.2.4   *Turkish returned migrant workers*

There is no agreement as to how many Turkish migrants have returned home

1 Böhning, 1970bE, pp. 193 and 199.

2 *Milliyet*, 24 Kasim (November) 1972.

3 Nonetheless, the proportion of the S.P.O. sample to have visited countries other than that for which they had initially departed was small (about 8% – Table A47).

because of the lack of any adequate statistical information on this subject. Since 1966, the number of workers entering Turkey who have alleged that they are returning permanently has been recorded in the State Institute of Statistics' annual *Tourism Statistics* (Table 19, column 6). However, with the exception of 1967, only about 5,000 per annum described themselves as permanent returnees (Table A8). This figure is not consistent with the German data on departures (Table A6) which suggest a figure of the order of 20—25,000 per annum since 1965, but which must be adjusted for strong cyclical variations and for a slight upward trend as the volume of migration increased. Adjustment for returnees from other host countries would raise the unadjusted figure to around 30,000. However, this figure includes all those who return to Turkey and then re-apply to work abroad again after a while. According to Böhning's estimate this group of returned migrants is fairly large: a 'guesstimate' of between one-sixth and one-third of total returned workers will be used here.[1] Adjustment for this (assuming that the propensity of Turks to return for a second or further work period does not depend on their past or prospective host countries) gives an estimate of between 25,000 and 20,000 for the annual average of permanent returnees between 1965 and 1973.

This would mean that many returning migrants who at the time of re-entry into Turkey planned to work abroad after a short holiday at home again cannot have done so. In other words, they did not plan to return permanently, and might well be harbouring the hope of a subsequent work-period abroad. If this is so, then it becomes important to distinguish between *deliberate* and *actual* permanently returned workers. Certainly a substantial majority (73%) of the ex-migrants in the S.P.O. sample reported that they were thinking of going abroad again, although all must have had an interval of *at least* 4-6 months between the time of their return and their interview and so would qualify as actual returnees. This question of whether the 'permanently returned worker' is, as Böhning would want to argue, a myth, is taken up in §3.6.14 below: for the time being the phrase 'actual returned worker' or just 'returned worker' or 'ex-migrant' will be used, without allusion to the question of permanency.

1 Böhning (1972bE p.36 and 1972aE Table 36) found that 40% of the Italians, Greeks, Spaniards and Turks who entered Germany during the first three quarters of 1968 had worked in Germany before. Assuming that the proportion for Turks taken separately is no higher than the average (because a smaller proportion of Turks than of other nationalities were made redundant in 1967 and because geography makes it more difficult for Turkish workers to return home and then change their mind about it), this gives an upper estimate of about 25,000 Turks who entered Germany in 1968 after working there previously, i.e. about one quarter of those who had left Germany in 1967 or earlier. A reasonable (but arbitrarily chosen) lower estimate would be about 15,000, giving a mean estimate of 20,000, i.e. about one-fifth of those who had left Germany in 1967 or earlier. Of course, this mean estimate of one-fifth only provides a lower limit for the propensity of *pre-1968* returnees to go abroad again since it includes only those who went abroad again in 1968 (as opposed to 1969, 1970 etc., and 1965, 1966 etc., if relevant). A reasonable upper limit would seem to be about two-fifths. If one then takes into account the fact that the proportion re-entering in 1968 was rather high as compared with previous years owing to certain redundancies during the 1967 recession when workers had been sent home on an 'extended holiday' without pay or had not had their contract renewed, a reasonable estimate of the annual average proportion of returnees who re-migrate would lie between one-sixth and one-third.

3.3 The procedure for a prospective migrant[1]

3.3.1 *Application and departure in the early 1970s*

The aspirant migrant worker would apply to the nearest local office of the T.E.S.,[2] where he was interviewed, after which his skills, experience and occupation (as determined from the interview) were recorded. Nothing further happened until the T.E.S. offered a vancancy suitable for this worker. He was then despatched to the host country directly by the local branch of the T.E.S. If he was going to Germany, he had to visit the German coordinating office in Istanbul for a final check, including a medical; if to Holland or Australia, the relevant office in Ankara. Normally his prospective employer paid his travelling expenses. An employer might recruit a particular worker directly (by name), in which case they notified their national employment commission so that the worker jumped the queue for despatch.

In either case, he had to pay T.L.90 (approximately £2.50)[3] for his passport, which was issued for one year, but which could be extended annually at the Turkish consulate abroad on payment of a small fee, for as many years as desired if his job contract had been renewed.[4] But in contrast to the official migrant, the non-official aspirant migrant had to pay T.L. 500 (approximately £14.30) per 3 months (T.L. 2000 – approximately £57 – for one year).[5]

All departing workers had normally to take with them $200 in foreign exchange, though sometimes the limit might be raised to $400, and in 1973 it was raised to $800.

This system was basically the same as the one described by Özşahin (1970C).[6] What did change, however, were the criteria for priority acceptance. During the late 1960s priority was given to workers who were

    (i) 'naturally and involuntarily' unemployed
    (ii) asked for by name
    (iii) conversant in the appropriate language
    (iv) applying jointly with their spouses
    (v) members of an agricultural producers' cooperative.

1 Information supplied by the General Secretary of the T.E.S., September 1972.

2 The T.E.S. has two regional directorates at Istanbul and Ankara, the former with twenty-five and the latter with forty-three regional offices.

3 Throughout this paper, a conversion rate of £1 = T.L. 35 has been used unless otherwise stated. This rate is slightly below that of the 1970 devaluation so as to compensate in part for the subsequent adjustments.

4 In the original Turkish-German agreement of 1961, the maximum residence period was limited to 2 years, but this stipulation was cancelled in 1964.

5 These rates applied if renewing an old passport. If obtaining a new passport, the cost in 1972 was T.L. 1000 (subsequently increased to T.L. 1500).

6 However, observers in the mid 1960s emphasised the migrants' transport costs to and living expenses in Istanbul and Ankara, and one expert estimated these at T.L. 400-500 in 1967. In the early years even officially recruited migrants sometimes paid *all* their transport costs. O.E.C.D. estimated that 20,000 out of 177,000 sent by the T.E.S. in 1965 travelled at their own expense.

In addition, a rotation system was operated so that different provinces (*iller*) had priority each year.

In April 1972, four principles for priority were recognised, and a new rotation system for the selection of unskilled workers established. Priority was to be accorded to

(i) members of producer cooperatives
(ii) applicants in areas of natural catastrophes
(iii) applicants with a close family member (normally a husband or wife) already abroad
(iv) applicants from less developed regions, for which purpose all areas of the country were classified as (a) less developed (b) developing or (c) developed. Less developed provinces were to receive two years' priority, developing provinces one year's priority.[1]

However, because of its relative failure (see below §3.6.11) the government considered terminating the producer cooperative scheme (Kayser 1972C), though it decided to continue with it after all.[2] Over 13,000 workers had departed under the scheme up until the end of 1971.

But in addition to the new principles for allocating priority, new restrictions on applicants were introduced at the same time, in order to keep the queue, which had reached one and a quarter million, down to manageable proportions. No applications would be accepted from male unskilled workers over the age of 25 (since they could be expected to have to wait for ten years before departure) or from skilled workers over 40. The T.E.S. would destroy the records of former male applicants who had not been placed by the age of 35. No strict age limits would be applied to female applicants since they could normally expect to be placed within a few months. Removal of the names of unskilled males over 35 reduced the queue to one million applicants, though by 1973 it had risen again to 1.2 million.

The existence of a queue with an estimated ten year wait, together with certain legitimate queue jumping practices, led to the growth of corrupt queue-jumping practices – in certain areas at least.[3] There, aspirant migrants have had to pay a bribe to the local employment office official. This might amount to as much as three or

---

1 The provinces alloted 2 years priority were:

Adıyaman,	Ağrı	Artvin,	Bingöl,	Bitlis,	Çankırı,
Çorum,	Diyarbakır,	Erzincan	Gümüşhane	Hakkâri,	Kars,
Kastamonu,	Kırşehir,	Malatya	Maraş,	Mardin,	Muş,
Nevşehir,	Niğde,	Siirt,	Sinop,	Sivas	Tunceli,
Urfa,	Van	Yozgat			

Those accorded 1 year priority were:

Afyon,	Antalya,	Bilecik,	Burdur,	Denizli	Edirne,
Erzurum,	Gaziantep,	Giresun,	Hatay,	Isparta,	Kırklareli,
Muğla,	Ordu,	Rize,	Samsun,	Tekirdağ	Tokat,
Trabzon,	Uşak.				

Source: Milliyet, 10 Nisan (April) 1972.

2 *Milliyet,* 13 Kasim (November) 1972.

3 This information was supplied to the author by departing workers. No information about this was available from official sources.

Priority of less developed provinces in the despatch of migrant workers, 1972

four thousand lira (about £86—£114). Unfortunately it has been impossible to discover just how widespread and systematic this system of bribes has been; it emerged during the last few years as the average wating-time prior to departure lengthened substantially, and must surely have been encouraged by the new age restrictions which meant that waiting one's turn was no longer sufficient to guarantee eventual departure. However, this spread of a bribery system has meant a reduction in the chances of acceptance of applications from those in greatest need such as the unemployed and the landless rural proletariat. As yet, however, there is no evidence that this corruption has occured on a national scale.

3.3.2   *The legal situation of Turkish workers abroad: permits and rights*

The legal situation of Turkish workers abroad normally depends on the bilateral agreement negotiated between Turkey and the particular host country. For although there is a large literature on the free movement of labour provisions of the E.E.C., these apply to E.E.C. nationals, not to recruited workers from non-E.E.C. countries (unless it is explicitly stated that the latter are included).[1] Of course, since Turkey has signed Articles of Association with the E.E.C., the free movement of labour provisions should ultimately apply to her. The situation at present is that these provisions will be introduced gradually between the end of the twelfth (1975) and the twenty-second (1985) year after the coming into effect of the Agreement signed in 1963 (Article 36). In the meantime (Article 37) each member country of the E.E.C. will treat Turkish workers employed in the Community without any discrimination as to conditions of work or remuneration. This means that Turkish workers in theory get the same rate for the job as do nationals (though this can be evaded by, for instance, introducing special grades for foreign workers, and there have been reports that unofficial migrants have been forced to accept lower wages); until late 1973 it also meant that employers could not refuse to give a notified job vacancy to a Turk on grounds of nationality.[2] However, it also means that certain forms of discrimination against Turks (as non-E.E.C. nationals) in the labour market and social and political spheres still persist. To illustrate the sort of controls which have been inforce, the situation in Germany (whose government has to some extent liberalized controls because of the large demand for foreign workers) will be described here.[3]

Although in theory migrants to Germany were required to get a labour permit and visa before their arrival, in practice this stipulation was not strictly enforced during periods of severe labour shortage; thus many non-official migrants would enter on tourist passports, and subsequently obtain a work permit after they had found a job. Until the policy change of March 1971 (see below), the permit normally

1 The free movement of labour provisions are published in Böhning and Stephen 1971E and summarized in Böhning 1972bE, Chapter 2.

2 Though in 1972 Italy demanded that her workers should be given preference over the other supplying countries on the ground that she was a full member of the E.E.C. This request was in effect granted when W. Germany and the Netherlands banned non-E.E.C. immigrant workers in late 1973.

3 For an excellent summary (on which these paragraphs are based) of the situation of migrant workers in Germany before March 1971, see Böhning, 1970aE.

allowed the migrant to work in a named workplace for one year, irrespective of any change in the labour market situation. The worker had to apply again to the employment authorities to renew the permit or to change his job. After two years employment with a particular firm, a worker could be given a renewed permit without a named workplace.

The longer the worker stayed the more rights he received. After five years of uninterrupted employment or a total of eight years residence, or after marriage to a German national, the foreign migrant was automatically entitled to stay and work for up to three years in whatever job he chose no matter how high the unemployment rate was. After ten years of residence, the worker could receive a work permit without any time limit.

The *Arbeitserlaubnisverordnung* of 2nd March, 1971, changed the policy as follows: (1) the labour permit was to be offered without constraints with respect to specific occupations or enterprises, (2) its geographical validity was to be enlarged, (3) it was to be offered for up to 2 years and in special cases, 5 years, and (4) the number of cases where a labour permit was not required for employment was to be increased (Hüfner 1972E, p. 143). In June 1973, the government introduced new regulations designed to discourage use of temporarily recruited workers. Employers would have to demonstrate that they could provide adequate housing, and would have to pay a much higher recruitment fee (£160 per worker instead of £50). And immigration into centres with an existing high concentration of foreign workers, such as Munich and Stuttgart, would be extremely strictly limited. A levy on employers of foreign workers to pay for such social infrastructural investment for immigrants as could be postponed no longer was also proposed. However, no change was made in the increased rights a worker obtains as he stays longer. In November 1973, recruitment of non-E.E.C. immigrant workers was banned, and in January 1974, it was proposed to encourage those already in Germany to return home by paying them a gratuity (p. 23, fn.1).

In contrast with the agreements negotiated with Spain, Greece, Portugal and Yugoslavia, the German-Turkish agreement did not mention sympathetic consideration for family members. Generally dependants have been admitted if the worker could show that he could provide suitable housing for them. Often, however, the worker has found that the simplest way was to find a job for his wife and obtain her entry that way. But although the worker pays taxes, local family allowances are only paid if the children are actually resident in the host country[1].

Thus in practice, even after the new controls of June and November 1973, if a worker has successfully lasted out the first few years it has been fairly easy for him to stay in Germany for life. Adjustment of the migrant stock in times of recession — one of the major advantages in using temporarily recruited migrants from the point of view of the host country — has to take place primarily through control of new arrivals. But as the absolute number of migrants successfully seeking permanent residence rises, the flexibility of the temporarily recruited migration system correspondingly falls. This reduction in flexibility is inevitable, given the general preference of employers for workers whom they have already employed but who,

1 However, in 1974 E.E.C member countries have been negotiating legislation to make social security provision for non–E.E.C. workers already imported comparable with that for workers from member states.

by continuous employment, obtain more and more rights. Consequently it is not surprising that Germany has been considering policy changes such as employing Turkish workers in German subsidiaries to be set up in Turkey,[1] or encouraging or enforcing their return home,[2] or settling those already there and taking few, if any more.

3.4   The socio-economic characteristics of Turkish migrant workers

3.4.1. *Distribution by sex*

During the period 1961–72 there has been a large rise in the proportion of women in official migrant departures – from 5% in 1961–2 to 16% in 1970–1 (and an even greater increase in the proportion of women in official departures to Germany (Table A11). Secondly, there has been a marked cyclical variation in the proportion of female departures, which rose sharply during the 1967 slump and declined as the cycle picked up again. In other words, the demand for female migrant workers has been much less sensitive to fluctuations abroad than has the demand for male migrant workers. This is shown very clearly by the change in the *stocks* of Turkish workers in Germany between September 1966 and March 1967: the number of men fell by almost 25,000 (19%) whereas the number of women fell by only 1,810 (7%). Comparison between German and Turkish sources suggests that the proportion of women in unofficial departures corresponds roughly to that in official ones. Two counter-balancing influences seem to be at work: men seem to have been more likely to go abroad unofficially in the hope of getting a job (which would tend to lead to a higher share of males among unofficial migrants), but women who have left to join their husbands as dependants, and not as workers, have often taken a job on arrival (so raising the proportion of female *workers* not despatched officially from Turkey).

However, the proportion of female migrant workers is still disproportionately low in view of their share in the economically active population, which amounted to 38% in 1965 and 37% in 1970.[3] On the other hand, according to the T.E.S. survey data, the proportion of female migrant workers who had previously been employed in the non-agricultural labour force was 29% in the 1968 survey, 19% in 1969 and 15% in 1971.[4] If only those females who were employed before departure are included (i.e. if housewives are excluded), these proportions rise to 94%, 87% and 87% respectively. In either case the results greatly exceed the share of women in Turkish non-agricultural employment which was 8% in 1965 and 11% in 1970. Particularly significant is the high proportion of skilled female migrant workers (see below §3.4.10), though this has declined somewhat now that the pioneer years of female migration are over and 'mass' migration of unskilled women become

---

1 Preliminary discussions on this issue were in progress during September 1972.

2 See p. 23, fn 1.

3 In 1965 56% of women aged 15 years and over were classed as economically active.

4 15% of the women in the S.P.O. survey had been employed in the non-agricultural labour force prior to departure.

established. So far, however, female migrants have been less representative of the female e.a.p. than their male counterparts.

Although the proportion of women among Turkish migrant workers has been rising and that of those from the longer established exporting countries declining slightly, Turkey still has a relatively low proportion of female workers in its migrant worker stock abroad (particularly when compared with Greece (Table A11).[1] Nonetheless, the migration of Turkish women is becoming increasingly important – and it is therefore unfortunate that most of the surveys of Turkish migrant workers have included a disproportionately small number of women[2] so that general statements about the socio-economic characteristics of female workers and about their situation on return are particularly liable to error.

3.4.2   *Regional origins*

Tables 7a and 7b show the regional distribution of Turkish migrant workers *before departure*. Table 7a is based on official departures only, whereas Table 7b is based on all arrivals in Germany. Although they are not strictly comparable owing to differences in the regional classification,[3] they tell the same story. The richer, more westernized and more conveniently located regions of Thrace and Marmara, and North Central Anatolia have had a dominant share throughout, not just absolutely but also relatively, in the sense that their share in supplying migrants greatly exceeds their share in the total population. Similarly the poorer regions – especially South-East Anatolia, but also East Central Anatolia and the Mediterranean, have always supplied a lower proportion of migrants than their share in the total population. The main changes over the decade can be seen most clearly from columns 15 and 16 of Table 7a. These show a region's share in supplying officially recruited migrants over the periods 1964–6 and 1969–71 as percentages of its share in the total population for the years 1965 and 1970 respectively. During the decade the relative shares of 7 of the 9 regions rose, the exceptions being Marmara whose relative share fell substantially, though she remained *absolutely* the largest supplier, and North-East Anatolia. Indeed even in those eastern and southern regions whose relative share did rise, the improvement was only slight – most noticeably in South-Eastern Anatolia. For even though priority was supposed to be given to less developed regions, in fact, over the period 1968–71 the group of provinces listed by the Turkish Employment Services as least developed (see footnote 1 p. 67) only just maintained their share in the total of official departures, while the share of the

1   The particularly low proportions in the surveys of returning or returned workers conducted by the T.E.S. and S.P.O. are partly explained by the fact that since women did not start to leave 'on mass' till later on in the 1960s, one would still expect a lower proportion among those returning. However, women may well be more likely to stay on and settle abroad.

2   There are, however, variations in the situation between the host countries. In 1969 the proportion of Turkish males to Turkish workers in Germany (79%) was very similar to that of all foreign workers (approximately 80%). On the other hand 97% of Turkish workers in France over the period 1968–70 were male, as compared with approximately 81% for all European migrant workers there.

3   The T.E.S. regional classifications have been used here unless otherwise stated. These are described in full after Table 7b.

Table 7a. *Percentage distribution of Turkish migrant workers and of Turkish population by province of residence and year*

Regions[1] (T.E.S. data)	Regional distribution of official migrant worker departures (%)												Total Population		Relative shares of provinces in despatching migrants	
	1963	1964	1965	1966	1967	1968	1969	1970	1971	1972	Average 1964–66	Average 1969–71	1965 Census	1970 Census	1964–6 (11/13) ×100	1969–70 (12/14) ×100
	1	2	3	4	5	6	7	8	9	10	11	12	13	14	15	16
Marmara	40	34	35	32	40	28	24	27	27		34	26	15	16	226	167
Aegean	13	12	18	17	14	14	16	14	17		16	16	15	15	101	104
Mediterranean	2	5	6	7	8	9	8	7	8		6	8	11	11	55	69
S.E. Anatolia	—	0	1	1	2	3	1	1	2		1	1	8	8	9	16
N.E. Anatolia	4	4	3	3	4	4	5	3	5		3	4	4	6	83	68
Black Sea	11	15	12	12	9	14	13	13	12		13	13	15	13	89	98
E. Central	3	5	5	5	3	6	6	6	5		5	6	9	8	57	68
N. Central	22	19	13	15	15	13	15	21	16		16	17	15	15	108	119
S. Central	6	7	7	9	5	9	11	9	10		7	10	7	9	97	114

Sources: Turkish Employment Service, *Yearly Labour Reports*
Republic of Turkey, State Institute of Statistics, *Census of Population 1965*, Ankara 1969, & *Genel Nüfus Sayımı 1970 (Telegraphed results)*, 1970

1 Key to regions used in T.E.S. data follows. Impossible to identify precise composition of regions used in German data.

Percentages may not add to 100 because of rounding.

Turkish Employment Service classification of regions

Marmara (7)	*Aegean* (9)	*North Central* (10)	*East Central* (7)	*South Central* (5)	*Mediterranean* (6)	*North East* (5)	*South East* (9)	*Black Sea* (9)
Bursa	Aydın	Ankara	Adıyaman	Afyon Karahisar	Adana	Ağrı	Bingöl	Giresun
Edirne	Balıkesir	Bilecik	Amasya	Kayseri	Antalya	Artvin	Bitlis	Gümüşhane
Istanbul	Burdur	Bolu	Elâzığ	Konya	Gaziantep	Erzincan	Diyarbakır	Kastamonu
Kırklareli	Çanakkale	Çankırı	Malatya	Nevşehir	Hatay	Erzurum	Hakkâri	Ordu
Kocaeli	Denizli	Çorum	Sivas	Niğde	İcel	Kars	Mardin	Rize
Sakarya	Isparta	Eskişehir	Tokat		Maraş		Muş	Samsun
Tekirdağ	İzmir	Kırşehir	Tunceli				Siirt	Sinop
	Manisa	Kütahya					Urfa	Trabzon
	Muğla	Uşak					Van	Zonguldak
		Yozgat						

Table 7b: *Percentage distribution of Turkish migrant worker arrivals in W. Germany by province of origin and year of arrival*

Regions[1]	1962	1963	1964	1965*	1966	1967	1968	1969	1970	1971
Istanbul & Thrace	53	41	32	34	37	44	24	20	21	22
Ankara & C. Anatolia	13	24	28	25	21	16	23	24	23	23
N. Anatolia	4	10	5	9	13	11	14	16	17	14
W. Anatolia	–	21	18	16	15	11	20	24	27	25
E. Anatolia	30	4	14	11	8	10	10	8	4	8
S. Anatolia	–	1	3	5	7	9	9	8	8	8

Source: W. Germany: Bundesanstalt für Arbeit, *Ausländische Arbeitnehmer 1962–1971*, Nürnberg 1963–1972.

1 Key to regions used in T.E.S. data as for Table 7a. Impossible to identify precise composition of regions used in German data.

* Estimated.

Percentages may not add to 100 because of rounding.

group of less developed provinces actually fell, (and that of the most developed provinces rose).

These figures do not take into account unofficial migration. *A priori*, one might expect a higher proportion of such migrants to have come from the richer provinces since they would have been more likely to be able to raise the necessary cash for departure, and would have had lower transport costs. On the other hand, they would have been more likely to have held a reasonably well-paid job and so might have had more to lose if they took a chance on finding employment abroad, whereas a landless peasant from Eastern Anatolia would have had almost everything to gain. Clearly the crucial factor has been the absolute cost of becoming an unofficial migrant. Assuming that the worker has had to buy a one year passport plus the $200 currency requirement, and has travelled by bus to Germany, where he has stayed without payment while he was seeking a job, the minimum cost in 1972 would still have been £160–170 – a sum out of the question for the urban unemployed or landless peasantry. It would therefore seem most unlikely that a higher proportion of actual (as opposed to aspirant) unofficial migrants have come from the poorer provinces.

There is a further reason why the apparent improvement in the share of the poorer provinces may be overstated (or, to put it another way, why during the early years of migration the share of the poorer provinces may have been understated). This is because the marked fall during the mid- and late-1960s in the proportion of migrants who lived in İstanbul before departure is to some extent due to improvements in recruitment procedures. There was no longer any need to use the urban centres (especially Istanbul) as 'staging-posts': prospective migrants stood as good a change of acceptance if they applied from their home village.[1]

1 It is however impossible to identify to what extent the much higher proportion of migrants leaving from (as compared with those born in) urban centres was due to deliberate or accidental use of the town as a migration 'staging post'. Abadan (1964A) for instance reported that although 41% of her sample cited İstanbul as place of residence prior to departure, only 17% had been born there. Similarly, in his 1966 survey of migrants who had returned to the Marmara region, Tuna (1967A) found that whereas 92% of the males reported Marmara as their place of origin prior to departure, only 66% had been born there.

To summarize: the vanguard migrants came from the richer provinces, and although the inter-regional distribution of migrants has moved closer to the inter-regional distribution of population, the gap is still substantial. A similar sort of experience occurred in Yugoslavia, though with a much narrower gap: in 1970 the ratio of migrants to total population in underdeveloped provinces was 3.1% as compared with a ratio of 3.4% in the rest of the country, 5.1% in the relatively developed province of Croatia, but only 2.8% in the comparatively rich province of Slovenia (Nikolić 1972a p. 4).

3.4.3 Rural or urban origins

The available information on the rural or urban origins of Turkish migrant workers has been gleaned directly or indirectly from surveys. Few surveys (e.g. Abadan 1964A, Aker 1972D, S.P.O. 1971A) have enquired into the actual size of the place of origin. More often surveys have merely enquired into the administrative title of the place concerned and inferred its size from that. Administratively Turkey is divided into 67 *iller*, or provinces, which are subdivided into a total of 572 provincial districts (*ilçeler*). These districts are further subdivided into a total of 887 sub-districts (*bucaklar*), each of which contains a number of villages (*köyler*). All province and district centres, together with towns of over 2000 inhabitants are designated municipalities (*belediyeler*). However, the size of provinces, districts, and their centres varies substantially.[1] Thus there is only a very crude correspondence between locations classified as villages and subdistricts, and those with a population of under 10 000, as often subdistrict centres have a higher population, and district (or even provincial[2]) centres a lower one.[3]

The various survey results are summarized in Tables A12a–c. By far the most significant trend has been the increase in those living in a village before departure. The proportion of village migrants rose substantially during the latter half of the 1960s, though it seems to have been falling off somewhat since then. This increase was of course partly attributable to improved recruitment procedures; indeed, the appearance of a recent decline may be due to the lengthening of the waiting list for unskilled male applicants (now estimated at about 10 years) – an increasing proportion of applicants from villages may have moved to urban areas in the hope of increasing their incomes before their applications to work abroad were accepted.

The same sort of qualifications apply to the comparison of migrants' places of birth and places of residence before departure, which, as would be expected, show

---

1 In 1970 the largest *il* was İstanbul with a population of almost 3 million; the smallest, Hakkari with 102 927; the population of these two province centres were 2 247 630 and 10 029 respectively.

2 In 1965 five, and in 1970 one *province* centre had a population of less than 10 000.

3 However, since the S.P.O.'s 1971 sample included few such 'intermediate' areas, the two distinctions correspond quite closely: 42.7% of the sample came from the 'country' as compared with 43.3% from villages or subdistricts.

a sizeable net inflow from rural to urban areas. However, the proportion of village-born migrants departing from urban areas has declined during the decade.[1]

But in spite of the increasing share of rural workers in migrant departures, this comes nowhere near to their share in the indigenous population or labour force. In 1965, 65%, and in 1970, 61% of the population lived in a sub-district centre or village, in addition to which there were 235 sub-province centres which had a population of under 5000 in 1970 (Turkey, S.I.S. 1965 and 1970).

3.4.4   *Age*

Unfortunately data on the age of applicant migrant workers are not available. It is usually possible to estimate age on departure only by subtracting from a worker's age at the time of interview the amount of time he has been working abroad. As would be expected, migrant workers have been concentrated in the 20—45 years old age group (Table A13), though certain variations in the distribution within this interval have taken place over the decade. Firstly, the increasing proportion of female migrants has tended to reduce the mean age, as female applicants tend to be concentrated in the younger age groups and then to have a much shorter waiting period prior to departure.[2] Secondly, the lengthening of the waiting period for unskilled male departures has entailed a corresponding increase in their age on departure. This latter effect outweighed the first until very recently: thus the mean age of Abadan's sample in 1963 was 28 years 11 months (or just under 28 years at the time of their departure from Turkey) as compared with a mean of 29 years 6 months at the time of departure in the Aker survey (1970/1). But the introduction in April 1972 of the new regulation according to which unskilled male applicants must be under 25 while skilled ones must be under 40 at the time of application has tended to check increases in the age of departing migrants (unless the regulations have led to widespread misreporting of age), as has the increasing proportion of skilled workers (who have normally been placed within a few months) among migrant departures.

As would be expected, the proportion of migrant workers in the younger age groups is substantially higher than that for the indigenous economically active population, with the exception of the 15—24 group where the reverse is the case (Table A13).

Although there seems to be little difference between the mean (or median) ages of Turkish and other nationalities of migrant workers, according to the German data the age distribution of the Turks is much more concentrated around the mean than

---

1   For instance, 24% of Tuna's Marmara sample (1967A) had been *born* in a village whereas only 8% were living in one prior to departure. The corresponding proportions from the S.P.O.'s 1971 survey are 57% and 50% respectively. The much smaller gap is to be explained chiefly by the wider coverage and later date of the survey.

2   32% of Turkish female workers in Germany in 1968 were under 25, and 55% under 30, as compared with 7% and 36% for male workers (Germany, Bundesanstalt für Arbeit, 1970B).

that of all other foreign workers taken together, and slightly more concentrated around the mean than that of other southern European exporting countries.[1]

In other words, although the Turkish migrant worker stock has 'aged' slightly while abroad as some of its members have stayed away for five or more years, Turkish (and to a lesser extent Yugoslav and Greek) workers abroad are a long time behind the Italians in the ageing process. It may be that at least a significant minority will not follow the same path but will return to work and settle in their home country rather than finish up as permanent immigrants abroad.[2]

3.4.5 *Marital status*

Roughly speaking, during the 1960s, the urban bachelor gave way to the rural family man. The proportion of unmarried workers amongst departing migrants fell substantially from about 40% in 1963 (Abadan) to 14% in 1970/1 (Aker). This corresponds reasonably well with a survey of the *stock* of Turkish workers in Germany in 1968 which found that 18% were unmarried,[3] (Table A14).

Thus even recently, when the proportion of single workers had fallen substantially, it was still somewhat higher than that for the comparable portion of the indigenous population; according to the preliminary 1% sample results of the 1970 census, 10% of the population aged 20 and over had never been married. Again, however, it is not possible to find out to what extent this narrowing of the differences between migrants and the native population was due to a change in the sort of workers applying and to what extent it was due to the fact that a large proportion of applicants had to wait a long time before departure (during which time they got married). However, the S.P.O. survey of returned workers (most of whom had departed before the 'queue' became so long) found that a much higher proportion of the rural sample were married before departure.[4] It therefore seems likely that the rise in the proportion of married migrants during the later 1960s was mainly due to the increase in village departures.

According to the German survey of 1968, the proportion of Turkish workers who were married exceeded that for any other nationality (82% as compared with 78% for Greece and Portugal, 76% for Yugoslavia and 71% for all foreign workers).

---

1 78% of Turkish male workers were between the ages of 25 and 40, as compared with 59% for all male foreign workers and 32% for German males. The age structure of female workers was much more 'normal': 55% of both Turks and all foreign workers were under 30, as compared with 48% for German women (*ibid*).

2 Böhning (1972bE chapter 4) argues that the steps from temporary migrant worker to permanent immigrant constitute a slippery slope from which there is virtually no return. Although the proportion of Turks who had in 1968 been continuously resident in Germany for 4 or more years is less than that of all foreign workers (for men, 43% as compared with 57%, and for women, 21% as compared with 39%), Böhning's view cannot be regarded as conclusively refuted (see §3.6.14).

3 The T.E.S. surveys report smaller proportions of bachelors, but this is largely attributable to the fact that the migrants were interviewed after working abroad.

4 96% of the rural sample were married prior to departure as compared with 65% of the urban sample. The proportion of female spinsters was much higher than that of male bachelors, but this result — as with all those for the female sub-sample in the S.P.O. results — must be treated with extreme caution.

On the other hand, the proportion of married Turks who left their wives in their home country was higher than that for any other nationality. According to the German survey of 1968, less than half of the male Turkish workers in Germany had their wives with them, as compared with 58% for all foreign workers.[1] This proportion has of course risen over the decade as migrants have established themselves abroad and sent for their wives (often so that they can both work and so attain their savings target more quickly).

3.4.6 Children

The available information about the children of married migrants has to be treated with care, as its interpretation depends on the time when it was obtained. Thus one would expect returned migrants to have more children than those interviewed before departure (assuming that they have taken their holidays at home in Turkey or taken their wives with them). Furthermore, the lengthening of the waiting list means that workers who have departed recently are likely to have more children at the time of departure than were those who left in the early 1960s, a supposition which seems to be confirmed by the available evidence.

Returned workers seem to have slightly smaller families than the indigenous population.[2] The S.P.O. survey found that the returned married migrants had an average of 2.9 children (2.3 in urban and 3.6 in rural areas (Table A15a)) *at the time of the survey*. This compares favourably with a mean of 3.1 children per married woman in the 20–39 age group in 1970.[3]

Since a smaller proportion of Turks than of other foreign workers have tended to be accompanied by their families, the ratio of Turkish children to workers abroad is comparatively low.[4] Among those Turks whose children were in Germany, the mean number of children per employed male was very close to that of all other nationalities taken together (being if anything slightly below (Table A15b)). On the other hand, the large and increasing number of Turkish children in Germany[5] has been causing serious social and educational difficulties.

3.4.7 Dependants

The S.P.O. survey enquired how many dependants the migrant workers had when the survey was conducted. The mean for all workers was 4.6, for males 4.8, for

1 Turkish surveys conducted in Turkey normally underestimate the proportion of workers joined by their wives, as such workers tend to be much less likely to return to Turkey (and be included in the survey). This particularly applies to the T.E.S. surveys.

2 For a discussion of the effect of migration on the birth rate see §2.2.3.

3 1970 census, sampling results.

4 According to the German survey of 1968, this was below the ratio for all foreign workers. But although the Turkish ratio was comparatively low (27%) it was over twice that for Yugoslavia (13%).

5 Estimated at 70 000–80 000 in 1972. A detailed survey of the problem is given in a series of articles in *Milliyet*, March 9th–13th, 1973.

workers in the urban sample 4.0, and for workers in the rural sample 5.3 (Table A16). This compares with an average household size for all Turkey of approximately 5.6 in 1965 and 6.4 in 1970. Since there may well be more than one income earner per household, migrant workers probably have an above average number of dependants (though the S.P.O. data overstate dependants before departure as 16% were unmarried before they left but married at the time of interview). Thus this may have contributed towards the economic pressure to earn a higher income by working abroad.

3.4.8 *Literacy*

The proportion of illiterates *rose* during the 1960s as the share of village and of female migrant workers increased:[1] the percentages of illiterates in the Abadan, Tuna, T.E.S. 1969, T.E.S. 1971 and Aker 1970/71 surveys respectively were 3%, 1%, 10%, 6% and 9%,[2] (Table A17).

Even so, the proportion of literates amongst Turkish migrants has been substantially higher than that for the indigenous population: in 1965, the illiteracy rate for males in the 15—65 age group was estimated at 33%, and that for females at 71%. The corresponding figure for 1970 (using the 1% sample results) are 27% and 63%. Even compared with the estimate of 46% illiterates in the e.a.p. between 20 and 40 years old in 1970 the proportion of illiterates among migrant workers is still extremely low.

It also compares quite favourably with that for some other migrant nationalities abroad. According to Livi-Bacci (1971C), for instance, the proportion of illiterates among Portuguese male emigrants ranged from 20% in the 20—24 age group to 13% in the 30—34 group and 22% in the 40—44 group, increasing still further with age[3] (1968 data). Yugoslav migrants, however, have tended like the Turks to be highly literate as compared with their indigenous population, although there are huge regional variations (Begtić 1972E, pp. 25—26). However, the low illiteracy rate among Turkish as compared with some other migrant nationalities is particularly striking since Turkey has a much higher illiteracy rate than the other main supplying countries. It is probably to be explained partly by the greater concentration of Turkish migrants in the younger age groups, partly by Turkey's late start (so that at any time it had a higher proportion of vanguard workers than most other exporting nationalities at that time), and perhaps partly by a less strict definition as to what constitutes literacy.

---

1 Though during the early years of 'vanguard' migration, the proportion of literate women tended to exceed that of men as only fairly well-educated women from urban areas went to work abroad. Also, whereas in the early years, older migrants tended to be illiterate, the length of the queue has effectively precluded their departure and so raised the proportion of literates, *ceteris paribus*.

2 This last figure also includes those whose level of education was unknown.

3 According to the O.E.C.D. data, 31% of the Portuguese labour force was unable to read in 1960 (O.E.C.D. 1969, p. 83). Since Turkish migrants have been more concentrated in the 25—35 age group, the impact of age on migrant illiteracy rates has hardly been able to show up.

3.4.9 Education

The same factors which brought about changes in the literacy level of departing migrants also affected their overall educational attainment. Thus the latter tended to decline over the decade as an increasing proportion of less well-educated migrants from rural areas were recruited.[1] On the other hand, there was an absolutely small but nonetheless important fall in the proportion of higher level manpower amongst the departing migrants.[2] 5% of the Abadan (1963) survey had had lycée education or higher as compared with an average of 3% for the T.E.S. surveys and with 4% for the Turkish e.a.p. in 1965, (Table A17).

Indeed the overall educational attainment of the migrants compares most favourably with that of the e.a.p.[3] Although the difference is greater at the lower levels of educational attainment, it persists through all levels, especially for women. Furthermore, even though it is narrowed when the older age groups are excluded, it is by no means eliminated.

Systematic information on the educational attainment of foreign workers by nationality is not available. Data on Yugoslav workers temporarily employed abroad show that only about 10% have no qualifications, while about 90% have at least completed elementary school and 25% secondary education, though there are significant differences between regions (Begtić 1972E and Nikolić 1972bE).

3.4.10 Vocational training and skills

Just as the educational levels of migrant workers have exceeded those for the e.a.p., though by decreasing amounts, so also has the amount of vocational training received. In Turkey, occupational training may be obtained through the school system, through special formal courses (e.g. those run by the Ministry of Industry for workers in small scale enterprises), through the guild (*esnaf*) system (whereby an apprentice (*çırak*) will be trained as a qualified workman (*kalfa*), and then may subsequently become a master workman (*usta*) and later a head master workman (*ustabaşı*), and through on-the-job training in the factory.

The proportion of migrants who had received vocational training through the school system at the beginning of the 1960s was particularly high — 14% for men and 24% for women (Table A17) — but this fell quite substantially over the decade, so that Aker, for instance, found that only 5% had graduated from and another 1% attended vocational schools.[4] In this respect the gap between the qualifications of

1 It is not as yet clear whether the recent shift back towards urban migrants has been accompanied by an improvement in educational levels.

2 Most of the 'brain drain' from Turkey went to the U.S. and Canada (Franck 1970).

3 In addition to the differential in illiteracy reported above, 64% of Aker's 1970—1971 sample had had elementary education as compared with 36% of the e.a.p. between 15 and 65 in 1970. The S.P.O. survey obtained similar results: 65% of the male and 40% of the female migrants had had elementary education as compared with 39% and 12% respectively for the e.a.p. (1965). Indeed 77% of the rural sample had had elementary education (though only 4% had had any higher level).

4 The S.P.O. survey results lie, as one would expect, between these two extremes: 7% of the total, 11% of the urban and 1% of the rural samples had completed intermediate level technical and vocational education (Table A17).

80

migrants and of the e.a.p. has narrowed. According to the sampling results of the 1970 census, 3% of the total (4% of the male and 2% of the female) population between the age of 20 and 40 had completed technical and vocational education at the intermediate level.

Information on the other methods of training is more sketchy. 29% of the Abadan sample (1964) and 27% of the S.P.O. sample (31% of the urban sub-sample) reported that they had attended some occupational training course,[1] (Table A18). Although explicit information on the other sources of training is not available, one can make a rough estimate of the proportion of workers who had had at least one form of occupational training by examining the proportion of workers who had held skilled positions prior to departure.

All surveys to date have brought out the relatively high proportion of skilled workers among the migrants,[2] though this has changed somewhat over the decade as on the supply side, the skilled vanguard flows were replaced by less skilled flows of 'mass migration', but on the demand side, increasing proportions of skilled migrants were requested. In the case of the Abadan survey in 1963 this was approximately 50%. According to the T.E.S. surveys of 1967, 1968, 1969 and 1971, skilled plus semi-skilled amounted to 60%, 55%, 54% and 50% respectively. The T.E.S. data based on official departures give a lower figure: about 41% in 1964—5,[3] around 30% during 1966—8, rising to 37% in 1970 and 36% in 1971.[4] The superficial discrepancy between these figures and the surveys is probably to be explained largely by the fact that the survey sample workers had departed some years previously. The S.P.O. survey found that 47% had held skilled positions prior to departure,[5] (Table A19) 69% of Aker's sample reported skilled or semi-skilled positions. Unfortunately, the failure of any of the surveys to distinguish between skilled and semi-skilled workers complicates the issue: Turkish sources have tended to aggregate the two categories whereas in the German data skilled workers are defined much more strictly. Consequently the Germans tend to report a smaller proportion of Turks as skilled[6] (16% of males in the 1968 survey), though a larger proportion (38%) as semi-skilled.

Nonetheless, despite the qualifications which must necessarily accompany attempts to measure skill level in an under-developed country (or in any country for that matter), there is no doubt that the migrants were relatively highly skilled as compared with the rest of the e.a.p. Only 33% of the 'urban' S.P.O. sample were

---

1 According to the S.P.O. survey, the average length of attendance at such a course was 8.4 months. (Table A18).

2 In addition to the laments of employers about the loss of workers whom they had just finished training (information supplied by the Turkish Employers' Confederation).

3 Migrants to Germany, Austria and Holland only are covered.

4 In which year the proportion for men was 39% as compared with 16% for women.

5 But this only included returned migrants who were likely to be less skilled than the migrant population abroad (§4.2.3).

6 However the situation is confused because the distinction between skill level in Turkey and skill level while employed in Germany is not always made. This is significant because of the propensity of skilled migrants to work in unskilled jobs abroad.

unskilled prior to departure[1] as compared with 64% of those employed in Turkish manufacturing industry in 1965 and 59% in 1967.[2]

The S.P.O. survey attempted to break down the 'skilled' category in considerable detail (See Table A19) and has consequently brought out the relatively high proportion of top skill levels in this sample of migrants. For instance, 10% were technicians or officials, as compared with 2% for the e.a.p. in manufacturing. This is an important finding since it had to some extent been assumed that the skilled migrants had been craftsmen such as carpenters, shoemakers and the like, or new industrial workers such as turners and welders. However, Aker found that only 5% of his sample were white collar workers, of whom three-quarters were unskilled — but this is to be expected from a survey which included a much smaller proportion of vanguard migrants. And although there was certainly some narrowing of the gap between the occupational skills of the migrants and those of the Turkish e.a.p. because of changes in the sort of workers who applied for work abroad, in the later 1960s and early 1970s, the host countries increasingly demanded skilled Turkish labour.

No simple verdict can be reached as to the impact of the loss of such skilled workers to the Turkish economy, since the ultimate effect depends on (1) the replaceability of the departed skilled workers and (2) the economic contribution of the workers themselves on return and of their savings and remittances from abroad. No general conclusion can be reached with respect to the first factor, chiefly because of the segmentation of Turkish labour markets: a shortage of a particular skill in one area may well coexist with a surplus in another. Altogether, the available evidence on the nature and extent of skilled labour shortages which is reviewed in §4.2.1 below seems to indicate that no large scale shortages have as yet emerged, although problems have arisen in certain industries.

3.4.11 *Employment status before departure*

A question of major interest is whether or not it has been the unemployed who attempt to migrate. However this necessitates knowing whether workers were unemployed *at the time of application*, not just before departure, although in the early 1960s when the post-application waiting period was very short, the latter can be taken as a rough approximation for the former. Furthermore, it is also necessary to know whether or not rural migrants came from areas with considerable disguised unemployment. Since no survey has satisfactorily overcome both these two

1 Note that this includes, for instance, agricultural workers who moved to urban areas on their return: 62% of the 'urban' sample had been employed in industry prior to departure. Over three-quarters of those from manufacturing industry were skilled.

2 The German data show that in 1968 the proportion skilled in the stock of Turkish workers was higher than for other labour-exporting countries, with the exception of Yugoslavia, (Bundesanstalt für Arbeit, 1970, p. 86). Indeed only 11% of those Yugoslavs with worker's status employed abroad in March 1971 were classified as unskilled. Unfortunately, however, data on the 59% of migrants who lacked worker's status are not available. (Begtić 1972). Since 1968, the proportion skilled among *new Turkish entrants* to Germany has been higher than for the other Mediterranean emigration countries, reaching 46.3% in 1971 as compared with an average of 29.2%. Turkish workers in France have tended to be more skilled than those from other emigration countries (*Le Monde Diplomatique*, Oct 1973).

difficulties[1] the following summary of the evidence should be taken as an attempt to make the best of the available data, rather than as a conclusive answer to the question posed above. However, data on unemployment before departure are useful for examining the impact of migration on unemployment.

In 1963, Abadan found 14% of her sample had been unemployed before departure and another 2% were new entrants to the labour force. Much lower rates of pre-departure unemployment were recorded in later surveys. The S.P.O. for instance found that only 4% of the total sample and 3% of the men had been unemployed *at the time of application*[2] (Table A20a), Aker found that only 3% of his sample were unemployed prior to departure. This would seem to suggest a declining trend, but it does not take into account changes in the percentage of disguised unemployed among those who migrate. It is possible that this has risen over the decade as the proportion of rural migrants increased. 92% of the rural S.P.O. sample cited insufficient income as their main reason for migration and this suggests unsatisfactory employment; on the other hand, their responses to the question on pre-departure income suggest that many were comparatively well off as compared with the indigenous rural population. One can therefore only point to a definite fall amongst departures of openly unemployed workers during the decade – any change in departures from the disguised unemployed is as yet a matter of guesswork. However, the fall in openly unemployed migrants is to some extent to be expected in view of the lengthening waiting list: in the early years a worker who became unemployed could apply to work abroad and leave soon afterwards. But as the waiting list grew, this course of action became impossible, so that it was in the interest of any workers contemplating employment abroad to apply in advance of any potential unemployment.

There is no doubt, however, that the extent of open unemployment among migrants compares most favourably with that among the indigenous population. Estimates of urban unemployment in 1968 range from 7 to 10% of the active population. The household labour force survey (1967/8) recorded unemployment rates of between 6 and 8% (mean 7%). And the official Turkish estimate in 1973 (see Table 3) was 1 600 000 (11%). Only the 1963 Abadan survey of vanguard migrants has found pre-departure unemployment rates greater than these levels.

Yugoslavia has had the same sort of experience in that urban migrants have tended to come from the skilled élite rather than the unemployed. Except in the early years of migration, Greece's problem has been to cut down the outflow of workers in the face of serious labour shortages, and has, like Yugoslavia, had no clear positive correlation between regions of high migration and those of high unemployment (Botas 1970). In any case, the types of skilled labour demanded by the importing countries preclude any mass export of the unemployed. For although exporting labour has important effects on employment in the home country these have *not* come about simply by exporting the unemployed.

The S.P.O. survey brings out the differences between urban and rural patterns of

1 In the latter case this would seem excusable in view of the fact that the extent of disguised unemployment in the Turkish countryside is unknown. There is also the additional problem that different surveys have used different definitions of unemployment (some for instance depending on the respondent's opinion, some on the interviewer's). Also since at one time the unemployed were supposedly accorded priority in T.E.S. despatch, some workers made false declarations of unemployment to jump the queue.

2 In 1966, 3% of the men in Tuna's sample were unemployed before departure.

employment (Table A20a): 55% of the urban sample were wage earners as compared with 16% of the rural. On the other hand, 79% of the rural sample were self-employed as compared with 38% of the urban. When these results are compared with those for the e.a.p. (1965), both wage earners and self employed workers were relatively over-represented at the expense of family workers[1] (Table A20b). Changes over the decade in the distribution of pre-departure employment status have been chiefly determined by the increase in the proportion of rural migrants (so bringing about a fall in the proportion of employees).

3.4.12 *Sector of employment before departure*

Over the decade the share of migrants from the agricultural sector rose, and that of migrants from the industrial sector fell. In 1963 Abadan found that 74% came from industry, 9% from mining, 11% from agriculture, 3% from professional services, 2% from private services. In the S.P.O. sample, 37% had been employed in agriculture, 45% in industry and 18% in services[2] (Table A21). The T.E.S. survey data show a steadily rising proportion from agriculture, increasing from 30% in their 1967 survey to 41% in 1971. But the T.E.S. surveys were carried out as migrants were returning to Turkey, so that these results describe their work status before departure some years earlier. For data on migrants actually departing in 1970—1 indicate a substantial fall in agricultural migrants. For instance, Aker found that only 17% of his sample had come from agriculture, of which 16% were small landowning peasants while 1% were agricultural labourers.[3] This turnaround can be attributed mainly to the increasing demand of host countries for skilled and for female unskilled workers (both more likely to be of urban origin), and partly to the influence of the quota system on departures. But given the structure of host country demand for labour, it seems unlikely to be reversed if large scale migration recommences.

However, there is no doubt that even at the peak of ex-agricultural migration during the late 1960s, migrants from this sector have been underrepresented when compared with its share in total employment; in 1972, 65% of the labour force were still employed in agriculture and only 11% in industry (Table 3).

3.4.13 *Occupation before departure*

The migrants' list of pre-departure occupations covers most of the jobs, trades and professions known in Turkey (Table 22a). Examination of the data confirms some of the tendencies noted earlier, particularly the high (but, until recently at least,

---

1 39% of male migrants in the S.P.O. survey were wage earners as compared with 33% of the male e.a.p. in 1965; the corresponding figure for the self-employed were 56% and 44%. The difference is made up chiefly by underrepresentation of unpaid family workers in the sample, with some underrepresentation of employers in addition.

2 Again, of course, there was a difference between the urban and rural pattern: 66% of the rural sample were engaged in agriculture, 62% of the urban sample in industry.

3 But despite the low proportion of ex-agricultural migrants in the Aker sample, 52% had been born in a village and 38% lived in one prior to departure.

declining[1]) proportion employed in manufacturing occupations, and the increasing proportion of housewives. The balance between occupations has of course been determined mainly by the demand side: thus there have been few changes in the occupational distribution of skilled workers prior to departure (Table A22b). The distribution has however been weighted heavily towards 'modern' industries as compared with the proportion of the manufacturing labour force employed in these industries (compare with Table 3).

One interesting feature of the S.P.O. survey was that nearly all of those working on the land classified themselves as farmers (*çiftçi*) not as agricultural workers (*tarim işçisi*) or sharecroppers (*yarici, ortakçı*).[2] If they really were farmers, then this means that the poorest, non-land owning peasants were not migrating. In other words, there is some evidence that in agriculture, as in industry, the most appropriate potential migrants — the less skilled labourers — have not been accepted for migration.[3] This is supported by Aker's results, in which 79 out of 92 migrants employed in agriculture were small farmers (rather than sharecroppers or agricultural labourers).

3.4.14 *Size of workplace before departure*

32% of urban males (53% of those who answered the question) reported that they had been employed in industrial establishments with 10 or more employees (Table A27). But although according to the 1963 manufacturing census only 2% of establishments fell into this scale group, 69% of industrial employees did. This means that despite the high representation of 'modern' occupations, the proportion of industrial migrants employed in 'large' enterprises was lower than that of the industrial labour force.

In the service sector workers reported working in establishments with 10 or more workers than in those with less than 10 workers.

3.4.15 *Earnings before departure*

The evidence received so far on migrants' occupations suggests that, as a group, they had been earning higher incomes than the rest of the population. This hypothesis is confirmed by such direct evidence on earnings as is available. According to the S.P.O. survey (Tables A23 and 10) the mean yearly net base income for the total sample of employed workers was TL 6226 (£178), supplemented by a mean side

---

1 Though in view of the increasing foreign demand for skilled or semi-skilled manufacturing workers, this proportion does not seem likely to decline much more. The T.E.S. surveys recorded a sharp rise (from 30% in 1967 to 38% in 1968) in the proportion of workers in agricultural occupations but subsequently increases have been small (in the 1971 survey the proportion was 44% but this refers to departure time some years ago). The Aker survey suggests that it has now fallen (above, §3.4.12).

2 Indeed only 4 workers had been sharecroppers.

3 This may partly be because the poorest families could not raise the basic capital requirements for successful completion of their application (e.g. transport to and residence in Ankara or İstanbul). On the other hand, foreign reluctance to accept completely unskilled migrants may equally be responsible.

85

income of TL 382 (£11), amounting to a total of TL 6608 (£187).[1] The rural sample
had earned a mean income of less than half that earned by the urban group (mean
base income was TL 3692 as compared with TL 8165; but mean side income was
somewhat higher — TL 454 as compared with TL 327. Tuna's estimates were higher:
the mean pre-departure income was TL 8352 p.a., though the urban-rural differential
was smaller (TL 8880 for migrants from *il* centres as compared with TL 6672 for
migrants from villages). This was probably because of the large proportion of workers
from urban districts in Marmara in his survey. But both surveys bring out how the
migrants tended to be better off than their fellow countrymen. According to the
estimates of the Ankara University Study[2] the mean annual income per employed
person after tax in 1968 (i.e. *at least* three years after 77% of the migrants in the
S.P.O. sample had departed) was TL 4065, which is slightly lower than the mean
total rural income (TL 4146) in the S.P.O. sample. Certainly those in the S.P.O.
'urban' migrant sub-group were relatively well off even when compared with
'registered' workers in industry. According to the Workers Insurance Institute data,
the gross average annual wage in insured workplaces for 1964—5 was about TL 6160
before tax.[3] According to a sample of 10 firms in İzmir, Kocaeli and Zonguldak in
1969, the mean yearly wage for an unskilled worker in 1965 was TL 3810,[4] that for
a skilled worker TL 4530, for a master worker TL 6255, for a chief master worker
(or foreman) TL 8670, and for technical personnel TL 13 845. This high premium
for skill explains the relatively high mean income reported by the urban sub-group
in the S.P.O. sample. Only 29% earned a basic income of less than TL 5000 — but
only 32% had reported that they were unskilled.

48% of the rural S.P.O. sub-sample reported that they had had a basic income of
less than TL 3000. Of course, agricultural incomes are notoriously difficult to
estimate:[5] according to a careful estimate made by John Enos (1963), the post-tax
income of a 'low-income' agricultural worker was TL 1280, of a 'middle-income'
worker, TL 8250 and of a 'high income' worker (or rather, landowner) TL 40 650.
Since *at least* 60—65% of agricultural labour fell into the 'low-income' group,[6]
those in the S.P.O. sub-sample seem to have been comparatively well off as compared

1 Using an exchange rate of TL35 = £1. These figures are not adjusted for inflation. 95% of the
   workers had departed before the rate of inflation began to accelerate in mid 1968, prior to
   which it remained around 5% per annum. Given the yearly frequency distribution of departures, it turns out that mean annual income at 1965 prices is roughly equal to the unadjusted
   value.

2 Bulutay, Timur, and Ersel, 1971. This survey covered households of more than one person
   where the wife was still under 45. For a discussion of the implications of this and other
   biases in the results, see Kryzaniak & Özmucur 1972.

3 Assuming a working year of 300 days. Although coverage is improving annually, the
   Workers Insurance Institute data chiefly include larger enterprises where wages tend to be
   higher and working conditions better than in small workshops (wages in such workshops
   are often below the legal minimum).

4 Again assuming a working year of 300 days.

5 The thorough study of this subject by Hirsch (1970) is unfortunately confined to the early
   1950s.

6 Using the Hirsch income distribution estimates adjusted to allow for inflation.

with the prevailing living standards in agriculture, though within the sub-sample it is the middle, not the high income group which is slightly over-represented.[1]

The same conclusion is reached if the data from the Ankara University study are used (Bulutay, Timur and Ersel 1971). According to this, the mean annual post-tax income per employed person in places with a population of under 2000 was TL 2167 in 1968 — indeed 79% earned less than TL 2500 p.a. and 74% under TL 2000 p.a. Thus in agriculture, as in industry, the middle rank workers seem to have obtained a disproportionate share of migration opportunities at the expense of the poorest proletariat.

Although one would expect female migrants to have received lower pre-departure incomes than their male comrades, in the S.P.O. survey an inverse differential appeared, attributable to the pioneer character of this sub-group. Tuna found a small but 'normal' differential (TL 8064 p.a. for men as compared with TL 7140 p.a. for women), which has persisted since the mass migration of women began.

3.4.16   Reasons for departure

All surveys have brought out the predominantly financial motivation of Turkish migrants. For instance, 81% of the S.P.O. sample cited their desire to earn a higher income as a reason for their departure (Table A24). But this was more important for the rural than for the urban sub-sample: 92% of the former explicitly stated it on interview as compared with 73% of the latter. Women on the other hand seemed less concerned with the financial side, less than half mentioning it as a reason for departure.

Similar results were reported both by Abadan and Tuna, notably the almost one-track financial motivation of the village migrant. 77% of the Aker sample reported some financial motive as their main motivation, and nearly all the remainder gave a financial reason as their secondary motivation. However, many more (62%) cited financial difficulties as their main motive than cited the desire to save up money (13%), an interesting difference in emphasis.[2]

On the other hand, Neuloh's group gave a slightly different response: only 40% mentioned a financial reason, while 22% cited unemployment or difficulties in finding work. In comparison, only 11% of the Aker sample[3] and only 5% of the S.P.O. sample mentioned this (and another 4% job dissatisfaction).[4] Furthermore only 12% of the S.P.O. sample and 1% of the Aker sample gave occupational or vocational reasons for departure. In other words, in these surveys the emphasis was on lack of or dissatisfaction with employment rather than on financial motives for

---

1   As was noted earlier, this is also supported by the high proportion of ex-agricultural migrants who described themselves as farmers, not as agricultural labourers or sharecroppers.

2   In fact, the differences between many of the 'reasons for departure' listed in the various surveys are more of emphasis than of substance (compare, for instance, 'financial necessity' and 'lack of work').

3   Only 0.3% of this sample were actually unemployed before their departure.

4   With the growth of the queue during the 1960s there emerged an increasing gap between motivation for applying to go abroad and personal circumstances prior to departure.

departure,[1] (though often workers wanted to save so as to change their type of employment on return by starting a small business or becoming an independent farmer).

One financial reason which merits special mention is the need to repay debts. In the S.P.O. sample four workers volunteered this as a reason for departure whereas 30 reported that they had spent foreign savings on this on their return (Table 13). Unfortunately no explicit question on debt was included in the survey so that unless the worker brought up the subject himself, no mention was made of it. (In view of this, and of the widespread prevalence of debt in villages, even the 8% figure given in Table 13 should probably be counted an under-estimate.)

Perhaps the most striking feature of survey results on Turkish migrants' motives for departures is that financial reasons were emphasized so much *even though the various sub-groups of migrants have tended to be relatively well-off.*[2] Given the lower living standards of many of their fellows, it is not surprising that the queue in Turkey reached one and a quarter million in 1971, and again in 1973.

3.4.17 *Expenditure incurred in order to leave to work abroad*

The expenses which unofficial migrants must incur have been described above (§3.2.1). But even officially recruited migrants find that departure abroad is by no means costless. Aker found that the migrants in his sample (who all departed officially) spent an average of TL 960 while 5% spent over TL 2100. This brings out clearly just how severe a barrier to departure are the financial costs of migration to the 'average' Anatolian peasant — where 74% of employed persons in villages with a population of less than 2000 earn less than TL 2000 *per annum* (§3.4.15). Migration abroad is virtually impossible for the really poor proletariat, unless they can borrow from more wealthy relatives.

3.4.18 *Summary table*

For convenience, a summary of selected characteristics of Turkish migrant workers as compared with the Turkish economically active population is given below. It is, however, important to bear in mind the qualifications to the various figures as indicated in the appropriate section above.

---

1 This seems also to be the case with Spanish migrant workers in Germany (Delgado 1966E). However, Lahalle (1972E) obtained a slightly different result in a survey of migrant workers in France, 44% of whom said they had come to escape unemployment (and as many as 71% of the Algerians and 58% of the Moroccans interviewed).

2 Though of course the financial motivation of applicants does not imply that international wage differentials determine the actual volume of the migratory flow between a particular host and exporting country. Owing to excess supply of potential migrants in the supplying countries, host countries introduced recruitment policies which ensured that the actual volume of migration depended on host country demand. (For an attempt to show this econometrically, see the study described above (§3.2.3) by Böhning (1970bE).

Table 8:   *Summary of selected socio-economic characteristics of Turkish migrant workers as compared with those of the economically active population*

Characteristic	Migrant workers	E.a.p.	Direction (if any) in which the characteristic has been changing for migrant workers before departure
% males	84[1]	62[1]	Declining
% from Marmara, Aegean and N.C. Anatolia	62[1]	46[1,2]	Declining
% from rural areas[3]	50[4]	61[1,2]	Increasing, but possibly stationary or falling during early 1970s
% aged between 20 and 45	96[5]	47[1]	Little change
% married	86[6]	90[1,7]	Increasing but fairly constant during early 1970s
Mean no. of children	2.9[8]	3.1[1,9]	?
Mean no. of dependants	4.6[8]	3.6[10]	?
% illiterate	8[5]	47[1]	Increasing, possibly declining during early 1970s
% with lycée education and above	3[5]	4[1]	Declining, possibly constant during early 1970s
% of non-agricultural skilled or semi-skilled workers	67[11]	41[12]	Declining until late 1960s, then increasing
% unemployed	4[13]	10[14]	?
% employed in agriculture	41[15]	67[1]	Rising – then constant (?)
Mean earnings	TL 6608[4]	TL 4065[15]	Rising
Mean industrial earnings	TL 8492[11]	TL 6160[16]	Rising

Notes

1. 1970
2. Whole population.
3. Defined as villages and sub-district centres.
4. S.P.O. survey, before departure (mainly mid-1960s).
5. T.E.S. survey 1969–1971 average.
6. Aker survey, at time of departure (1970/71).
7. Population aged 20 and over.
8. S.P.O. survey, on return (mainly mid-late 1960s).
9. Married women aged 20 to 39.
10. Assuming 2 income earners per household; 1965
11. S.P.O. urban sample.
12. Turkish manufacturing industry, 1965.
13. S.P.O. survey at time of application.
14. 1971 – official estimate which understates agricultural unemployment.
15. Per *employed* person after tax, 1968.
16. Gross for insured workplaces 1964–5.

3.5   Information about Turkish migrants' work and life abroad

3.5.1   *Duration of stay*

When a migration system is becoming established, the later the year in which a survey of migrant workers has been conducted, the higher the mean length of stay abroad which it reports. The S.P.O. survey reported a mean length of stay abroad of 2 years 4 months, higher than that of Tuna's Marmara survey in 1966, nearly two-thirds of whom had remained abroad for one year or less (Table A25a). The T.E.S. found that workers' mean length of stay rose substantially between their

1967 and 1969 surveys but had fallen again in their 1971 survey.[1] However, only 34% of Aker's sample planned to spend less than five years in Germany, while 11% planned to spend 10—15 years and another 3% never to return.[2] This survey was based on a sample of *all* departing migrants, in contrast to the T.E.S. ones which only covered supposed returned workers, automatically excluding those who had stayed abroad, as did the results of the S.P.O. survey. So one would expect these latter surveys to provide an underestimate of the mean length of stay abroad[3] — certainly this seems to be the case, since the German survey of the migrant worker stock in 1968 found that only 20% of Turkish men (35% of women) had stayed less than 2 years while 43% had already stayed for 4 or more as compared with 57% for all foreign males. This supports Böhning's hypothesis that after the initial vanguard flows, temporarily recruited migrants tend to try to remain permanently, even if initially they did not intend to do so.

Furthermore, the Turkish S.P.O. survey data seem to support another of Böhning's hypotheses — that skilled migrant workers tend to remain abroad longer. Table A25b gives the mean duration of work abroad by skill category and shows clearly how those in the higher grades tend to stay abroad longer. In fact, the data cited by Böhning (1972aE p. 245) show only that skilled Turks tend to stay longer in one job than unskilled — though less so than for other migrant worker nationalities,[4] so that the S.P.O. results provide important confirmatory material.

The S.P.O. survey gave additional information on the number of work periods abroad, home visits, etc. 94% of the migrants had worked abroad only once, with little variation for the rural, urban, male and female sub-groups. Only 28% had never returned home during their work abroad, and these tended to be either short-stay workers, or married with family accompanying, or bachelors. Of those who mentioned the time and reason for their home visit, the majority said that they had returned for their summer holiday. Twice as many returned for New Year as for the main religious festival (Paine 1972D).

3.5.2 *Sector of employment while abroad*

Even more so than other migrant worker nationalities abroad, Turks are highly concentrated in the manufacturing and construction sectors. In 1970 and 1971,

1 20% of the 1967 sample had worked abroad for 3 or more years as compared with 62% of the 1969 one and 36% of the 1971 one.

2 8% of Delgado's sample of Spanish workers in Germany wanted, if possible, never to return. Skilled workers and female workers were more likely to want to remain permanently abroad (Delgado 1966E).

3 Though the data based on *intentions* might also be on the low side as migrants tend to underestimate how long it will take them to accumulate their target savings. On the other hand, they probably also underestimate the probability of their repatriation because of cyclical unemployment abroad.

4 He also uses Delgado's data to show that skilled Spanish males want to stay longer than unskilled, suggesting that this is because of their better earnings and employment situation. However, unskilled workers may well *have* to *try* to stay longer since their smaller wage packets mean that they cannot save as much. The point is that the host countries are most likely to *permit* skilled workers to stay.

90

84% and 81% respectively of Turkish workers in Germany were employed in these sectors (Table A26) as compared with under 50% of the indigenous German labour force. Less than 1% were employed in agriculture. Furthermore, they have tended to be employed in larger enterprises. According to the German survey of 1968, 53% of both male and female Turkish workers worked in enterprises with over 500 employees (as compared with 43% for all foreign workers).

There have, however, been some changes in the sector of employment over the decade. Firstly, the proportion of Turkish migrants working in mining abroad has fallen substantially. In 1963, 13% of migrants to Germany and over half those to Belgium worked as miners.[1] By 1970 only 7% of those in Germany were working as miners, whereas migration to Belgium had almost ceased. Secondly, the proportion employed in German manufacturing has risen from 59% in 1963 to 69% in 1969 and 1970, and 66% in 1971. Within manufacturing, the metal industries have remained the dominant employer, though more female migrant workers have been employed in the non-metal manufacturing industries − the metal industries taking second place.[2] Indeed, a higher proportion of female than of male migrants were employed in manufacturing in the early 1970s.

The most striking feature about the distribution of migrants' sector of employment while abroad is how much it differs from that before departure and how much more it differs from that of the Turkish e.a.p. (see Table 3). Indeed, as the gap between the pre-migration sectoral distribution and that of the Turkish e.a.p. has narrowed, that between the pre-migration distribution and the sectoral distribution abroad has widened.

3.5.3   *Occupation while abroad*

Turkish migrant workers abroad are concentrated in industrial occupations and in building trades as compared with the labour force in their host countries, with the Turkish e.a.p., and with their occupations prior to departure and on return (Tables A22a, A22b and A28). Of course, the data by occupation bring out many features similar to those observed from the data classified by sector of employment.

However, the S.P.O. survey raw data enable inter-temporal comparisons of the occupational profiles of individual workers to be made (Table 9), though these figures must be treated as rough approximations owing to the often tenuous correspondence between job description and job content. Only 20% (27% for the urban and 10% for the rural sub-groups) reported that they had been employed in the same occupations before departure and while away,[3] even though the proportion of those in industrial employment before departure was much higher than for the

---

1 In 1964 the proportion for Germany reached 15%.

2 In 1970 as many as 32 513 Turkish women − 42% of Turkish female migrants and one in five of the total industry's labour force − were employed in German metal industries. However, this change in the type of women's employment abroad is only in part brought out by the S.P.O. survey, in which half of the women were engaged in the more traditional type 'female' jobs.

3 The Aker survey provides information on the occupations of labourers before departure and on return and found that as many as two thirds had similar jobs.

Table 9: *Percentage distribution of Turkish migrant workers according to job similarity before departure, while abroad and on return, S.P.O. survey, 1971*

	Total %	Urban %	Rural %
a) Same job –			
Before departure and while away	7	10	6
Before departure and on return	37	30	47
While away and on return	6	10	2
Before departure, while away and on return	12	17	4
b) Different job before departure, while away and on return	38	33	41

total Turkish e.a.p. This change in employment can be treated as potentially advantageous (in that the worker may gain experience of a new job in a disciplined industrial environment) or as disadvantageous (in that skilled workers (at least) may not only be failing to develop their talents, but actually allowing them to fall into decline). On the whole (see § §3.6.7, 4.2.1 and 4.2.3), it seems that the latter probably did not completely offset the former, but that the total net outflow was so great that some loss of skills did occur, a problem which is discussed below.

3.5.4   *Number of jobs abroad*

The longer migrant workers have been away, the more one would expect them to have changed their jobs: 31% of the migrants in the S.P.O. survey (who had been away for an average of 2 years 4 months) had had more than one job while they were away (Table A27). The individual questionnaire results show distinct patterns of job change: for instance, those who began work as miners often changed their job even if this meant accepting a lower wage. Secondly, workers who had held skilled positions in Turkey but unskilled jobs abroad would sometimes manage to find and move to a job in which they could utilize their former training.[1] Thirdly, unskilled workers would move between factories, presumably in an attempt to obtain better pay and conditions, since those that did so normally reported higher earnings after their move – though other non-quantifiable factors like job satisfaction, proximity to friends and family etc. could equally have prompted such changes.

The mean duration of jobs held by migrants in the S.P.O. sample was 1 year 8 months. Even when this is adjusted to allow for the fact that some workers moved to different jobs while continuing with the same occupation, it still represents a disappointingly high rate of turnover from the point of view of worker training[2]

1 This is the explanation underlying the occasional spectacular promotions (e.g. from unskilled to official (Table A29b)). However, according to the T.E.S. surveys, the proportion of workers who had held skilled jobs in Turkey but who were employed in unskilled jobs while abroad has declined substantially (Tables A22b and A28).

2 Only 18 of the 49 workers who were abroad for 4 years or more held only one job during their stay, and of these, 7 were women. (Table A27).

(given that German employers reckon that at least 2 years employment is necessary to train an unskilled migrant) — though there is no evidence that it was the cause of the low rate of such training. Rather the reluctance of employers to train their foreign workers[1] probably contributed to the high rate of turnover. Certainly the German surveys in 1966 and 1968 found that male migrants employed in skilled positions tended to remain longer in a particular job than did unskilled, though this tendency was much less marked for Turks than for other migrant nationalities.

3.5.5   Skill level abroad

Despite variation between sources, there is no doubt that the proportion of migrants doing skilled jobs abroad has changed over the decade. This is reflected in movements in the ratio of skilled vacancies to total vacancies handled through the T.E.S. This fell from 47% in 1965 to 24% in 1966, rising gradually thereafter (though with an exceptional increase in 1967 owing to the German recession). Correspondingly the proportion of skilled Turks amongst total arrivals in Germany has risen since the mid-1960s, reaching 34% in 1970 (according to German sources), though these may not have been employed as skilled workers there, for the proportion of skilled migrant workers in Germany has normally been lower than that in Turkey before departure (Table A22b). (Indeed Neuloh (p. 117) referred to the complaints by skilled workers who had to take on a different profession in Germany).

The S.P.O. survey provided more detailed information (Table A29a). 44% of the urban, 68% of the rural and 54% of the total sample reported that they were employed in unskilled positions during their first year abroad, as compared with 32%, 75% and 51% respectively before departure.[2] The figure of 46% initially in skilled or semi-skilled positions abroad is consistent with the German estimate for the stock of Turkish migrants in 1968 (43% for men and 62% for women). The apparently surprising result is that more of the rural sub-group reported skilled employment in Germany than in Turkey. In fact, this only arises if the unskilled are treated separately: the proportion of unskilled *plus* semi-skilled in Germany (83%) exceeds that in Turkey (75%). Since it is extremely unlikely that unskilled rural workers were *initially* taken on except as unskilled workers abroad,[3] this result is probably explained by upgrading of their initial skills by workers who had become semi-skilled by the time of departure.[4]

The survey also found that the difference between the migrant's skill level before departure and abroad was greatest at the higher levels: in Turkey, 28% had worked as a master workman or higher whereas the corresponding percentage

---

1 Vocational training in Germany is designed for school-leavers without family responsibilities but with a comprehensive knowledge of the German language. It is therefore most unsuitable for temporarily recruited workers.

2 The figure of 51% refers only to the first year, when the proportion of unskilled was highest; when adjusted for the later years, the result is much closer to the German estimate for the stock of Turkish migrants.

3 Neuloh for instance (p. 11) emphasises the unsuitability of Turkish agricultural labour for work in many industries *even if* they were trained.

4 This would also help to account for the surprisingly low proportion of promotions (see below).

abroad was 16%.[1] This means that relatively highly skilled workers have taken less skilled jobs abroad. However, one way in which such loss of skilled workers has *not* been compensated for in any significant degree is through the training of migrants abroad. Indeed in 1963 as many as 34% of the Abadan sample said that they had learnt *nothing* new in their work abroad. Remarkably few workers in the S.P.O. sample (less than 10%) had reported receiving any formal training, although in Germany at least they were concentrated in those industries in which jobs normally presuppose at least some previous training, even in 'unskilled' occupations such as the mechanical engineering, steel, automobile and electrical industries, and the building, textile and clothing trades. Furthermore, it was only amongst first-year migrants that a majority were completely unskilled — yet only 20% of the migrants had the same job classification while away as before departure. Consequently it seems reasonable to infer the under-reporting of basic initial training.[2] For instance, workers may have only reported formal training schemes, ignoring on-the-job training of an informal nature.

However, under-reporting of any sustained *subsequent* training to enable unskilled workers to become skilled is less likely. This is brought out by the low number of workers who raised their skill classification while abroad[3] (even when adjusted to allow for possible under-estimation of the numbers of unskilled who became semi-skilled), particularly when allowance is made for those skilled workers initially employed abroad as unskilled who moved to jobs more suited to their qualifications[4] (Table A29b).

This low estimate of training abroad during the 1960s is also supported by the findings of other surveys,[5] although with the increasing demand by foreign employers

1 There are serious difficulties in comparing skill levels in Turkey and abroad, for in Turkey the traditional *çırak – kalfa – usta – ustabaşı* hierarchy coexists with the modern unskilled – semi-skilled – skilled classifications, with *usta* being used to mean foreman as well, whereas abroad most of the former classification is redundant.

2 Or under-reporting of the proportion of migrants who had been trained as skilled workers prior to departure.

3 Certainly the Turks themselves seem to have been pessimistic about the prospect of any promotion while abroad. According to the Ankara University survey reported in Grandjeat (1966), 37% attributed this to linguistic differences and absence of training opportunities.

4 Similarly, the reported cases of 'demotion' are in fact of workers who moved to less skilled jobs.

5 For instance, only 2 of those in the Selcen survey qualified as skilled workers during their time in Germany, though the 1966 German survey found that some workers had succeeded in changing from the position of unskilled worker to that of partly instructed worker. This promotion to semi-skilled positions was also reported in the German survey of 1968: about one-quarter of unskilled males from the Mediterranean countries had attained semi-skilled status.

for skilled workers, various organized migrant-worker training schemes have been established during recent years,[1] (as compared with the previous piecemeal attempts).

3.5.6   *Learning*

Despite this pessimistic evidence on the extent of formal training abroad, it has been argued that migrants have nonetheless benefited through learning.[2] This view has been advanced by Monson (1972) in his study on experience-generated learning in Turkey and Germany. Since this is the only available source material on this subject, the results will be discussed in detail here. He examined the behaviour of Turkish workers employed as machine operators, welders, die casters or assemblers in five Turkish firms and in five German firms in 1971.[3] Altogether, data on 67 workers in Germany and 78 workers plus eleven groups of workers in Turkey were used (groups were used when it was impossible to disaggregate to obtain learning curves for individual workers).

The first step of his analysis involved the estimation of the parameters giving the shape and level of each worker's learning curve. He found that 81% of the German and 59% of the Turkish sample fitted his logarithmic learning pattern.

The function which he used to represent *each worker's* learning curve was

---

1 For instance, in 1971 it was announced that D.M.3m would be allocated for the vocational training of Turks in Germany, and courses in the automotive, machine and electronics industries were started at Nürnberg, followed by similar courses in Cologne. The German trade unions have also introduced training schemes for foreign migrant workers. In addition in 1972, 22 workers were selected and trained for 9 months in Germany in management skills, plus another 3 to 4 months in Turkey, with the aim of subsequently employing them in German subsidiaries in Turkey. A further group were trained in a similar way in 1973. The scheme was operated, under a German director, by the Turkish Management Centre in İstanbul (*Sunday Times*, July 22nd 1973).

2 No attempt was made in the S.P.O. survey to enquire into either the 'learning' or the 'discipline' aspects of migrants' skill acquisition.

3 He obtained data from fourteen Turkish and sixteen German firms, but could only use five from each group. The firms covered were:

	Commodities produced	Employment	of which (i) foreign	of which (ii) Turkish
German	1. autoparts & electrical equipment	12 000	4669	609
	2. metal products	21 000	700	178
	3. industrial & transport equipment	18 000	3250	1332
	4. automobiles	6000 blue collar	5000	4000
	5. industrial & construction equipment	1800 blue collar	450	58
Turkish	1. compressors, electric motors and parts	500	American subsidiary	
	2. stoves, fridges, hot water heaters, gas cookers	2100		
	3. light fixtures & electrical equipment	300	German subsidiary	
	4. electric motors	400	German subsidiary	
	5. lighting	550		

95

$$\log X_t = \log X_1 + E\log t \quad \text{where } X_t = \text{productivity at } t$$

$$X_1 = \text{productivity on day 1}$$

$$E = \text{'elasticity of learning', i.e. influence of length of experience in that job on productivity}$$

or, writing productivity in index form,[1]

$$\log I_t = \log I_1 + E\log t \quad \text{where } I_t = \text{productivity index at } t$$

$$I_1 = \text{productivity index on day 1}$$

Turkish workers in Germany had higher initial productivity, higher absolute productivity changes, but lower 'elasticities of learning' than their counterparts in Turkey. Learning was more systematic in Germany than in Turkey, and the learning period was much shorter (59 days as compared with 334 days).

The eleven individuals in Germany who did not fit the function were spread over all occupations, though eight had had previous experience. There were, however, some differences between the learning behaviour of different occupations; die casters learnt least (20% gain) and machine operators and welders most (29% gain). Such differences also existed between firms. In Turkey the data fitted much less well. Indeed only 19 assemblers and 6 groups of assemblers, plus 11 machinists and one group of machinists fitted the data (out of 63 individuals and 11 groups). In some cases the initial productivity of those who did learn was the same as that of those who did not.

Monson explained the higher initial productivities but lower 'elasticities of learning' in Germany by suggesting that the former were higher because of the influence of highly disciplined work and of skilled colleagues, while the latter were lower because of language barriers and difficult social adjustments. He then proceeded to stage two of his analysis in which he attempted to estimate the influence of occupation, education, experience, etc. on learning behaviour. These results were much less satisfactory. His main results were: (1) education, whether vocational or general, had little effect on industrial learning behaviour: this he explained by suggesting that employers gave more educated workers more difficult jobs. (2) Experience, whether in a similar job or of a more general nature was a valuable influence when applied *in* Germany *if* acquired in Germany. But experience acquired in Turkey was either insignificant or even had a significantly negative coefficient, whether applied in Turkey of Germany. The influence of German experience when applied in Turkey could not be tested because none of the Turkish sample had worked in Germany. He found the fact that general experience in Turkey was associated with a negative effect on initial productivity in Germany rather difficult to explain, suggesting that employers gave more experienced workers more difficult jobs, or that such Turkish experience may have been a disadvantage, given the different systems of work organization in German factories. (3) An *inexperienced*

---

1 The index was computed by taking $\hat{I}_t = \dfrac{\hat{X}_t}{\bar{w}}$ where $\bar{w} = $ the normal wage for that occupation and is taken to represent the worker's normal productivity.

worker in Germany was likely to have *lower* initial productivity and lower rates of learning if the labour force he worked with was more skilled. This, he suggests, can be explained by the fact that firms with a high proportion of skilled workers were more technically advanced, employing few semi-skilled workers and tending to keep in menial positions those workers who became potentially classifiable as semi-skilled. But since he obtained the opposite result for Turkey (i.e. an improvement in the skill mix raised initial productivity) he had to argue that there, shortages of skilled labour meant that semi-skilled workers were used in skilled positions. (4) Technological differences were significant influences on learning behaviour across countries but not within each country. This he explained by suggesting that because of differences in the availability of skilled labour, improved technologies tended to change the Turkish occupational structure in a different way from that in Germany. Finally (5) he found that changes in the experience mix were important influences on learning behaviour – an improvement in a firm's experience mix tended to cause a parallel upward shift in the learning curve with a slight positive effect on rates of learning.

Many of these results seem rather implausible[1] and their explanations extremely far-fetched. The main trouble is that Monson's entire econometric edifice was built on extremely shaky statistical foundations. Because he could not obtain any individual productivity data from the German firms, he used wage data instead (deflating for any automatic increase because of in-plant experience premiums and trade union negotiated increase). In other words, what his results really show is that money wages in Germany (deflated as described above) went up during the period under observation, and that they went up more systematically than did productivity in Turkey. Now there is no doubt that money wages were, to some extent, linked to productivity (one firm, for instance, offered a piecework system, while two others offered incentive schemes). But in most cases this was at the group rather than at the individual level: firms paid higher wages to a particular individual either because he belonged to a group whose productivity increased or because they had a fairly fixed idea of the 'normal' increments of a migrant worker's wage as he became more experienced on the job. Of course, this implies that migrant workers as a group *do* tend to learn (which is what one would expect), but it also implies that such learning may not have been so systematic at the level of the individual as Monson would have us believe.

Furthermore, if the fact that wages were used to represent productivity is explicitly taken into account, some of his other findings seem much more reasonable. Monson's finding that experience acquired in Turkey had no – or even a negative – effect on productivity in Germany means in fact that the effect was on *wages* in Germany. Most of his 'perverse' results become more acceptable when re-interpreted in this way.[2]

More seriously, however, he hardly tackles the main point about Turkish workers'

---

1 For instance, if vocational training and experience acquired in Turkey have virtually no (or even a negative) effect on productivity in Germany, why have German employers kept on demanding workers who have got them?

2 Though some difficulties remain, particularly with the Turkish results, owing to unavoidable inaccuracies and inconsistencies in the data.

learning in Germany, except to mention that none of his Turkish sample had had German experience, and that most of the Turkish firms which he contacted were not keen to employ returned migrants (§3.6.4). For acquisition of 'learning' is an *actual* economic benefit only insofar as it is subsequently utilized – which, given the evidence to date, does not seem to have happened in Turkey (§3.6.6). In other words, in the final analysis, Monson's study does little more than point out that Turkish migrant workers may 'learn' while working in Germany.

Indeed, he does not even consider the extent to which workers' learning possibilities abroad are realized abroad. Yet the evidence on job changes, work satisfaction etc, suggests that many migrants are frustrated in their work and so are much less likely to realise such learning opportunities as there are (Böhning 1972aE, Castles and Kosack 1973E).

3.5.7 *Linguistic skills*

All enquiries bring out the reputedly poor linguistic skills of Turkish migrants abroad. In the S.P.O. survey only 61% claimed that they could understand a foreign language, 21% that they could read one and 19% that they could write one, despite the fact that they had been abroad for an average of 2 years 4 months, and that the respondents themselves were assessing their linguistic standards (Table A30a & A30b) Few had ever had any formal instruction (4% in Turkey and 16% abroad). The T.E.S. surveys tell the same story. The proportion who claimed that they knew a foreign language well varied from 7% in 1967 to 9% in both 1969 and 1971. Indeed in 1967 and 1971 more claimed that they knew only little of a foreign language than that they knew a moderate amount. Furthermore, the German survey in the autumn of 1968 showed that the Turks' linguistic skills were worse than those of Italians, Greeks and Spaniards, even though according to Hentschel's survey in 1967, 77% of Turks wanted to participate in a language course as compared with an average of 61% for all Mediterranean nationalities in Germany. Yet since linguistic skill is an important element both in work promotion and social adjustment, Turkish migrants' poor language ability seriously affects their life and work abroad.

3.5.8 *Factory life, work organizations*

Neuloh's study pays considerable attention to workers' conditions in and feelings about their place of employment. 46% of Turks said that they were positively pleased about their work situation while only 10% specifically complained. Similar opinions about work discipline and work time were recorded, though there was a substantial shift from those who were previously neutral to the discontented group on the question of feelings about working conditions such as noise and dirt (Table A31). This apparent satisfaction with factory life[1] and compliance with factory

1 In 1963 Abadan's sample of workers were less satisfied with their work: 27% wanted to work on all stages of production, 21% wanted to work in a small workshop and 12% to be independent. However, her sample only covered 'vanguard' workers who had only been abroad a short time and so were less likely to have adjusted to assembly-line conditions. In 1967 Hentschel found that Turks were more frustrated in their work in Germany than other migrant worker nationalities – indeed nearly one-half preferred their job in Turkey. Thus the favourable picture given by many survey replies may reflect Turks' reluctance to criticize their current work situation rather than their approval of it.

discipline surely underlies the frequently-reported preference of German employers for Turkish workers during the late 1960s.[1] But the fact that nearly half the workers sampled were positively pleased with assembly-line conditions in German industry is a powerful indictment of the sort of existence which they must have had in Turkey. Indeed two-thirds of the workers in his sample had not previously been in contact with industry.

For many, work abroad was their first introduction to the trade union movement. In the S.P.O. survey for example (Table A32), whereas 45% had worked in industry before departure, only 24% had belonged to a union or to an employees' organization.[2] 53% however joined a union while abroad[3] (the proportion for the rural sub-group (57%) being somewhat higher than that for the urban (50%) — a differential which still persisted when women were excluded). Of course unions abroad have been extremely suspicious of immigrant labour. Only relatively recently did the German unions really try to recruit foreign migrants and set up services to advise them.[4] Indeed many workers in the Neuloh survey were unaware that there was a union which they could join.

3.5.9 *Earnings abroad*

Officially recruited migrant workers abroad receive the going-rate for whatever job they are doing. But since they tend to be employed in unskilled occupations and to be placed within the lower grades for any particular job, they tend to earn lower wages than host country nationals — and in the case of illegal migrants, may actually be forced to accept less than the normal rate of pay if they work for certain unscrupulous employers. According to the German survey of 1968, the average wage for all male immigrants from S. Europe was D.M. 4.51 per hour, while the national average was D.M. 5.18 per hour (though this probably understates the differential because of underrepresentation of the worst paid immigrants in the sample).

Wages have of course risen substantially in the host countries during the period 1960—73, though with some variations between host countries.[5] In 1963, Abadan found that the mean net monthly income of Turkish workers in Germany was D.M. 516.80, i.e. approximately T.L. 1300. By 1969, 59% and by 1971, 88% of the

1 Similarly Minces (1973E) reported that French employers preferred Turkish workers. In Germany, Turks have on occasion been preferred to German employees when dismissals have become unavoidable. This can be attributed partly to their greater willingness to accept whatever working and housing conditions their employer chooses to offer — and partly to their comparative lack of unionization. (§3.2.3). But German employers might well have changed their views after the Ford strike at Cologne in the autumn of 1973.

2 Though this was high when compared with the Turkish non-agricultural e.a.p., of whom only about half a million belonged to a union in 1970.

3 This is substantially higher than the results of the early Abadan survey, where only 15% of the sample had joined a union.

4 For a very useful summary of trade union attitudes and policies towards immigrant labour in the host countries, see Castles and Kosack 1973E, Ch. 4.

5 For instance, Turkish workers in Germany, Switzerland and Belgium have tended to earn more than those in France, Austria and Holland (T.E.S. survey data).

T.E.S. survey workers earned more than T.L. 2000 a month, while in 1971, 15% earned more than T.L. 4000. Özşahin (1970C) put average monthly net income at $206.40 (about T.L. 2477).[1]

The S.P.O. data, reflecting as they do migrant departures up to 10 or more years before the survey date, provide a useful basis for comparisons with the Turkish e.a.p.[2] Mean average monthly net earnings amounted to T.L. 2165 (T.L. 2181 for men and T.L. 1873 for women — Table 10).[3] On average, migrants from the urban sample earned about two and a quarter times, and those from the rural sample about four times the total amount which they had earned before departure. The mean data per migrant in Table 10 are of course affected by the fact that a higher proportion of migrants from the urban sample went abroad in the earlier years when wages were lower. Some idea of the magnitude of the annual differential is given in Table A35 which shows the proportion of each sub-sample earning more than T.L. 2000 (net per month) for each year. Here the urban-rural differential is quite clear, as would be expected from the higher proportion of the urban sample in skilled jobs.

The S.P.O. survey did not enquire into wage rates so that it is not possible to find out to what extent migrants worked overtime to boost their income. Also, since the data are presented net, they include such child allowances as were paid to those eligible (about D.M. 50 per child per month) but this has little influence on the results[4] since only 9% had their family with them at any time.[5]

Both the 1963 Abadan and the Neuloh surveys emphasized how workers who spoke and understood German were more likely to be employed in higher grade positions and so receive higher wages. Thus the difficulty which most Turks encounter when trying to learn the German language (§3.5.7) often acts as a serious

---

1 Using an exchange rate of T.L. 12 = $1, since this was roughly what workers were obtaining for their foreign currency.

2 Though the precise totals recorded should be regarded as rough and not as strictly accurate estimates. This is because the S.P.O. chose insufficiently high income groups when framing the survey questionnaire, so that almost half the respondents fell into the top interval group. All estimates are therefore crucially dependent on which mid-interval value is used for this group. Fortunately, details of total net monthly earnings were given for some workers, so that the mid-interval value for this known sample could be calculated for each of the 4 sub-samples (i.e. urban men, rural men, urban women and rural women). Assuming that the earnings distribution of the known and of the total workers in the top interval group in each sub-sample was the same, mean monthly earnings per migrant (unadjusted for the year of migration) could be calculated. Since the rate of inflation in the host countries has been somewhat higher during the later 1960s, this means that the unadjusted mean is somewhat higher than a mean calculated from earnings adjusted for inflation or, to put it another way, that more weight is given to the more recent earnings. Taking this into account, the S.P.O. results are consistent with those from other surveys — for instance, the proportion earning more than T.L. 2000 rose from 50% in 1961 to 80% (100% of men) in 1970.

3 Note, however, the small number of women (20) in the sample. In the early years, there was an inverse male–female wage differential which persisted until 1965, when substantial flows of unskilled women began to leave and work abroad.

4 Adjustment for this would lead to a slight reduction in the urban-rural and male–female income differentials.

5 The issue raised by the fact that migrant workers normally pay a more than proportionate share of tax and social security contributions is not discussed here (see Özşahin 1970C).

100

barrier to obtaining higher earnings. This comes out clearly from the German data relating wage rates to linguistic ability in 1968. One third of foreign male workers who spoke German fluently obtained more than D.M. 5 per hour as compared with 10% or more who spoke no German (Bundesanstalt für Arbeit 1970, p. 83).

3.5.10 *Expenditure abroad*

Since the chief purpose of migration for most workers has been to save some target amount as quickly as possible, the cost of living is just as important to them as their income. The S.P.O. survey again provides the only detailed data about this, though again the results must be treated with caution owing to under-estimation by the S.P.O. of suitable expenditure interval groups.[1]

The mean for the whole group was T.L. 932 a month, i.e. approximately £41 at the official rate for the mid-1960s and about £31 using the black market rate for conversion. In either case the result is very low, since all expenditure on housing, food and 'necessary expenses' was included. Indeed about 10% of the sample reckoned that they had spent £13 or less (£18 at the official rate) which, even in the early 1960s, was incredibly low.

Excluding the 2 rural women, the average proportion of income spent abroad on housing, food and necessities was virtually identical for all the sub-samples (43%) despite the existence of urban–rural[2] and male–female differentials in absolute expenditure. To obtain overall propensities to consume abroad, it is necessary to estimate non-essential expenditure. If this is treated as a statistical residual after savings and remittances have been deducted,[3] then the estimates for the total, urban and rural groups respectively are T.L. 2708, T.L. 4366 and T.L. 563 (Table 10). The corresponding average propensities to spend on non-essential commodities while abroad are 10%, 16% and 3%, thus the average propensities to consume are 54%, 59% and 43% respectively. Here the urban-rural differential is striking, particularly in view of the lower rural incomes. But even if it is assumed that all remittances to Turkey for family maintenance are consumed, the propensities for all the groups are well below the average propensity to consume out of personal disposable income in Turkey itself, which was around 88% in the mid-1960s.[4] Indeed they may be somewhat overestimated as non-essential expenditure as defined here would include any purchases of capital goods effected while abroad which, according to the data in Table 13, although few, were not zero.

1 The same method as for the income data was used to enable estimation of mean monthly net expenditure per migrant (p. 100 fn. 2). However, only 25% were included in the top interval group (over T.L. 1000) as compared with 45% in the income question.

2 Mean expenditure by the rural group was about 86% of that of the urban when the figures unadjusted for year are used. However, the first two and the last years contain exceptional readings: the differential over the period 1963–9 is shown clearly by the fact that the proportion who spent more than T.L. 1000 was three or four times as great (depending on the year) for the urban sample than for the rural (see Table A35).

3 The survey asked for totals of savings, remittances, work investment and non-work expenditure separately. However, it is quite clear from the responses that expenditure on work ventures after return was included in, and not additional to, savings.

4 S.P.O. data. The ratio of total domestic savings to G.D.P. was about 16% in the mid-1960s and 20% in 1970 (O.E.C.D. 1972).

Table 10: *Comparative data on income, savings and remittances of Turkish migrant workers, S.P.O. survey, 1971*

T.L. per annum		Total	Urban	Rural	Male	Female
Income before departure[1]	Total	6608	8492	4146	6607	6611
	Basic	6226	8165	3692	6215	6611
	Side	382	327	454	392	0
Income while abroad		25 980	27 636	23 856	26 172	22 476
Basic expenditure while abroad		11 184	11 880	10 248	11 268	9600
Savings while abroad		9221	9130	9390	9510	6200
Remittances while abroad		2867	2260	3655	2910	1535
Non-essential expenditure while abroad		2708	4366	563	2484	5141
Income on return[1]	Total	11 279	13 678	7896	11 203	13 432
	Basic	10 089	12 514	6670	10 068	10 705
	Side	1190	1164	1226	1135	2727
Mean expenditure abroad as % of mean income abroad	(%)	43	43	43	43	43
Mean savings as % of mean income abroad	(%)	36	33	39	36	28
Mean remittances as % of mean income abroad	(%)	11	8	15	11	7
Residual (i.e. percentage of earnings abroad spent on non-basic expenditure	(%)	10	16	3	10	22

Note: Calculated from Tables A23, A33, A34, and 11.

1 Employed workers only.

3.5.11 *Savings*[1]

The official data on foreign exchange repatriated by migrants include both savings and remittances to maintain the living standards of dependents, but cannot be disaggregated to obtain the proportions of each. Information about savings and family maintenance expenditure taken separately is only available from surveys. The available data on savings will be described in this section and those on remittances for family maintenance and on total repatriated earnings in the following section.

Both the proportion of migrants saving and the proportion of income which they have saved have been very high. In 1963, Abadan found that 80% of her sample had accumulated financial assets in Germany (slightly higher for men and lower for women). Migrants who had worked in agriculture or mining in Turkey were particularly likely to have saved abroad. In 1966, Tuna found that 78% of the men and

1 See fn. 3, p. 101.

74% of the women in his sample had saved,[1] and that those from villages and those who were married were more likely to have done so.

The S.P.O. survey obtained similar results (Table 11).[2] 96% of the rural sample and 88% of the urban sample had saved at some time while working abroad. The mean annual total of savings per migrant (unadjusted for year) was T.L. 9221, i.e. of the order of £340,[3] so that on average, a migrant saved a total of about T.L. 22 000 (over £900 — or more than twice the mean annual income of migrants before departure, *before* allowance has been made for any remittances sent home and consumer durable expenditures). The receipt of such high savings is of course the fundamental raison d'être for the emigration country of the whole labour export system, just as the effect of the utilization of these savings on the development process is the main criterion of its success. These data, relating mainly as they do to the mid-1960s when incomes were lower and no special official encouragement of saving abroad had been introduced, do not suggest that there is any serious difficulty in ensuring that high rates of saving take place: workers saved an *average* of 36% of their income abroad and remitted an average of 11% in addition to this. The proportion of income saved, as was that remitted, was particularly high for the rural sub-sample (39% and 15% respectively, i.e. over half the total income).

The S.P.O. survey shows how savings per worker have increased steadily over the decade as incomes rose absolutely and as workers stayed abroad longer, so accumulating more savings by the time they returned home.[4] It also shows the changes in workers' propensity to save during their stay abroad: normally serious saving commenced in the second year, often rising again substantially in the third year, but then levelling off. The workers who did not save had often spent one year or less abroad.

The S.P.O. survey also provided information about the form and transfer of savings. For instance, resistance to banks declined during the decade. In the 1963 Abadan survey one-third of the workers had avoided banks; whereas in the S.P.O. survey 87% of rural and 72% of urban savers had kept at least some savings in a bank (Table A36a).

1 One would expect the proportion of savers to be higher out of a sample of returned workers than one of migrants still employed abroad because in the former case those who had saved in *any* year are included, whereas in the latter case only those saving in that particular year are included.

2 Unfortunately the savings data from the S.P.O. survey are subject to quite a high margin of error. This arose indirectly from the fact that the savings intervals noted on the questionnaire were too low. The interviewers tried to write in the higher amounts but did not always make clear whether total savings or savings per annum were given. In many cases the matter could be settled by inspection of a worker's earnings and expenditure, but ambiguous instances still remained. (The same problem applied to the data on remittances also). The data presented in Table 11 have been checked for consistency, but should nonetheless be regarded as fairly crude estimates.

3 Using the official rate adjusted for the worker premium.

4 For instance, the T.E.S. data show how 78% of ex-village migrants were bringing back more than T.L. 25 000 by 1969 and 85% were doing so by 1971. However, it is important to bear in mind that many official sources of data on repatriated earnings understate total earnings during the 1960s because of the extent to which money was transferred through the black market. This applies particularly to Central Bank data, but seems to have applied less so to surveys — for instance, some workers in the S.P.O. one were certainly prepared to admit their use of the black market.

Table 11: *Percentage distribution of Turkish migrant workers by range of average annual savings and of average annual remittances, S.P.O. survey, 1971*

Range (T.L.)	Savings			Remittances		
	Total	Urban	Rural	Total	Urban	Rural
0	8	12	4	19	26	10
1–2500	7	8	3	34	32	36
2501–5000	16	17	15	25	22	29
5001–7500	14	9	20	9	9	10
7501–10 000	16	13	19	4	3	4
10 001–12 500	12	13	9	1	1	1
12 501–15 000	11	9	15	1	1	2
15 001–20 000	9	9	8	1	1	1
20 001–30 000	6	7	4	–	–	1
30 001–40 000	1	1	1	–	–	–
40 001–50 000	–	1	–	–	–	–
over 50 000	–	1	–	–	–	–
unknown	1	2	1	6	7	4
Mean amount per annum (T.L.)	9221	9130	9390	2867	2260	3655
Mean amount per annum as percentage of mean annual income	36	33	39	11	8	15

See p. 103, fn. 2.

Percentages may not add to 100 because of rounding.

On return, over half of the total (44% of the rural and 61% of the urban sample) had brought back a combination of money and goods (Table A36b); 52% of the rural sample brought back all savings in monetary form as compared with 35% of the urban sample (Table A36c).

55% had brought back their savings themselves. Failure to use the available official channels may be partly explained by attempts to obtain a better exchange rate than was officially available (even after the government had introduced a special premium rate for workers); over-valuation of the lira led many migrants to change their foreign exchange through unofficial channels. As the government has become increasingly dependent on workers' savings and remittances as a source of foreign exchange, the need to secure the use of official channels of transfer increased in priority. Since the devaluation of 1970 broke the back of the black market, most workers have used the official channels.

3.5.12 *Remittances*

In this paper the term 'remittances' has been used to refer to earnings sent home for family maintenance purposes, as distinct from foreign exchange repatriated from workers' savings abroad. But usually, official data on 'remittances' refer to all foreign exchange repatriated for whatever purpose. From the migrant workers' point of view, both savings and remittances (in the narrow sense) require abstinence from *his* current consumption. Consequently remittances have, to some extent, been subject to the same sort of variation as savings during the worker's stay abroad, increasing somewhat as the worker settled down, but being more likely than savings to be made during the first year if the worker had a family at home.

Data on remittances for family standard of living maintenance are only available from surveys. Only 59% of migrant workers who responded to the question in the 1963 Abadan survey reported that they had sent money to their families. This comparatively low proportion is probably to be explained by the high proportion of relatively new arrivals. The proportions remitting earnings were much higher in the S.P.O. survey — 79% of the urban and 90% of the rural sub-groups (Table 11). This differential can be explained by the higher proportion of bachelors and of migrants accompanied by their families in the urban sample. Furthermore, despite the lower absolute incomes, the mean remittance of the rural sub-group (T.L. 3655) was higher than that of the urban (T.L. 2260),[1] representing 15% of the mean rural income while abroad as compared with 8% of the mean urban income. This is probably to be explained in part by the higher number of dependants per worker in the rural sample. These mean remittance levels (even when adjusted to exclude non-remitting migrants) are not very high, particularly for the urban sub-group, where the mean (adjusted) annual remittance was just over one quarter of mean total pre-departure income, as compared with a proportion of just under two-thirds for the rural sub-group. Thus from this survey it looks as if workers remitted little more than the minimum necessary for the maintenance of their family's standard of living. However, annual savings plus annual remittances per worker in the S.P.O. survey (T.L. 12 088) exceed the mean repatriated earnings of all workers (T.L. 8000) during the 1966—68 period.[2]

The volume of remittances (in the sense of total repatriated earnings) has been affected very much by the exchange rate: while this was overvalued, it paid workers to send home as little as possible (as this normally had to take place through official channels) and to bring home all non-consumed earnings in foreign exchange to change on the black market. The less overvalued the exchange rate has been, the more willing workers have been to send home foreign exchange on a regular basis (as this has to be done through official channels).[3] Thus there was a substantial increase after the 27% foreign exchange premium for repatriated earnings was introduced in 1964.[4] Much more striking has been the increase which followed the 1970 devaluation — itself partly forced by the deliberate refusal of many workers to repatriate foreign exchange at the prevailing exchange rate.

Recent data on repatriated earnings show just how much higher they have been

1 The absolute differential was a bit lower if only those workers who had remitted were included in the sub-groups. But note that the remittance data are subject to the same liability to error as to the savings data.

2 This suggests that the surprisingly low mean level of the S.P.O. survey workers' remittances may have arisen because money used for family maintenance was classified under savings (if, say, it was repatriated in a lump sum rather than at weekly or monthly intervals). Totals may in any case have been underestimated. (see p. 103, fn. 2).

3 The failure to take this into consideration is a serious defect of the Miller model of remittance determination, in which remittances are assumed to be dependent only on the number of dependants at home and the domestic Turkish per capita income (Miller 1971C).

4 Subsequently increased to 33½% in 1969.

in recent years. In 1970, the T.E.S. data showed a total of T.L. 4095m,[1] in 1971, T.L. 7071m, in 1972, T.L. 8880m, and in 1973, T.L. 14 000m. The corresponding crude estimates per capita are T.L. 9400, T.L. 12 900 and T.L. 14 000 and T.L. 17 000. These figures include both savings and family maintenance. But it is virtually impossible to estimate the family maintenance element with any degree of accuracy. The figures can be adjusted to exclude the summer peak months when migrants return on holiday, often bringing their savings with them,[2] but no non-arbitrary allowance can be made to exclude the regular flow of savings throughout the year as workers return after completing their work period abroad. Yet it is this regular flow which is likely to be quantitatively the more important, as until they finally return, workers tend to keep their savings abroad where they can earn interest in foreign exchange, and prevent their relatives from spending them. However, the amount which migrants send for family maintenance has undoubtedly risen substantially since the mid-1960s and probably approximates reasonably closely to income forgone by departure abroad.

The importance to Turkey of repatriated foreign exchange can hardly be overestimated. In 1972 and 1973 for instance, it amounted to 84% and 89% respectively of export earnings and to 47% and 57% respectively of the cost of imports: in 1972, it amounted to about 5% of G.N.P. The success of the third 5 year development plan (1973—8) is crucially dependent on the maintenance of repatriated earnings at a level of about T.L. 10 000m per annum.

3.5.13   *Family status while abroad*[3]

It has already been observed (§3.4.4) that although a higher proportion of Turkish than of other migrant worker nationalities tended to be married, a lower proportion had been joined by their wives. This comes out very clearly from the results of the S.P.O. sample. Only 3% of those migrants who were married were accompanied by their spouses when they left, and all these came from the urban sample. Another 9% were later joined by their families. This is comparable with the results of T.E.S. surveys which also cover returnees, but lower than the results of both the Abadan and the 1968 German survey, both of which estimate that about 30% of Turkish workers were accompanied by their families. The difference between these results suggests that migrants who have been joined by their families are less likely to return to Turkey.[4]

---

1 Of which 45% was remitted during the last 4 months of the year (in August 1970 the Turkish lira was devalued by two-thirds from T.L. 9 = $1 to T.L. 15 = $1 and the premium rate for repatriated earnings from T.L. 12 = $1 to T.L. 15 = $1.) Data on workers' foreign exchange is presented in §4.2.2 below.

2 The adjusted annual average from the autumn of 1970 to 1972 was T.L. 10 400.

3 The detailed results on the sociological aspects of the S.P.O. survey are reported in Paine 1972D.

4 Of course, the chain of causation may work either way — workers who have decided to remain abroad will seek 'suitable housing' and summon their wives and families, while workers who perhaps summon their wives so they can both work to earn their target savings faster are more likely to want to settle. They can then enjoy normal family life abroad.

One implication of these results is that most Turkish migrant workers did not seem to have felt a need to summon their wives so they could both work and so save more quickly, as Böhning has suggested is the normal pattern for migrant workers,[1] (for the S.P.O. workers had in most cases completed their saving and returned home): one might try to explain this by saying that the S.P.O. sample contained a relatively high proportion of skilled urban migrants who were more likely to get well paid jobs, but this is hardly adequate since most were in unskilled positions and given little, if any, promotion. Rather it seems to be the case that as yet Turkish migrant workers do not fit neatly into Böhning's pattern.

3.5.14 Wives' employment abroad

According to the S.P.O. survey, only 9 out of the 26 workers who had reported that their wives had joined them at some stage also reported that she had been working, and 8 of these came from the urban sub-group.[2] There was certainly considerable resistance to women's employment. Of those who gave reasons for their wife not working, 31% reported that this was because they were opposed, 25% 'that she could not find work'. Urban males were considerably more opposed to their wives' taking employment.[3] The most popular reason given was unsuitability of the wife's health, which covers pregnancy, (and probably prejudice on the part of those unwilling to admit that they forbade their wives to work). However, 7% of the men said that their wives were not working because others disapproved.

Perhaps the most significant feature here is the fact that about three-quarters of the men were prepared to give a reason for their wives not working.[4] The results certainly seem to indicate a favourable change of attitude towards women's employment, as did those in the Neuloh survey. And this is confirmed by the fact that 17% of the men reported that their wives were employed at the time the survey was conducted (i.e. after their return to Turkey).

3.5.15 Life abroad

Considerable sociological research has been carried out into migrant workers' life abroad, most of which lies outside the scope of this study.[5] Therefore all I shall attempt to do in this section is to sketch some of the main points, utilizing the S.P.O. survey data where appropriate.

1 Unless the reason for wives' remaining in Turkey was stringent immigration control in the host country. However, in Germany at least the regulations were such that any worker determined to bring his family could usually find a way to do so (§ 3.3.2).

2 Although the questions technically asked about *spouse's* employment, both the phraseology of the questions (e.g. did you put your spouse to work?) and the options listed (e.g. women's employment disapproved of) made it clear that in fact *wives'* employment only was being investigated.

3 In Turkey, female employment in agriculture is the rule rather than the exception, in contrast to the towns where, except in Ankara and Istanbul, the reverse is normally the case.

4 18% described their wives as housewives implying that they would therefore not be working.

5 See for instance Böhning 1972bE and Castles and Kosack 1973E, and the references cited therein.

Many unaccompanied migrant workers live in factory hostels, particularly when they first arrive. According to the S.P.O. survey, 77% had at some time lived in accommodation provided by the workplace. This percentage is high compared with the German data on place of residence, according to which 48% of Turkish male workers[1] (and 62% of females) were living in private accommodation. If workers tend to live in factory accommodation in their early years abroad, moving into private houses after they have become semi-settled, this could explain the lower proportion of returned workers who had lived in private homes in the S.P.O. survey.

Various opinions have been expressed about place of residence abroad: an O.E.C.D. mission[2] praised the 'high standard' of the accommodation provided by the Ford factories in Cologne; others,[3] however, have argued (quoting German employers) that it is partly because the Turks can be given inferior accommodation that they make desirable employees (e.g. Abadan in Kayser 1972C); indeed others have gone on to argue that the provision of factory accommodation has merely been a means to increase control over the workers. Unfortunately the S.P.O. survey does not provide information relevant to the assessment of any of these views. On the other hand, there is little doubt that the frustrations brought about by accommodation problems have an important influence on the migrant's ability to settle down abroad (Böhning 1972bE).

The S.P.O. survey does, however, bring out the Turks' lack of integration with other nationalities while abroad. Only about one in seven had lived either in hostels or houses with non-Turkish citizens during their first year abroad, and this proportion tended to decline the longer they remained away. Furthermore, 45% of the rural sample and 29% of the urban sample reported that they had made no non-Turkish friends during their stay abroad. This social isolation is quite striking in view of the fact that 77% were abroad for over one year, and it is probably to be explained by their rather modest linguistic skills (§3.5.7) since many surveys have reported how most male migrants want more contact with the local population. As would be expected, those who made friends did so with their workmates; Germans first, then fellow migrant workers — Italians, Spaniards, Greeks and Yugoslavs. However, by the early 1970s many (often left-wing) organizations for Turks abroad came into existence.

The lack of integration with other nationalities extended also to entertainment, with many Turkish migrants listening only to Turkish language broadcasts on the radio (or perhaps television). In the S.P.O. survey 90% of the rural sample and 76.3% of the urban sample listened to broadcasts by Turkish radio, while about half listened

---

1 Though this figure was lower than for all other groups of migrant nationals except for the Portuguese.

2 Norwegian joint team to the Federal Republic of Germany and Switzerland, October 1966C.

3 For instance, Castles & Kosack 1972E. They cite a representative of Germany mining employers who was reported to have said: 'So far as we are concerned, hostel and works represent parts of single whole. The hostels belong to the mines, so the foreign workers are in our charge from start to finish'. (Magnet Bundesrepublik 1966, p. 81).

to broadcasts from Western European radio stations,[1] a habit which about one-third continued after returning to Turkey. In view of the anti-communist political climate,[2] it is most striking that 36% of the total (almost half of the rural sample) admitted to listening to Eastern European broadcasts and 13% to continuing to do so after their return. But the significance of this should not be over exaggerated. The most likely explanation is that the lonely workers abroad listened to all available broadcasts in their native language,[3] and continued out of habit on return.

Since the host countries have on the whole done little[4] to improve the ghetto conditions in which many Turkish workers live, it is not surprising that problems have arisen. The crime rate is higher for immigrants than for the indigenous population, and particularly so for Turks. At the end of 1972 there were at least 70 000 Turkish children in Germany but no special schools for them to go to.[5] They would either stay away or be educated in German and in the Christian faith. Not surprisingly, many Turkish parents opted for the former. Finally, immigrants tend to be blamed by the indigenous population for social problems for which they are not responsible, the most notable example to date being the anti-Turkish riots (because of the housing shortage) in Rotterdam of August 1972.[6] Although these social problems do not strictly lie within the scope of this analysis, it should be borne in mind that they constitute the main underlying cause of the change of mind on the part of certain host country governments about the desirability of importing substantial numbers of temporarily recruited foreign workers — and particularly Turks, who are culturally more distant.

3.6   Information about those Turkish migrants who have returned home

3.6.1   *Reasons for return*

Only two detailed surveys have been made of migrants after their return — Tuna's in 1966 and the S.P.O.'s in 1971 — though others have enquired into migrants' post-return intentions (e.g. T.E.S., Aker 1970/1), and Abadan (1971C) compiled a few short case histories of returned workers. Both surveys agree that family problems

1 The survey does not enquire into the language of the broadcasts listened to, but in view of their poor linguistic ability it is probable that the special programmes in Turkish are the ones referred to; some of these were made on a local basis (e.g. at Cologne) and were very popular.

2 Note that the questionnaire refers to Eastern European Countries as 'Iron Curtain' countries.

3 Indeed it was the rural group, whom one would expect to be less politically conscious, but who had greater difficulty in making friends, who listened more to Eastern European broadcasts.

4 It is outside the scope of this study to survey the social conditions of migrants abroad and host country policies in this field. An excellent review, which adds up to a serious indictment of host country governments, is given in Castles and Kosack, 1973E. Germany set up an organization called Türk-Daniş, (Information for Turks) which employs social workers chosen from among Turkish citizens with the consultation of the Turkish embassy.

5 In 1973 attempts were made to improve this situation (see also *Milliyet* March 9–13th, 1973A).

6 Another instance is the anti-Algerian riots in Marseilles in September 1973.

were the main reason for return, the proportion reporting this in the S.P.O. survey being 44% (Table A37a). Of the remainder, about half returned because they had succeeded in what they set out to do (e.g. save a certain sum of money) and about half because they had failed (e.g. inability to adapt to surroundings).[1] Amongst the reasons volunteered by the interviewees (as opposed to those stated on the questionnaire) were unhappiness with life and work abroad and/or illness therefrom, passport problems and, in 3 cases, recall for military service. Illness was particularly common amongst miners. Only 3% said that they returned because of unemployment.

These results are similar to those obtained in Tuna's Marmara survey (except that he found that the proportion of those who came from villages who returned because of adaptation problems was significantly higher than those from towns)[2]. In both surveys relatively few stated that they had returned because of activities which they wanted to do *in Turkey*. Nearly three-quarters of the S.P.O. sample had come back simply because for some reason or other they were not able to continue living and working abroad any longer.

3.6.2 *Change of residence on return*

According to the S.P.O. survey 34% were living in a different town or village at the time of the survey from that before departure (Table A37b). Less than half of these gave a reason for their change in residence, and of these, 89% came from the urban sample.[3] The main reason given for moving was the worker's employment situation — as one would expect. Unfortunately, the replies hardly shed any light on the motives for internal migration within Turkey since (quite apart from the poor response) they do not permit distinction between, say, workers who moved because they wanted to set up their business or earn their living in some particular place, and workers who moved because they could not do this in the place in which they had lived formerly.

More of the rural group than of the urban group went back to their place of residence before departure and even more of the rural group went back to their birthplace. Altogether 43.3% were living in a *bucak* or *köy* at the time of the survey, while 42.7% were living in a place with under 10 000 inhabitants.[4] Given the dominant share of urban dwellers in the early and mid-1960s migration flows, the proportion of village origin in this sample of migrants (who had departed from 1–12 years previously) is higher than one would expect on the assumption that workers' origins have no influence on their propensity to return and settle in Turkey. In other

1 Abadan (in Kayser 1972C) has suggested that returned workers include a high proportion of short-stay migrants who could not adapt to life abroad. This cannot however be the main explanation as the mean length of stay abroad is not short enough.

2 Abadan (1972D) also emphasizes the adaptation problems which Turkish ex-rural migrants face, and argues that Yugoslav ex-rural migrants adapt themselves more easily to an industrial society because they have had a technically orientated education.

3 It should be remembered that 'rural' and 'urban' refer to residence place at the time of the survey.

4 In contrast to Tuna's urban dominated survey, where only 8% returned to villages (33% of those of village birth).

110

words, it would seem that a higher proportion of village origin migrants have returned to Turkey and tried to settle down.[1]

3.6.3   Desired employment status on return

The S.P.O., T.E.S., Tuna and Aker surveys all agree on migrants workers' preference for self-employment and dislike for wage employment.[2] In the S.P.O. survey (Table A38) only 17% wanted to take up wage or salaried employment on return (and of these, 4% wanted to become white-collar employees). The urban sample were much more willing to consider wage employment than were the rural, the respective percentages being 20% and 3%. Approximately half of the total (and also of the urban and rural sub-samples) wanted to become employers; the remainder chiefly aspired to some type of self-employment – often to becoming independent farmers.[3] Although these preferences could have serious effects if they were to be realized, as yet, such aspirations have rarely been fulfilled, though their non-fulfillment may have contributed towards many returned workers' intentions to go abroad again.

3.6.4   Actual employment status on return

All surveys have found that actual employment status on return bore little relation to the desired status but considerable similarity to the pre-departure situation. In fact in the S.P.O. survey *more* workers were wage earners on return than before departure (chiefly because some of those previously self-employed in agriculture took up wage employment in the town on return, so that overall the self-employed group fell, Table A38).

12% of the rural and 3% of the urban sample were unemployed. Thus the overall proportion of unemployed (7%) was twice as high on return as before departure (particularly when males only are compared), and the sectoral incidence was reversed (before departure the unemployed came mainly from the urban sub-sample). This unemployment occurred even though all the workers in the sample had been back for at least six months, and many for much longer. Furthermore, the unemployment rate for returned migrants was almost as high as that for the e.a.p. (estimates of open unemployment during the late 1960s range from 7 to 10%). This bears out other reports of migrants' employment problems on return. For instance 23% of the men in Tuna's Marmara sample were unemployed on return; both the Turkish Employers'

---

1 This is not necessarily in conflict with the survey's finding that a higher proportion of the rural sample were considering returning to work abroad, for this may merely indicate the greater dissatisfaction of the rural sample with their life in Turkey on their return.

2 In the T.E.S. surveys, only 328 men and 46 women out of over 13 000 surveyed during 1967, 1968 and 1969 wanted a factory job.

3 Tuna's Marmara survey, which gives desired sector of employment on return, is strongly biased towards industry (69%) and away from agriculture (8%) because of its urban composition. It also brings out the greater willingness of urban migrants to take wage employment; nonetheless, 74% of the men wanted to be employers or self-employed.

Confederation and Monson[1] have mentioned the reluctance of many employers to take on ex-migrants.[2] One would expect unemployment to be lower in the S.P.O. sample since most of the returned migrants had had much longer to find a job. In fact, the reported figure of 7% is probably an under-estimate as the unemployed were less likely to have been located and included in the survey (see Appendix 3).

Since two-thirds of the women in the S.P.O. survey had worked before departure, this survey does not bring out the marked increase in female participation rates on return as compared with before departure which is implied by responses to the T.E.S. and the Aker surveys.

3.6.5   *Finding a job and starting work*

In contrast to the optimistic views expressed in the Abadan survey in the early 1960s, Turkish migrant workers have become increasingly pessimistic about finding work on return (Neuloh 1970D, Kayser 1972C). The S.P.O. results show that their fears were to some extent justified.

Although a fairly high proportion of migrants were able to find a job and start work[3] within a month of their return, nearly one quarter of those who replied reported that it had taken more than 6 months (Table A39a). This of course means that savings accumulated while abroad would have been required for basic subsistence. It also provides further evidence of the unsatisfactory reintegration arrangements for returning migrants, as does the response to a later question which shows that only 1% of migrants (about 3% of those answering the question) had found their employment through official channels like the T.E.S. (Table A39b). The remainder of those who replied had found employment through their own or their relatives' efforts.

3.6.6   *Occupation on return*

Both the S.P.O. and Tuna samples reported similar results. In both cases approximately half of the sample did the same job on return as they had prior to departure (Table 9). Work experience abroad seems to have been of little subsequent use for most workers — only 6% of the S.P.O. survey workers continued on their return to Turkey with a job which they had learnt for the first time while abroad, while another 12% had the same job (or rather job title) before departure, while abroad and on return. The detailed occupational comparison is given in Table A22a. As would be expected, there was a fall in traditional occupations, especially in agriculture

---

1 'In general, most Turkish firms contacted did not have a policy of actively seeking returned migrants for employment, citing their demands for high wages and overstatement of their skills as reasons. In fact, several firms consciously avoided hiring returned migrants.' (Monson 1972D).

2 Krahenbuhl also brings up this point, but reports instances of workers returning to their old jobs (Kayser 1971C).

3 More reported starting work within 1 month than did finding a job because (1) temporary work was counted for the former but not the latter and (2) some self-employed who did not reply to the latter did so to the former.

112

but also in tailoring, shoemaking and the like.[1] But there was also a change within industrial occupations: the number employed in certain skilled occupations fell slightly, but this was compensated for by a substantial increase in the number of foremen and chief master workmen. There was no net loss in industrial skills.

3.6.7   Skill level on return

Only the S.P.O. survey obtained information about this. Whereas the occupational data from this survey show that there was no net loss in skilled industrial occupations, the skill level data show that there was actually a net increase in the skill level of the returned migrants (Table A19). This is seen clearly from the proportion of foremen and higher, which before departure was 36% but on return was just over half of those who replied to the question. However two qualifications should perhaps be made to the above. The first is that the general improvement of skills was most disappointing, given the potential. For while half were unskilled before departure, 40% of those who replied to this question were still in unskilled jobs on return. Secondly, the reported skill improvement may be greater than the actual if, for instance, some Turkish employers regard experience abroad as a reason for employing a worker at a higher level.[2]

3.6.8   Use of linguistic skills

According to the S.P.O. survey (Table A40) such linguistic skills as the returning migrants had managed to acquire were only of limited use to them on their return: 7% claimed that their knowledge of a foreign language had helped them to find a job, while 10% said that they were currently using it at work. The rural sub-group reported approximately the same proportion of linguistically competent workers as the urban sub-group, even though they had received considerably less formal instruction. But as would be expected, fewer from the rural than from the urban sub-group reported that their language knowledge had been of any use since their return.

3.6.9   Participation in work organisations

Migration had the expected effect on membership of work organisations. Whereas only 24% of the S.P.O. survey had belonged to a union or employees' organisation before departure, 53% had done while away, and 42% did so on return. (Table A32). The survey does not of course cover the question of the potential effects of the increased unionization in Turkey — nor did it even enquire whether they had joined the major federation, Türk-İş or the more militant DİSK.

---

1 One quarter of those who changed jobs were ex-farmers or farm workers who moved to the towns.

2 Or if workers have reported an inflated skill level, an event which employers allege is normal with returned migrants. Certainly some employers have been wary of taking on returned migrant workers (§ 3.6.4).

3.6.10 *Earnings on return*

According to the S.P.O. survey (Table A24) the average mean basic income per employed migrant on return (i.e. income from his main occupation) was 43% higher than that before departure (adjusted to allow for inflation at 5% p.a.); mean side income was 176% higher, so that the mean total was 51% higher (again including the inflation adjustment). This arose partly because of the sectoral shift in employment and partly because of earnings increases within sectors. Mean total rural incomes for the employed were as much as 69% higher, and the whole distribution shifted up — indeed 77% were in the under T.L. 5000 a month base income group before departure as compared with 43% on return.[1]

In money terms, mean total income rose by 80%, mean total urban income by 61% and mean total rural income by 89%. These figures compare with an annual average money wage increase for workers covered by the Social Insurance Institute of 14% between 1962 and 1970. Since the S.P.O. migrants were abroad on average for 2.4 years, the average money wage for these workers would have risen by about 36%. Thus even though the migrants had, relatively speaking, been an élite before departure, how much more so they were on return, earning a mean annual income of nearly T.L. 11 300.[2] Despite this, the majority were thinking of returning abroad because they considered their income insufficient. (§3.6.14).

3.6.11 *Investments in work ventures*

The Turkish government has long been hoping that workers' savings will be invested in industry or agriculture rather than spent on consumer goods or on small service sector ventures. However, there is as yet no evidence that such investment has taken place on any significant scale. The S.P.O. survey found that 46% of the rural sample and 27% of the urban sample had put savings into a work venture (Table 12a). The mean amount invested was just over T.L. 25 000[3] — slightly higher for the urban and lower for the rural sub-groups[4] (Table 12b). Unfortunately however, the survey did not enquire directly into the nature of the investment, into its success or

---

1 These reported increases may be underestimates if workers concealed the true magnitude of the income (especially their side income) for fear of having to pay higher taxes. On the other hand, in real terms they may be slightly overestimated as the inflation adjustment is a little on the conservative side — inflation only remained at around 5% per annum until the end of 1968.

2 Though it should be noted that this figure is for *employed* workers. If the unemployed are included in the denominator, total mean income is T.L. 9 475.

3 It could not be estimated precisely because the size of ventures in the largest group was not given, so that the mid-interval had to be selected on the basis of such information as was available about the probable cost of the venture.

4 This works out at T.L. 8418 per migrant. Inspection of the income, expenditure, savings and remittance data presented so far shows that most, if not all respondents must have included work-related investment under the savings data given in Table 10 (otherwise expenditure plus savings plus remittances plus work-related investment would have more than exhausted income). This also applies to Table 13, where the evidence of overlapping is much clearer, various examples of agricultural machinery and the like being given despite the fact that the question asked for non-work-related purchases.

114

failure — or even into its financing (e.g. had the Halk Bank Loan scheme been used?).[1]

It does however bring out how few workers invested their savings in projects in which others participate and how many invested them in individual or family concerns. The two main 'participatory' type investments which have been encouraged by the government are the joint industrial partnership, in which workers abroad invest their savings so as to form a company in which they can work on their return to Turkey, and the cooperative. About 200 industrial partnership companies were established by workers abroad,[2] but nearly all failed — chiefly because the workers were frequently defrauded of their money in Germany.[3] The only exceptions have

Table 12a. *Percentage of returned Turkish migrant workers who put savings into a work venture, S.P.O. survey, 1971*

	Total %	Urban %	Rural %
Yes	35	27	46
No	58	63	50
n/a	8	10	5

Table 12b. *Amount of investment in work ventures by returned Turkish migrant workers, S.P.O. survey, 1971*

T.L.	Total No.	Urban No.	Rural No.
10 000–15 000	30	11	19
15 001–20 000	14	10	4
20 001–25 000	21	9	12
25 001–30 000	10	4	6
30 001–35 000	9	2	7
35 001–40 000	7	4	3
40 001–45 000	5	3	2
45 001–50 000	4	–	4
50 001–55 000	4	–	4
Over 55 001	17	11	6
Total	121		67
Amount not stated	4	1	3
Mean amount invested	25 116	27 130	23 492

1 The Halk Bank operated a loan scheme whereby a returned worker could borrow from three to five times his deposit up to a limit to T.L. 75 000. The loan was repayable over 5 years at interest of 1% with a one year grace period.

2 e.g. Türksan (based on Cologne), İşbir, Kartaş, Türkar, Türk Al (based on Wuppertal), Türk Yap (based on Frankfurt), and Birsan (based on Berlin).

3 Information supplied by the Turkish Employment Service. It is quite likely that the villains were unscrupulous compatriots.

been Turksan (making paper),[1] İşbir (making nylon sacks) and the Bursa and Balikeşir cement factories, which are all actually in operation employing 100–200 workers each.[2] Not surprisingly, after all these frauds, workers' enthusiasm about establishing industrial joint ventures waned considerably. Recently however, the Ministry of Industry (which has to approve such projects) reported a resurgence of applications, though almost exclusively from workers in relatively prosperous towns in Western Turkey. In any case, the Ministry has at least recognised the poor prospects for the success of industrial joint ventures established by returned migrants lacking any management experience. For although it is implementing a new law giving substantial investment incentives[3] aimed, inter alia, at encouraging such joint ventures, it is now trying to persuade workers to put their savings into large public investment projects.[4] This makes an important difference to the returnee shareholder, however, for much of the attraction of the joint venture lay in the fact that it would provide *employment* as well as dividends to participants (though the achievements of the joint ventures established so far in the employment field have been rather modest).

Returned migrants have also been most reluctant to put their savings into cooperatives. There are various types of cooperatives in Turkey, including agricultural producer, credit and marketing cooperatives and small industry cooperatives.[5] However, only 6% of the urban sample and about 9% of the rural sample in the S.P.O. survey had invested any of their savings in a cooperative; and even fewer (about 3%) had put any savings in an industrial partnership (Table A41a). Since 32% of these migrants (and 56% of those in the Tuna survey) had planned to participate in a cooperative or partnership, this raised the question of why they had not done so, in addition to the question of why under a third were planning to do so in the first place. The replies to a question in the S.P.O. survey which tackled these issues were not very revealing, except to bring out the general level of ignorance and

1 Türksan was based on a group of workers in Cologne, who in 1967 transferred over $1m to establish a wallpaper factory at İzmit. The initial capital was fixed at $3m, of which the balance was raised in Turkey. The factory began operations in Sept. 1967, and employed a combination of local labour and returned workers.

2 At the end of 1972 it was reported that two more such ventures would be established in Konya. (*Milliyet*, Dec. 13th 1972).

3 The proposals include a customs duty discount on imported equipment and supplies of 40–60%, a tax holiday of 3–4 years, lower export duty and priority credit facilities at a lower rate of interest. (Information supplied by the Ministry of Industry, September 1972. See also *Milliyet*, October 8th 1972).

4 In late 1972 three large projects were under consideration; electronic equipment (probably to be built at Balikeşir or İsmit), shipbuilding (probably to be built at Pendik) and diesel engines (probably to be built at Bursa). Whether or not this scheme will meet the fate of the one proposed in September 1971 is yet to be seen. Then shares in seven factories were to be reserved especially for workers (Türk Otomobil, Akdeniz Gübre, Perkins Motorlar, Ünye Çimento, Mardin Çimento, Bolu Çimento, and Göller Bolgesi Çimento Sanayi ve Ticaret, A.S.; see T.E.S. circular of 17th Sept. 1971). But nothing had come of the scheme by the beginning of 1973.

5 A comprehensive survey of cooperatives in Turkey is given in Turkey S.P.O. 1972. In 1973, there were about 1750 agricultural credit and marketing cooperatives.

116

mistrust about these organisations, (Table A41b). For whereas the T.E.S. have developed a highly organised system to cope with workers' applications and despatch, nothing similar operates as yet in the field of informing those returning about work and investment possibilities etc., and of assisting them to take advantage of these.

But even more disappointing has been Turkey's experience with migrants who actually belonged to cooperatives prior to their departure. These were given priority in selection for migration, and special concessions as to the goods which they could import on return.[1] Altogether about 13 000 workers went abroad under the scheme between 1965 and 1971.[2] But many of these had joined only to jump the queue for departure, and failed to keep up their dues once they had left. Indeed between 1964 and 1970 the money transfers under the scheme hardly covered 40% of the planned programmes. Half the cooperatives involved did virtually nothing and only 8% prepared projects of any size (Kayser 1972C).

Furthermore, few machines were imported under the concession scheme. According to data provided by the Central Bank, 118 items of agricultural machinery were imported under this scheme in 1970, 261 in 1971 and 487 up to July 1972. The corresponding figures for industrial machinery were 58, 120 and 92. But the available survey data show that not only did few migrants spend their savings on imported machinery, but also that few purchased Turkish machinery either. For instance, 10% of the unmarried workers and 16% of the married workers in the Tuna survey had spent savings on machinery of some kind (whether imported from abroad or purchased in Turkey). Only 2% of the Abadan survey in 1970 had spent savings on agricultural machinery (though 29% had spent savings on business ventures of some sort, which probably includes some expenditure on purchase of machines). In the S.P.O. survey information about imported machinery was not collected explicitly but was usually volunteered when respondents were listing non-work-related purchases (Table 13). Frequencies reported should therefore be regarded as minima — though in fact it is clear from the replies that the interviewers attempted to compile a comprehensive list of all expenditures out of savings. 5% reported buying agricultural machinery and 7% buying industrial machinery. Most of these machines had been bought in Turkey and not imported. Normally such a purchase took most of a worker's savings, sample prices quoted for tractors (at the time of purchase) being about T.L. 45 000—50 000 and for industrial machines, T.L. 20 000—80 000.

Altogether about one-third of the migrants listed work-related expenditure.[3] Half of these spent their savings on buying land or farm stock in order to set

1 These concessions have varied somewhat, but roughly speaking the main extra advantage of belonging to a cooperative is the right to import investment goods without applying for a foreign exchange allocation, subject to certain limits on their value and on the amount of residence abroad required to qualify. These have been altered quite often; at the end of 1972 a member of a cooperative could import machinery up to a limit of T.L. 20 000 after working for two years abroad, plus an extra T.L. 1000 for every additional month.

2 *Milliyet* (April 11th, 1972) reported that altogether 12 678 cooperative members had been sent abroad.

3 Since 35% had previously alleged that they had spent savings on a work venture, these results give quite a good picture of the type of work ventures selected.

themselves up as small farmers. Just under one quarter spent their savings on items required for establishing a small scale manufacturing workshop, the remainder on items required for a small-scale retail or commercial business of some sort (including those who bought cars for business purposes).[1]

These results correspond well with those of the Tuna survey of returned migrants. Aker, however, found a higher proportion of his sample intended to purchase agricultural or industrial equipment (24%). But this discrepancy is perfectly reasonable given the known discrepancy between intended and actual work status on return (§3.6.3 and §3.6.4).

Reviewing the evidence of this section, it seems that about one third of returned migrants have spent a fairly substantial part of their savings on items related to work, though the rural migrant was much more likely to have done so than the urban. The former would have tended to buy the requisites for setting himself up as a small farmer, the latter to have established himself as a small businessman, more probably in a service than in a manufacturing activity. Both would have been unlikely to join any cooperative scheme.

3.6.12   *Other purchases*

All surveys of returned workers agree that the most popular large item purchased is a house or a building plot for one. About two-fifths of the S.P.O. survey said that they had spent savings in this way[2] (Table 13). This corresponds with results from other surveys — about one-fifth of the Tuna survey, two-fifths of the Aker survey and almost one half of the Abadan survey, two-fifths of the Neuloh survey, reported planned or actual expenditure of savings on a house or building plot.

After this came consumer durables. Half the S.P.O. migrants said that they had bought a radio. Relatively few mentioned purchase of a car, although in the mid-1960s this was a major item amongst imports with waiver. The Ministry of Finance data[3] on car imports by returned migrants show a rise from 5506 in 1964 to 23 000 in 1967. Many migrants used to sell their permits to import cars to Turkish middlemen who would then import batches of two hundred or more. But after 1967, the Turkish government wanted to stop car imports in order to protect the infant car assembly plant. In 1968 therefore, the number of imported cars fell to 1085, rising slowly to 1840 in 1969, 2334 in 1970 and 3000 in 1971. But whereas car imports were controlled, imports of other consumer durables were normally classified under personal household effects which were allowed in without restriction. Some idea of the variety reported by members of the S.P.O. survey is given in Table 13. This is less a comprehensive list of purchases (as the migrants selected the goods mentioned) than a list of those purchases to which the owners attached significance, so that the detailed specification of consumer goods is of some interest.

---

1   Business purpose was assumed if the worker was subsequently employed as a driver.

2   Allowing for the fact that some of those who bought agricultural land would build a house on a small part of it.

3   Supplied by Mr. Haldun Akin.

Table 13: *Percentage of returned Turkish migrant workers who reported buying certain goods with their savings, S.P.O. survey, 1971*

		Total		Urban		Rural	
		No.	%	No.	%	No.	%
Building plot		23	6	12	6	6	4
House	A	2	1	2	1	–	–
	T	107	30	56	27	51	33
Property		12	33	3	2	9	6
Marriage		19	5	16	8	3	2
Household	A	61	17	47	23	14	9
	T	19	5	6	3	13	8
Car	A	22	6	17	8	5	3
	T	9	3	7	3	2	1
Clothes		140	39	82	40	58	38
Radio	A	138	38	61	30	57	37
Tape recorder /TV/ Record player		54	15	41	20	13	9
Camera/Watch		6	2	3	2	3	2
Cooker/Fridge/ Sewing machine		4	1	1	1	3	2
Presents		5	1	5	2	–	–
Field/Orchard		41	11	7	3	34	22
Tractor		4	1	–	–	4	3
Agricultural mach.	A	3	1	–	–	3	2
	T	11	3	–	–	11	7
Farmstock: Livestock/ Bees/Wheat		6	2	1	1	8	3
Shop		9	3	6	3	3	2
Cafe/Hotel		3	1	2	1	1	1
Buying stock		7	2	3	1	4	3
Workshop		3	1	3	1	–	–
Industrial mach.	A	6	2	8	2	1	1
	T	20	6	12	6	8	5
Bicycle		3	1	3	2	–	–
Motorcycle		5	1	2	1	3	2
Bus/Lorry		8	2	2	1	6	4
Bank		14	4	10	5	3	2
Debts		30	8	14	7	16	10
Illness/Doctor		5	1	4	2	1	1
Tourism		8	2	7	3	1	1
Children's education		1	–	–	–	1	1

N.B. (1) The data in this table represent *minimum* frequencies.
(2) Percentages are of workers who chose to mention that they had bought good in question. They therefore do *not* add to 100.

A Abroad
T In Turkey

Sample prices reported

House	TL 25 000
	15 000
Lorry	40 000
Car	30 000
	63 000
Industrial machine	80 000
Loom	20 000
Building plot	60 000
Shop	40 000
	70 000
Debts	10 000
	15 000
Tractor	45 000
Marriage	20 000
Field	20–30 000

119

As many as 30 workers (10% of the rural sample and 7% of the urban) had spent savings on the repayment of debt, and where amounts were stated, these were often quite high (well over pre-departure rural incomes). Since this is a minimum estimate of the proportion who paid off debts on their return, it is suggestive of a quite serious problem, particularly since it was given as the *main* use to which savings would be put by 4% in the Aker survey and mentioned prominently in the Tuna survey.

Only 4% said that they had put savings into the bank. Although others may not have spent theirs, a rough estimate would be that between one-half and two-thirds had done so (at least). The expenditure lists usually included clothes, selected household goods and consumer durables plus one 'major' item of expenditure such as a house, shop, tractor, weaving loom, etc. This suggests that the migrants worked until they had saved up for the main item plus a few semi-luxuries as well, all of which were bought on return (if not already purchased abroad). Not all workers indicated whether they had bought their acquisitions at home or abroad: in general, consumer durables were purchased abroad, but more of the work-related investment goods were purchased in Turkey than abroad.

In other words, the results suggest a high propensity to spend out of savings but only a moderate propensity to spend on imported goods (though higher than the national average propensity to import).[1] But a significant part of this expenditure would be on work-related commodities. A crude estimate from the S.P.O. survey data suggests that about 37% of the total savings brought back by the returned migrants was spent on such work-related goods, and about 50% was spent while away or soon after return on consumer goods of some sort.

3.6.13 *Life on return*

The migrants were naturally less interested in comparing their new life in Turkey with what they had known before than with what they had become accustomed to abroad. And they certainly felt that in real terms they were worse off. Only a quarter of those in the S.P.O. survey felt that their housing, food, clothing and entertainment were at least as good in Turkey as abroad, despite the fact that they had been living virtually on the breadline (by European standards) while away (Table A42a). Entertainment — or the lack of it — in Turkey was a particular source of complaint (Table A42b).

3.6.14 *Permanency of return*

Consequently it is not surprising that 83% of the rural and 65% of the urban sample said that they were thinking of going abroad again (Table A43a).[2] This is one of the most revealing statistics of the survey, since the respondents were supposed to have

---

1 Imports amounted to just over 7% of GNP in 1965 and 8.4% in 1970 (using $1 = T.L. 12 to allow for the 1970 devaluation).

2 About 80% of the Tuna sample reported that they were pleased to be back, chiefly because of reunion with their families. This is of course perfectly consistent with the subsequent disillusionment reported here. Indeed over half wanted to go abroad again.

returned permanently. Nearly two-thirds of the total sample (and 78% of the rural sub-sample) said that insufficient income in Turkey was the main reason (Table A43b). However some of the rural sample were planning to return, not because they preferred life abroad, but because they felt that it was the only way in which they could save enough to make new investments to expand their farms. On the other hand, inability to find suitable work in Turkey was cited by 9% of the total sample but by 18% of the rural sub-sample.

Altogether the answers to these 2 questions indicate severe migrant reintegration problems. For they suggest that the 'permanently returned migrant' is a myth. The majority of the migrants were so dissatisfied with life at home on their return that they were proposing to go back even though this would often entail abandoning any work venture they had so far set up, (though a few hoped to return to save money for expansion of their business, and others to save up again because their ventures had gone bankrupt). Of course, some were thinking of returning because of their unemployment. However, in the case of the others, the sort of faith (as reported, for instance, in the Neuloh survey) that hard work would solve both their own and Turkey's problems seems to have evaporated, and disillusionment set in.

However, as yet this tendency for ex-migrants not to settle down but to try to return abroad has been less of a problem in Turkey than in the other countries of migration, as fewer Turkish migrants have actually had more than one distinct work period abroad. For instance, German data for 1968 and 1969 show that the proportion of Turks with previous experience in W. Germany (27% and 14% respectively) is much lower than for other nationalities. This may partly be explained by the fact that it has been more difficult for Turks to go abroad again if they wished to do so. Only a skilled worker could have reapplied officially with the chance of being accepted within a year. Unskilled males would have had to leave on tourist passports − an expensive procedure (§3.2.1 and §3.4.17) − and have had to pay all their transport costs. Yet to have afforded this, they must have been comparatively well-off. Consequently although the proportion of returned workers who wish to go abroad again may well be as high in Turkey as in the other Mediterranean countries of emigration, the extra difficulties which have been faced by the Turkish second-time migrant have meant that the actual rate of second-time migration has been lower.[1] But this in turn means that since Turkey's frustrated returned migrants cannot easily resolve their situation by returning abroad, particularly since the worker immigration ban by the main host countries, it is even more important for Turkey to reintegrate her returned migrants successfully.

3.7   Summary

3.7.1   *The system (pp. 56–71)*

Although a late starter amongst the Mediterranean labour exporting countries, Turkey

---

1 It may also be partly explained by Turks' greater reluctance to consider return in the first place because of the greater difficulties which they face if they subsequently wish to return, and because of the lower level of development of the Turkish economy as compared with that of the other emigration countries, for this has in general meant much less attractive employment prospects on return than has been the case, say, for Italian migrant workers.

became a major supplier of new worker arrivals in W. Europe, though the stock of Turkish migrants abroad (about 850 000 at the end of 1973), has not caught up with that of earlier starters such as Italy, and the ratio of migrant workers to the indigenous labour force, (about one in sixteen), is still very much lower than that for the smaller supplying countries of Yugoslavia and Greece (pp. 56–60). Fluctuations in European demand have led to severe fluctuations in the volume of the Turkish migratory flow, and in the proportion of unofficial migrants, which has been lowest in 'bad' years, (pp. 59–64). Before 1974 the flow of returned migrants had been low – in the order of 20–25 000 p.a. from 1965 to 1973 (pp. 64–65) – though somewhat higher than that for some of the other supplying countries (notably Greece and Yugoslavia).

There has been a highly organised system for despatching aspirant migrants from Turkey, (pp. 66–69), though in the early 1970s, the excess supply of applicants had led to the formation of a queue of well over one million. Since 1972 applicants have faced age limits and those from less developed regions supposedly have had priority in selection for despatch. While abroad, migrants are subject to various controls and cannot change jobs or bring their families as of right. However, the longer the worker stays the more rights he obtains, and he may manage to remain there long enough to receive an unrestricted work permit which permits permanent settlement, (pp. 69–71).

3.7.2 The socio-economic characteristics of migrants[1] (pp. 71–89)

During the last ten years, the socio-economic characteristics of migrants have become more like those of the Turkish active population. The proportion of female workers has risen substantially. The regional distribution of migrants before departure has become less unequal and the share of migrants from rural areas has risen substantially. The age distribution has become less concentrated. The proportion of married migrants has risen substantially, as has the proportion of those who have been joined by their families. Levels of literacy and education have fallen as the proportion of unskilled rural migrants has risen. The proportion of skilled migrants also has fallen with the increase in unskilled applicants until this was offset by the increasing host country demand for skilled migrants – estimates of the proportion of skilled migrants leaving in 1970 range from one third to one half. The proportion unemployed at the time of departure has also declined, though this may have been higher at the time of application.[2] The share of ex-agricultural migrant workers has risen at the expense of those from industry. The mean level of pre-departure earnings has risen less than wages of workers covered by the Social Insurance Institute because the magnitude of the rise has been limited by the increasing representation of less well-off rural migrants. The predominant reported motive for departure has been financial, though there is no doubt that in many case the financial motive was prompted by less than satisfactory employment conditions.

These changes over the decade mean that recent migrant departures have been less

---

1 Since many of the following results are of a tentative rather than a definite character, it is important to refer back to the appropriate section of the text and to bear in mind any qualifications about the reliability of the primary source data.

2 Because the queue for departure encouraged all new entrants to the labour force to apply for migration.

unrepresentative of the Turkish labour force than were their forerunners of ten years ago. Nonetheless, they are still a relatively élite group, though less so now than formerly. They are better educated, more skilled, financially better off, employed in more modern occupations, and suffering from less unemployment than their fellow workers in Turkey. They have come mainly from the middle and upper middle ranks of the peasantry and urban labour force.

The Turkish migrant labour flow has differed in certain respects from that of other Mediterranean supplying nations. This is partly attributable to Turkey's later start, but partly to intrinsic differences in the Turkish situation. Thus Turkey seems to be catching up in the proportion of female migrants and in the proportion of workers who bring their families to join them abroad. But Turkish migrants are still much more of an élite, *as compared with the indigenous population*, than are migrants from the other Mediterranean exporting countries, where a higher proportion of migrants tend to come from the poorest areas and to be unemployed or only in part-time employment before departure.

3.7.3   *While abroad (pp. 89–109)*

Most Turkish migrant workers have gone for one work period, the average length of which has increased during the 1960s and which in the early 1970s, was about 3½–4 years. Normally this would have been interrupted by occasional visits home (pp. 89–90).

While abroad they have worked mainly in unskilled jobs in manufacturing or construction, their occupational distribution being completely different from that before departure and from that of the host country's economically active population. Well over three-quarters of the women have been employed in the manufacturing sector, (pp. 90–92). Many of the men have held less skilled jobs than before departure, and few have been promoted, although some moved to semi-skilled positions and some to more skilled jobs which were more suitable given their previous experience. Few have received any formal training abroad either in industrial skills or in the language of their host country. Consequently quite a few felt frustrated with their work situation; this probably contributed to the fairly high rate of job changes. On the other hand, many migrants have undoubtedly learnt some new skills, and nearly all have acquired considerable experience of factory production methods, (pp. 92–99).

Their earnings abroad have been much higher than in Turkey – around two or three times higher for a typical urban migrant, and four or even five times higher for his poorer rural counterpart. Of this sum they would on average spend about 43% on necessities (housing, food, etc.), save about 35% and remit to their families about 11% – the residual normally being spent abroad. But this high saving propensity would have permitted only an extremely low living standard as compared with that of the host country, (pp. 99–106).

Hardly any of the migrants have taken their family with them initially, though up to one-third have done so later. Over three-quarters have lived in accommodation provided by their factory. On the whole they have tended to live with their compatriots and to remain rather isolated socially, often making no non-Turkish friends. Indeed certain serious social problems have arisen, particularly over the education of their children and the relatively high proportion of legal convictions, (pp. 106–109).

Although this picture is, roughly speaking, applicable for most of the decade, some changes have taken place. Concentration in manufacturing and construction has tended to increase. Employment of female labour has also risen sharply. The proportion of migrants employed in skilled positions started to rise because of the increasing host country demand for skilled labour, and reports of training schemes suggest that a more serious attempt has recently been made to train temporarily recruited workers.

The work and life of Turkish workers abroad is very similar to that of those from the other Mediterranean exporting countries. Certain scraps of evidence suggest a few differences: Turks have tended to be more willing to accept – and to make fewer complaints about–their work situation. Migrants from other countries unfamiliar with the hardships of life in Anatolia have been less willing to accept meekly whatever conditions the employer chooses to offer. But Turks seem to have found social integration more difficult: held back by their poor linguistic abilities, and their different culture and religion, they have tended to become very isolated and to make few contacts with the host country population outside work, (pp. 107–109).

3.7.4   *On return (pp. 109–121)*

Information about migrants after their return is much scarcer and less reliable than that concerned with their situation before departure or while abroad, so that the following statements should be treated more as statements of probability than as statements of fact applicable to all returned migrants.

Most Turkish workers returned for family reasons (pp. 109–110). Although a substantial majority have wanted to set up a business of some sort, in fact most have failed to do so. Indeed the S.P.O. survey found more workers in wage employment on return than prior to departure (pp. 111–112). They had not, however, all found it easy to get work on return – nearly one-quarter of the S.P.O. respondents having taken over six months to find a job and 9% having failed completely. In fact, nearly half went back to the same occupation on return as they had held before departure; the chief change was a decline in traditional occupations, notably in agriculture (pp. 112–113). There was an overall increase in the level of skills reported, though nearly 40% of the respondents still held unskilled jobs. 10% reported that their linguistic knowledge was useful in their current job (p. 113). Correspondingly their mean incomes were considerably higher, those of the rural sample being over two-thirds as much again (even after some allowance has been made for inflation) (p. 114). Nonetheless, most compared their living standard on return unfavourably with that abroad (p. 120).

About one-third of the S.P.O. sample spent a fairly substantial part of their savings on items related to work, though the rural migrant was much more likely to have done so than the urban (pp. 114–118). The former tended to buy the requisite. for setting himself up as a small farmer, the latter to set himself up as a small business man, perhaps with a small manufacturing workshop, but more probably in a service activity. Both tended to concentrate on individual or family concerns and

124

were unlikely to have joined a cooperative scheme. As yet both industrial and agricultural cooperative ventures have had little success with migrant workers. Those who put their savings in industrial joint ventures with a view to setting up a factory (and working in it) on their return to Turkey were mostly defrauded of their money abroad. Those who went abroad through the agricultural cooperative scheme often failed to keep up their dues, and few imported machinery under the concession scheme.

All surveys of returned workers agree that the most popular 'large' expenditure unconnected with work which they make on return is a house or a building plot for one. About two-fifths of the S.P.O. respondents said that they had spent savings in this way. Nearly all bought some less expensive sort of consumer durable, and until the introduction of stricter import controls on cars, most workers would either bring one back themselves or sell their permit to do so. The S.P.O. results suggest that about 50% of migrants' savings were spent while abroad or after return on consumer goods of some sort, and about 37% on work-related goods, which were more likely to have been purchased in Turkey, (pp. 118–120).

The survey did not enquire into the success of these work ventures, but the fact that nearly three-quarters of all respondents were thinking of going abroad again does not suggest encouraging results. However, the additional difficulties faced by Turks who wish to return abroad mean that the permanently returned migrant is less of a myth in the Turkish situation than is the case in many of the other Mediterranean exporting countries. Nonetheless, for a substantial number of Turkish workers, migration abroad cannot be treated as a temporary interruption of life and work in Turkey which permits a worker to embark on a better work career on return; it must rather be regarded as initiating a new kind of life style according to which work and life abroad become the desired norm, to be preserved as long as possible.

4
The impact of labour export on Turkish economic development

4.1 Introduction

In Chapter 2 it was argued that there were certain factors which were the most important determinants of the impact of a labour export policy on economic growth. In this chapter these factors will be examined for the Turkish case in the light of the evidence reviewed in Chapter 3. Finally the impact of the system on the migrant workers themselves and on members of the non-migrant indigenous population is discussed.

4.2 The main determinants of the impact of labour export

4.2.1 *The occupational composition of migrants and the magnitude of output forgone*

All surveys have shown substantial migration of skilled industrial workers (§ § 3.4.10 – 3.4.14). However, the impact of this on the economy has to be assessed from various fragments of information. The first of these is employers' reports to the Turkish Employers' Confederation. During recent years these have been quite clear: the migration system has creamed off skilled workers.[1] What is not known is how representative these complaints are. For the second source, that is the Turkish Employment Service's recent surveys of labour vacancies, gives a somewhat different picture (T.E.S. 1970–1972). The surveys suggest that skilled manpower requirements have exceeded the supply, but do not on the other hand give the impression that there has been a serious and persistent skilled labour shortage since most of the vacancies notified to the T.E.S. have been filled comparatively quickly – usually in the first three months after notification.

A third source is the survey work carried out by members of the Social Planning Department of the State Planning Organization. They found that serious shortages of certain types of skilled labour had arisen in the shipbuilding, mining and construction industries, though there was no overall shortage of skilled labour in general. Recently there have been reports of more general shortages of all kinds of skilled

---

1 Information supplied by Mr. Saver of the Social Planning Department of the State Planning Organization, September 1972.

2 *Ibid.*

foremen and of small entrepreneurs.[1]

An indirect indicator of changes in the demand for certain types of labour is given by changes in wage rates and in differentials between skilled and unskilled workers. Table 14 shows the movement of the wage index by skill for five of the more common occupations of migrants employed in manufacturing before their departure.[2] In all five occupations the mean wages of unskilled workers rose faster than those of skilled workers or foremen when the data from all registration centres are considered together.[3] There is little change in this general picture when data from particular centres are considered separately — though, for instance, the wages of foremen and skilled fitters, of foremen and skilled carpenters and of foremen and skilled bricklayers in İstanbul rose faster than those of unskilled fitters, carpenters and bricklayers respectively. This suggests that although there has been no increase in skill differentials in general, there has been one for certain occupations in selected labour markets such as İstanbul, which may be the result of particular skilled labour shortages brought about by workers' migration. Indeed elsewhere skilled labour losses may have had an increasing impact on skill differentials, though of an amount insufficient to offset institutionally determined increases in the minimum wage. But although employers seem to have avoided raising skill premiums when faced with specific labour shortages, this is probably because these have not yet become sufficiently severe to force them to try to bid back skilled workers from abroad.

The above evidence on skill differentials tends to support the picture of the labour market situation obtained by the S.P.O., and also is very similar to that given by Krahenbuhl (in Kayser 1971C) in his report on the impact of emigration on three local labour markets in Turkey. Krahenbuhl found that forty-six out of fifty-four firms surveyed in 1968 in İzmir, Kocaeli and Zonguldak reported that workers had left for work abroad (though in only two cases had *no* workers at all *definitely* left for work abroad). Of these forty-six firms, eleven reported that they had had difficulty in filling some of the jobs vacated by emigrant workers, and thirty-five answered that they had had no difficulty.

> "Positions most frequently reported difficult to fill were of two types:
> (1) specialised types of machine operators peculiar to the textile industry and (2) general types of machine operators required by many industries for maintenance purposes if not for the production process itself. In the latter category we refer in particular to lathes, both setters and operators on millers and planing machines. Also mentioned were electricians, welders, moulders, blacksmiths, and two types of skilled worker required for mining." (Kayser 1971C, pp. 123—4).

1 *Sunday Times,* July 22nd, 1973; see also 'Turkey', *Financial Times* supplement, October 29th, 1973.

2 According to the T.E.S. surveys, carpenter and bricklayer were the most common pre-departure occupations of migrants, accounting for 6.6% and 6.4% respectively over the years 1967, 1968, 1969 and 1971. Lathe operators, fitters and electric welders were among the most frequent 'modern' manufacturing occupations reported amongst migrant departures.

3 In fact, actual skill differentials probably narrowed even more when the influence of side payments such as food, child-birth, death, marriage and clothing allowances have been taken into account. Most unionized workers in the modern sector receive such allowances.

Table 14:   Index of wages by selected occupation skill and province centre, June 1972 (June 1965 = 100)

Tornacı – Lathe Operator

	Usta-Foreman			Skilled Worker			Unskilled Worker		
	Min	Max	Mean	Min	Max	Mean	Min	Max	Mean
Adana	120	125	183	200	171	183	183	200	192
Ankara	200	250	200	200	180	175	313	250	220
Bursa	379	220	236	455	187	323	403	162	333
İstanbul	181	276	157	145	161	147	186	156	173
İzmir	194	200	208	179	175	162	180	154	165
Mean[1]	173	186	171	207	179	196	238	191	210

Tesviyeci – Fitter

	Usta-Foreman			Skilled Worker			Unskilled Worker		
	Min	Max	Mean	Min	Max	Mean	Min	Max	Mean
Adana	125	167	140	250	200	220	220	231	227
Ankara	175	200	180	320	225	240	225	240	200
Bursa	324	190	236	560	222	417	536	187	357
İstanbul	157	280	175	144	163	146	182	164	159
İzmir	194	200	208	179	175	162	180	154	165
Mean[1]	176	189	183	216	193	204	226	194	205

Elektrik Kaynakçı – Electric Welder

	Usta-Foreman			Skilled Worker			Unskilled Worker		
	Min	Max	Mean	Min	Max	Mean	Min	Max	Mean
Adana	150	160	186	190	143	160	182	250	209
Ankara	180	233	180	173	175	167	180	167	154
Bursa	243	156	168	298	136	212	n.a.	n.a.	n.a.
İstanbul	100	172	144	109	121	125	160	166	150
İzmir	200	188	180	188	188	179	180	167	173
Mean[1]	159	167	164	165	158	162	210	186	191

Marangoz – Carpenter

	Usta-Foreman			Skilled Worker			Unskilled Worker		
	Min	Max	Mean	Min	Max	Mean	Min	Max	Mean
Adana	171	167	150	225	200	220	200	227	220
Ankara	200	267	260	267	260	250	313	333	350
Bursa	273	164	240	289	139	200	300	138	333
İstanbul	172	195	200	182	172	173	143	119	135
İzmir	200	150	152	177	177	167	180	167	173
Mean[1]	191	189	196	206	200	217	230	193	225

Duvarcı – Bricklayer

	Usta-Foreman			Skilled Worker			Unskilled Worker		
	Min	Max	Mean	Min	Max	Mean	Min	Max	Mean
Adana	250	250	229	250	280	261	227	250	231
Ankara	367	250	260	450	275	333	375	267	350
Bursa	213	170	205	163	146	167	n.a.	n.a.	n.a.
İstanbul	227	235	250	147	200	191	154	139	153
İzmir	278	171	185	267	250	250	250	233	231
Mean[1]	225	203	212	219	219	216	227	229	242

Source: İş ve İşçi Bulma Kurumu (Turkish Employment Service), İş ve İşgücü Bülteni, 1965–1972.

Note: 1   Mean is of workers registered in Adana, Ankara, Bursa, Diyarbakır, Eskişehir, İstanbul, İzmir, Kayseri, Samsun, Trabzon.

Krahenbuhl not only obtained information about vacancies left by emigrant workers, but also about the extent to which these had been filled by ex-migrants. Whereas a total of 503 jobs had been vacated by emigrant workers, 375 jobs had been filled by returned workers, although some of the latter jobs were newly created because of expansion rather than because of vacancies created by departing migrants.

The 1971 S.P.O. survey tends to confirm this picture of returned workers filling some of the jobs created by those newly departing. The survey obtained information about migrants' occupations before departure and on return. About half (47% of the urban sub-sample and 51% of the rural sub-sample) took up the same occupation on return as before departure (§3.6.6). As the same modern sector industries tended to lose labour through emigration during the 1960s, this meant that to some extent ex-migrants were filling skilled occupational vacancies created by those leaving. In addition, 6% of returned workers switched on return to a job learnt abroad, which usually meant some form of semi-skilled manufacturing wage employment. However, since the ratio of those returning to those leaving to work abroad has been low,[1] there is no doubt that even after ex-migrants have been taken into account, there has been a net loss of skilled workers because of emigration.[2]

But has the outflow of workers — particularly that of skilled workers — led to output losses? Unfortunately there is no direct evidence to settle this question conclusively. Certainly given the notoriously high rate of underemployment in agriculture (§1.2.3) it is extremely unlikely that emigration has led to any significant losses in agricultural output.[3] And although the quantity of new machinery brought back has been very low, this has probably raised output to some extent.

It is less easy to estimate the impact of emigration on industrial output, though again there is no reason to suggest that there have been any substantial output losses.[4] Indeed it is probably more likely that by increasing the demand for industrial commodities (by returned workers), emigration has enabled firms to work closer to full capacity, and that this has more than offset any decrease caused by supply bottlenecks because of skilled labour shortages.[5] In addition, certain ex-migrants have set up new industrial workshops on their return (§3.6.11). But in the

1 About one to four or one to five during recent years (excluding the 1971 recession).

2 This is not contradicted by the finding in the S.P.O. survey that among returned migrants there was if anything, a net gain of skills because, as is shown below (§4.2.3), it is the skilled workers who are more likely to settle permanently abroad and, by definition, these were not included in the survey.

3 Emigration may have affected agricultural output indirectly through its contribution to devaluation and to urban inflation, thus affecting agricultural incomes and the terms of trade between agriculture and industry (though in 1970 the exchange rate for the main agricultural commodities was devalued by only half as much as was the official exchange rate). But the output changes in response to these price and income changes are likely to be small when compared with changes caused by the main determinant of Anatolian farm output — the weather.

4 Though there may have been production delays because of skilled labour shortages in 1972 and 1973.

5 Though it is possible that the increase in demand has been greatest in those industries which have the most skilled labour shortages. This may have been the case in the construction industry in 1972.

absence of any detailed evidence, no more precise conclusion can be drawn as to the change in industrial output.

Service sector output has probably increased as a result of emigration. This is because the migration of a service sector worker is unlikely to lead to an unfillable vacancy because of loss of skills which cannot quickly be replaced. All surveys show that it is mainly low, not high level service sector workers who have left for work abroad, and these are easily replaced from the ranks of the un- or underemployed. Furthermore, many ex-migrants have set up service sector businesses (§3.6.11). Insofar as these represent an increment to (not just a replacement of) existing services, output will rise. Casual observation suggests that they have done both.

In summary, therefore, the Turkish economy has certainly lost some scarce skilled manpower, but this does not as yet seem to have been accompanied by serious output losses – indeed emigration may have led to an overall output increase. On the other hand, emigration has led to the loss of the resources which were used to train the emigrating skilled manpower. And such losses are not inconsequential. For example it takes three years as an apprentice (*çırak*) and three years as a qualified worker (*kalfa*) to produce a master worker (*usta*) in many industrial occupations, and it takes about four years to train a welder, and the same or more to train a planer or turner – the last three all being high emigration occupations. This means that in the short term supply cannot be increased quickly. Yet since only selective labour shortages have as yet emerged, this means that there must have been either a surplus of such skilled workers, or that employers have learnt to make do without them either by upgrading other workers or using more mechanized techniques. Since the data on registered workers have not shown high unemployment of skilled workers during the 1960s, the latter alternative – that in one way or another employers managed without them – seems the more likely, particularly in view of the interest rate structure and over-valued exchange rate which together encouraged the utilization of more mechanized techniques before the 1970 devaluation.

The loss of the resources utilized in the training of skilled workers who migrate may be wiped out if they return[1] or be offset if unskilled migrants return with new skills, or if the migrants repay their training costs plus any other costs incurred until a replacement worker can be produced. But none of these alternatives seems to have been the case in Turkey (§4.2.3).

According to one view, migrant workers' training costs can be regarded not as a means of helping them to get better jobs, but as an investment by the state in human capital, the return on which is obtained when the worker repatriates savings and remittances from abroad. The argument is that if the social rate of return is higher on investing in human capital for export than on other activities, it pays the Turkish government to do this. But apart from the impersonal character of this argument, and its failure to take into account the impact of labour export on the migrants themselves, it is in practice false to assume that the flow of savings and remittances will continue at the same rate over an emigrant's lifetime. If the emigrant worker is joined by his wife and family and settles permanently in the host country then the flow of his repatriated earnings will almost certainly fall sharply. In other

---

1 It would not be fair to assess the output forgone in Turkey during their absence as a net loss because this is normally offset by their savings and remittances unless they settle abroad permanently.

words, the discounted sum of his total repatriated earnings over the years is not likely to exceed the discounted sum of his contribution to output in Turkey had he not emigrated, unless a very short time period is chosen for the comparison. More importantly, it is a mistake to treat the sum of repatriated earnings as representing the return on labour export without allowing for its effects on the rest of the economy. At this point it is worth pointing out the policy dilemma which has faced the Turkish government: the more it trains potential migrants, the more likely are they to be accepted and given better wages etc. while abroad, and so be able to repatriate more savings, but the less likely they are ever to return home (see Chapter 5).

4.2.2 The propensity to repatriate earnings while abroad

The magnitude of Turkish workers' savings and remittances has already been described (§3.5.11–12). Workers in the S.P.O. survey had saved an average of 36% of their income abroad and remitted an average of 11% in addition to this. But although the devaluation of 1970 led to a substantial increase in the proportion of savings and remittances repatriated through official channels rather than through the black market, a new sort of problem has emerged. This is that as an increasing proportion of Turkish migrant workers abroad has been attempting to settle there, this has increased the proportion of earnings which are invested in Europe rather than repatriated to Turkey.[1]

Table 15: *Workers' repatriated foreign exchange and workers' imports*[1] *($m) 1963–73*

	Workers foreign exchange ($m)	% Imports	% Exports	%Total official capital transactions[2]	Workers imports[1] ($m)	Imports C.i.f
1963	–	–	–	–	5	688
1964	8.1	3	3	4	7	537
1965	69.8	20	25	23	6	572
1966	115.3	28	39	45	11	718
1967	93.0	22	30	38	12	685
1968	107.3	23	36	39	22	764
1969	140.6	31	44	44	20	801
1970	273.0	43	64	65	35	948
1971	471.4	43	72	129	27	1 171
1972	740.0	47	84	206	39	1 563
1973*	1200.0	57	89	n.a.	n.a.	2 100

Sources: Workers' foreign exchange: *Turkish Employment Service.*
Imports, exports, capital transactions and workers' imports:US.A.I.D. *Economic and Social Indicators – Turkey,* Ankara, 1972 and 1973; 1973 estimates: Economist Intelligence Unit, *Turkey* No. 4, 1973.

* Estimated figures.
1 Workers' imports (*bedeisiz ithalat*) are the commodities which returning workers could import without allocation of foreign exchange.
2 Project assistance, programme assistance and agricultural surpluses.

Note: Data during certain years during the 1960s may be underestimates because of the use of black market channels (see p. 103 fn. 4).

1 In the autumn of 1971 it was estimated that savings of Turkish workers held in German banks amounted to $230 million (*Economic News Digest,* October 15th 1971). The total in all host country banks was estimated at around $350 million (*Economic News Digest,* July 1st, 1971). A pre-devaluation estimate was much higher – the I.K.A. News Agency put Turkish savings in foreign banks at the equivalent of about T.L.4 billion (June 9th, 1970, p. 3). Özşahin (1970C) estimated that only 67% of Turkish workers' savings abroad were repatriated either officially or unofficially.

Despite this, repatriated earnings amounted to $740 million in 1972, which was 84% of a record export total of $888 million, and 47% of total imports (compared with 72% and 43% respectively in 1971 and estimated values of 89% and 57% respectively in 1973 (Table 15)). Receipt of repatriated earnings has meant that Turkey has been able to reduce her dependence on foreign aid from what would otherwise have been the case. Thus the estimated total of foreign credits required over the Third Five Year Plan is only $932 million, as compared with an annual average of over $300 million in consortium credits and other foreign aid during the Second Plan. This will in time reduce the high level of interest and debt repayments which Turkey has to make each year, and which reached $205 million in 1970.

In 1972 and 1973, repatriated earnings amounted to 5% and 7% respectively of the Turkish G.N.P., while approximately 4.7% and 5.2% respectively of Turkey's economically active population were working abroad. In other words, migrant workers contributed a more than proportionate share in G.N.P. through their repatriated earnings alone; that is, excluding their consumption expenditure abroad which is counted under the G.N.P. of their host country.

In summary, therefore, although Turkish migrant workers' propensity to save and remit earnings from abroad has been high, with many living on the poverty line to achieve this, Turkey is extremely dependent on the despatch of new migrant workers to sustain this flow, for as members of the existing stock abroad settle, their propensity to repatriate their earnings declines.

4.2.3   *The acquisition and utilization of new skills*

The impact of exporting labour to work temporarily abroad on the acquisition and utilization of skills in the home economy depends on (1) whether its nationals do learn new skills while abroad (2) whether the new skills learned are relevant to the needs of the home country (3) whether such relevant new skills learned abroad are ever actually utilized in the home country.

There is no doubt that the Turkish experience to date is unfavourable on all three counts. Less than 10% of the S.P.O. sample reported that they had received any formal training and 11% had worked in less skilled occupations abroad than they had held in Turkey before departure. Even if under-reporting of initial training is assumed, (see §3.5.5 above) remarkably few workers managed to raise their skill level while abroad (Table A29b).

However, it is possible that the S.P.O. sample data under-rated training received abroad because only those who had returned to Turkey were included in the sample. But as Table A25b shows, the more skilled a position a worker obtained, the more likely he was to work for a longer period abroad; the less skilled he was, the more likely he was to return to Turkey after only one or two years abroad. Of course it is not surprising that the more skilled stay abroad longer; it is in employers' interests to renew the contracts of those whom they have trained.

But it may then be argued that even those foreign workers who have received no formal training at all will at least have obtained experience of work discipline on the production line. In other words, although they may bring back little in the way of new skills, they will at least be usable as the core of a disciplined industrial labour force. But although this may seem promising in theory, in practice at least some

132

Turkish employers have found that ex-migrants' difficulties in settling down more than offset their experience on the production line. Evidence cited above (§3.6.4) indicates that some employers have avoided recruiting returned migrant workers mainly because these expected better pay and conditions – and might be more likely to organize trade union activity to agitate for them. There is also the suggestion that whereas the migrants were prepared to work under others on the production line while abroad, they were much less willing to do so on return. But whatever the reason, the net effect has been the same: employers have found that there is no special advantage in employing ex-migrants and that, from their point of view, there may even be disadvantages.

But what of the workers who did learn new skills? The problem here is that there is virtually no information about those who have learnt new skills abroad but have not returned to Turkey. All that is known is that workers in the S.P.O. survey who were skilled in Turkey were more likely to be employed in skilled jobs abroad or to receive training there, and were more likely to remain abroad longer. This suggests that those who do learn new skills may not return to Turkey to utilize them.

However, some at least have returned. Are the skills learnt in foreign factories relevant for work in Turkey? In some cases yes, in others no. For many of the workers will be producing commodities abroad which are unsuitable for the current Turkish market. However, the new scheme whereby selected Turks are trained in Germany and then again on their return to Turkey as a preliminary to employment there in German subsidiaries shows that skills relevant for work on return can in very special instances be obtained abroad (see p. 95 fn. 1).

Furthermore, workers who have returned have often not utilized their new skills. Indeed half the S.P.O. sample did the same job on return as before departure, of whom three-quarters did a different job while abroad (Table 9). Only 6% changed to a new job learned abroad. Some of the former had however improved their skills while away. All the same, although there was a net increase in reported skills on return, this was rather disappointing given the potential. For while half were un-skilled before departure, 40% were in unskilled jobs on return (excluding the unem-ployed) (Table A19).

Altogether, therefore, the impact of labour export on the acquisition and utili-zation of new skills has not been very favourable. Comparatively few Turkish workers learnt new relevant skills and of those who actually returned to Turkey, not all made use of them. Yet in many years during the last decade, the outflow of skilled migrants has exceeded total returned workers.

4.2.4   *The proportion of savings and remittances invested in producer goods on return*

The only detailed information on the fate of savings and remittances after return is given in the S.P.O. survey. Since the more sketchy information given in the Tuna survey (1966) is consistent with this, the S.P.O. data will be used below.

In this survey the estimated proportion of savings spent on consumption goods while away or soon after return was about 50%, and so was substantially less than the share of consumption in Turkish G.N.P.[1] (which fell from about 85% to 80% during the two Five Year Plans).[2] On the other hand, the proportion of savings spent on producer goods was rather small, as was the amount of agricultural and industrial machinery brought in under the concession scheme (§3.6.11). Both the industrial and agricultural co-operative schemes have as yet met with little success, though the government is persevering with both.[3] Furthermore, an expert from the Ministry of Industry reported that there were often serious problems in the comparatively rare cases where returned workers planned to put their savings into some form of industrial venture. The basic problem was their lack of information about potentially profitable ventures and their lack of managerial skills and know-how. Thus there had been a mass of applications from workers who wanted to set up fruit juice processing plants to emulate the success of the firm Meysu, which had been an early entrant into the field. Apart from attempts to dissuade the aspirant worker-investors from all setting up the same kind of plant when the market would not stand it, there is little other official assistance for which the workers can apply. In theory, an institute in Ankara can provide them with technical assistance, but according to the expert from the Ministry of Industry, workers rarely know of its existence. And its resources would be totally inadequate if workers attempted to use it on a substantial scale.

Because of the difficulty in providing technical and managerial guidance on the scale required for ex-migrants to set up industrial ventures to any significant extent, the Ministry of Industry has switched its policy to encouraging workers to purchase shares in certain new large public sector projects. As yet, however, there is no indication to suggest that this scheme will be any more successful than a previous scheme mooted in September 1971, whereby shares in seven selected factories were to be reserved for investments by returnee workers[4] (see p. 116 fn. 4).

In summary, therefore, the proportion of migrant workers' repatriated savings which have been invested in producer goods has been disappointingly low as compared with governmental hopes, and there is little reason to expect any substantial improvement in the future. It is of course not surprising that workers have been reluctant to invest directly in production. However, in the absence of a developed

---

1 And would be even lower if expenditure on housing were excluded.

2 During the Third Five Year Plan it is planned to raise domestic savings from 19.6% in 1972 to 25.5% in 1977.

3 For instance 684 persons left under the village co-operative scheme in March 1973 (*Milliyet,* 16th May 1973).

4 Another scheme involved the foundation of a Workers' Investment Bank to attract the savings of Turkish workers abroad. This was to have an initial capital of T.L. 400 million. Of its total share certificates, 51% were to be set aside for the state and public organizations, 34% for workers employed abroad and 15% for persons and legal entities in Turkey. The state would guarantee a profit of 12% to the worker shareholders. The aim of the bank was not just to attract savings, but to assist in the preparation of suitable investment projects for returned workers and to provide guidance and technical assistance. (*Economic News Digest,* October 15th 1971).

system of financial intermediaries suitable for the small saver, combined with the extremely low (or even negative) real rates of interest which have been paid on savings accounts, the relative failure of the special government sponsored schemes to persuade workers to invest in co-operatives, joint ventures, shares or stocks indicates a failure to persuade workers to invest at all since these productive investment opportunities were often more accessible and financially attractive than those provided through the banking system.[1]

4.2.5 *The proportion of savings and remittances spent on imported commodities on return*

Although repatriated savings provide the Turkish government with additional foreign exchange, this is reduced by the amount which ex-migrants spend on imported commodities. Turkey operates strict controls on imports so that only items on the liberalized list can usually be imported without a special allocation of foreign exchange. However, to encourage migrant workers to return to Turkey and bring back their savings with them, the government introduced a special facility whereby such workers could import certain commodities without allocation of foreign exchange (*bedelsiz ithalat*).

The increasing importance of such workers' imports is shown in Table 15.[2] These imports rose from $5 million in 1963 to $27 million in 1971. This increase is not just attributable to the number of returned workers utilizing the scheme but also to the additional commodities — notably consumer goods — which the government has permitted over the years as further inducements. Indeed the government even proposed to establish duty-free shops at customs posts where workers could purchase for payment in foreign exchange not just industrial machinery but also a wide variety of consumer goods and possibly even cars.[3]

The composition of workers' imports over the period 1969—71 is given in Table 16. The main categories have been vehicles and machinery (including consumer durables). In 1969, television and radio sets amounted to over half of the electrical machinery category and cars amounted to 83% of the vehicles category. But although workers' imports consist largely of consumer goods, such imports can hardly be considered a serious problem as long as the overall total remains so low when compared with workers repatriated earnings ($471 million in 1971) or with the total import bill ($1171 million in 1971).

The only evidence on the extent to which returned workers purchase imported commodities after their return home is that provided in the 1971 S.P.O survey. But

---

1 This raises the question of whether the government should be encouraging investment from migrants' savings in particular rather that of all Turkish savers in general. The pragmatic justification for this is that ex-migrants constitute a high saving group whose actions the government feels it may be able to influence. But all special incentive schemes for ex-migrants make them into even more of an élite group.

2 The item *bedelsiz ithalat* in the Turkish balance of payments is not exclusively workers' imports; it is however estimated that about 90—95% of *bedelsiz ithalat* are workers' imports. Imports obtained through grants and which are therefore obtained without allocation of foreign exchange have not been included in the figures presented in Table 16.

3 *Economic News Digest*, July 1st 1971.

Table 16: *Composition of imports with waiver into Turkey,*[1] *1969–71* (T.L. 1 000)

Commodity	1969	1970	1971
Food & Food products	930	3180	9090
Chemicals & Pharmaceuticals	3010	1130	2460
Rubber products	90	–	60
Wood products & Paper	310	570	110
Textiles & Clothing	970	230	50
Stone, Ceramic, Glass	150	10	50
Metal products	830	1300	930
Agricultural products	710	180	220
Base metal products	20	–	20
Machines	4980	4390	5600
Vehicles & parts	6850	18650	8090
Precision instruments etc.	590	280	720
Other goods	150	5110	40
Total	19580	35020	27420

Source: Türkıye Ticaret Odaları, Sanayi Odaları ve Ticaret Borsaları Birliği, *İktisadî Rapor 1972*, p. 407. Figures rounded to nearest ten.

1 See p. 135, fn. 2.

this can only give a rough indication since it refers only to commodities purchased out of savings accumulated abroad: thus it includes goods bought while abroad and brought back under the imports with waiver scheme and excludes goods purchased from other sources of funds after return. On the whole, the survey found that most consumer durables purchased out of savings had been bought abroad while more of the work-related investment goods had been purchased in Turkey than abroad. Since most imported consumer durables will have been brought back under the imports with waiver scheme, this means that after return, savings were spent predominantly on home-produced goods or, in other words, that the propensity to spend repatriated savings on imports was low.

There is no information at all as to whether or not workers' families used the remittances received to purchase imported goods, or as to whether or not returned workers have a higher propensity to spend their income on imported goods after their return. However, the government can exert some control over the actual propensity to import through its manipulation of the import regime. Import licenses are issued freely only for goods on an annual list of liberalized commodities; the import of other commodities is either prohibited or subject to global quotas. Consequently both the type and amount of imports can be adjusted annually and, in theory at least, any tendency for ex-migrants to switch to imported consumer goods can be checked.[1]

1 In fact, according to the State Institute of Statistics definition, imports of consumer goods have remained at around 5% of the total value of imports since 1963 (State Institute of Statistics, *Annual Foreign Trade Statistics*). However, a study on Greece (Nikolinakos 1971E) found that because of the growth of imports from Germany as familiarisation with German goods increased, the increasing volume of remittances covered a decreasing proportion of the growing trade deficit.

4.2.6 The change which expenditure from savings and remittances brings to the domestic price level.

Receipt of savings and remittances after the introduction of a labour export policy need not have an inflationary impact, at least in the medium term. If the government uses the foreign exchange equivalent of the savings and remittances to create the capacity to supply the commodities demanded by those spending the domestic currency equivalent, then, except in the very short run, prices need not rise. Alternatively if the government were able to reduce the level of public expenditure to compensate for the additional demand created by expenditure from the domestic currency equivalent of repatriated earnings, then the overall price level need not rise or, it there are structural rigidities, need not rise much. On the other hand, if the domestic currency equivalent of repatriated earnings is spent without additional capacity being created or if it is too difficult to estimate, let alone effect a compensating reduction in public expenditure, then prices can be expected to rise. Thus it is not so much the receipt of repatriated earnings, but their unexpected increase which is likely to have an inflationary impact. And since during the later 1960s and, more especially, the early 1970s, repatriated earnings have continually exceeded forecasts, the possibility of such an inflationary impact cannot be ruled out.

However it is not possible to distinguish with any precision to what extent this potentially inflationary role has actually been realised. Since 1968 Turkey has experienced a serious inflationary problem. The rate of inflation began to accelerate from around 5% in the middle of 1968 and continued to accelerate until 1972. The origins of this inflation are complex. First of all the government had done nothing to stem the basic sources of inflation in the Turkish economy during the First Plan (see above p. 31). Despite an attempt at more stringent credit control in 1970, the situation deteriorated because, after the devaluation, the higher lira cost of imports was normally passed on to end users. On top of this, the government granted large salary increases to public employees in the December of 1970. Then in 1971 there was a 15–20% increase in government support prices for cereals which affected industrial wage levels because of the cost of living element in organized labour's wage determination. The overall result of the large deterioration in purchasing power since the 1970 devaluation was wage settlements mainly of the order of 30% higher in 1971.[1] The general wholesale price index rose by 23% between December 1970 and December 1971; and the cost of living indices for Ankara and Istanbul rose by almost as much. The situation was again worsened by increases in the prices of the products of many state economic enterprises which were approved in July 1971. However in 1972 there was some improvement. The general index for wholesale prices rose by 15% while the Ankara and Istanbul cost of living indices rose by 13% and 11% respectively. But prices again started to rise more quickly at the beginning of 1973, during which the wholesale price index increased by 25%.

To what extent has expenditure from repatriated earnings contributed to this inflation? As described above (§§3.6.11–3.6.12), the main purchases by ex-migrants were housing and consumer durables, and agricultural land and small shops. There

---

1 Indeed in August 1971 the government raised the wages of a total of 57 000 workers in the railways, metal manufacturing and cement industries by an average of 35%.

is little doubt that the additional demand from returned workers has contributed to the very high rate of inflation of land prices in urban areas. For instance, Table A44 shows the large increases in the prices of certain plots in the Ankara area during recent years. Unfortunately, there are no representative data on other urban areas, particularly the smaller towns of Anatolia where increases have been much less severe. However, since (1) a significant proportion of urban ex-migrants[1] bought a house, building plot or property of some sort, and (2) they spent a substantial part of their savings in so doing,[2] this suggests that their demand has contributed to the rise in urban land prices.

Similarly, demand from returned workers has probably stimulated the expansion of the construction industry. Employment in construction has risen from 305 000 in 1962 to 433 000 in 1972, and of this about 75% was in housing in both years. However, the number of houses built has increased much faster as can be seen from Table 17. And although the cost per square metre rose by 68% between 1962 and 1971, this was considerably less than the rise in the general wage index for insured workers in the construction industry, which increased by 91% between 1963 and 1971.

If anything, returned workers' demand for housing may have had a countercycical effect as the large post-devaluation repatriation of earnings whose lira equivalents fueled aggregate demand coincided with a serious recession in the construction industry.[3] Furthermore, the price range which the S.P.O. survey returned workers quoted for their house purchase (around T.L. 25 000 in urban areas) lies below the mean cost of building a house in urban areas in the mid-1960s (Table 17), implying that the ex-migrants had on the whole bought modest properties (perhaps more so than they had intended if they had failed to allow for inflation during their absence). There is no evidence that returned workers' demand has yet had an inflationary effect on house-building prices.

There is also not very much evidence as to whether or not returned workers' demand for other commodities has had an inflationary impact. Excess capacity has been a perennial problem for many Turkish industries, so that often an unexpected increase in demand can be met with existing resources. And in the longer term, the required capacity to supply demand for machinery and consumer durables is being created as part of Turkey's planned development.

However, there is no doubt that the post-devaluation resurgence of repatriated earnings led to a substantial unexpected increase in demand which contributed to the current inflationary environment (and so possibly to the social and political unrest which culminated in the fall of the Demirel government). The smaller unexpected increases in repatriated earnings in other years may have had a similar inflationary effect, though except perhaps in the urban land market this is unlikely to have been strong.

1 At least 34% in the S.P.O. survey (36% of the men).

2 Returned workers in the S.P.O. survey had saved an average of T.L. 22 000, while sample prices quoted for the amount which had been spent on house purchase were often in the region of T.L. 5 000–25 000.

3 The annual growth rate of the construction industry fell from 9% in 1969 to 5% in 1970 and 2% in 1971 (Yaşer, B, 1972).

138

4.2.7   *The impact which employment of migrant labour abroad has on the actual and the potential trade between the host and the exporting country.*

If the host country cannot obtain migrant labour at no extra cost elsewhere, so that employment of a particular country's workers has a dampening influence on host country prices, and/or if emigration exacerbates inflation in the emigration country, the latter may find that its workers are producing abroad commodities which could have been produced domestically for export, and that it is importing commodities which it could have produced domestically for its own consumption. Although it could put a tariff on host country imports and subsidise exports, the emigration country would still have to choose a combination of commodity flows and labour flows because action to offset the price effects of labour export would in turn tend to reduce host country demand for labour.

However, although the evidence reviewed in Chapter 1 clearly demonstrates the general disinflationary impact on wages which use of migrant labour has brought about in the host countries, the use of *Turkish* labour has had limited influence in bringing it about. If Turkey had not participated in the system of temporarily re-cruited migration, the host country would have recruited elsewhere. But since Turkey has provided a large proportion of migrant workers in some host countries (e.g. Germany, where Turks are now the largest migrant worker nationality, and the Netherlands), it is unlikely that these countries would have been able to obtain sub-stitutes from other countries without incurring some extra cost, because it would have been necessary to recruit from even more distant lands, so increasing recruit-ment expenses because of the higher cost of transport. Consequently it seems likely that in the host countries which have high proportions of Turkish workers, the use of *Turkish* labour has made some — albeit small — contribution to keeping down inflation, with a consequent, though small, effect on the pattern of trade between them and Turkey.

Obviously such an effect is extremely hard to detect. Commodity trade between Turkey and the country most dependent on Turkish labour, Germany, is given in Table 18. The importance of this trade to Turkey can be seen from Table 19 which shows that Germany is her main trading partner (taking 19% of Turkish exports and sending 18% of Turkish imports in 1971). Table 18 shows that Turkey is im-porting commodities from industries where Turkish workers are employed in Germany and is exporting to Germany commodities produced in Turkey. The most obvious example of this is textiles. About 6% of the Turkish workers in Germany were employed in the textile industry in 1971 and of these 38% were women, who tend to be employed at the lowest grades on the pay scale. Consequently it might be suggested that the observed tendency for use of migrant labour to have a disin-flationary effect on wages in German industry as a whole, applies to the use of Turkish labour in the textile industry taken separately, If this has been passed on to commodity prices, exporting labour would dampen the prospects for Turkish textile exports and improve those for German exports to Turkey. However, any such effect has probably been insignificant, because it depends on Turkish workers in Germany producing the *same* kind of textiles as those produced for export in Turkey. This assessment seems to be supported by the data in Table 18, which show rapid increases in Turkish textile exports since 1968. However, although Turkish

Table 17: Selected Turkish Housing statistics, 1962–71

	1962	1963	1964	1965	1966	1967	1968	1969	1970	1971
No.of houses built (to nearest 100)	58700	57300	60800	80500	91200	99400	110300	132100	155100	150400
Index (1962 = 100)	100	98	103	137	155	170	188	225	264	256
Mean area (square meters)	105	103	100	99	99	97	96	98	98	93
Index (1962 = 100)	100	98	95	94	94	92	91	93	93	89
Mean cost of building (T.L.) (to nearest 100)	26800	26700	25800	26000	27400	29300	30800	32200	39300	40000
Index (1962 = 100)	100	100	96	97	102	110	115	135	147	149
Cost/sq met. (T.L.)	254	259	258	262	276	302	322	370	399	426
Index (1962 = 100)	100	102	102	103	109	119	127	146	157	168
Total value in TLm	1572	1528	1567	2095	2495	2914	3394	4786	5988	6009

Source: State Institute of Statistics.

140

Table 18: *Turkey's imports from and exports to W. Germany ($m), 1967–71*

	Imports					Exports				
	1967	1968	1969	1970	1971	1967	1968	1969	1970	1971
Food & live animals	–	–	2	4	–	52	50	75	62	65
Beverages & Tobacco	–	–	–	2	–	9	14	12	16	16
Crude materials	1	1	2	2	2	22	18	21	31	30
Mineral fuels	1	1	1	1	1	–	–	–	–	2
Animal & veg. fats	–	1	1	–	–	–	–	–	–	–
Chemicals	30	35	40	42	52	–	–	1	–	2
Manufactured goods	22	19	17	34	37	1	4	4	7	13
Textiles		3	3	3	4	–	1	4	6	11
Metal products		3	3	3	4		–	–	–	–
Machinery & transport equipment	75	94	74	77	95	–	–	–	–	–
Non-electrical	n.a.	63	50	54	59		–	–	–	–
Electrical	n.a.	14	14	15	20		–	–	–	–
Transport	n.a.	17	10	8	17		–	–	–	–
Misc.manufactures & commodities N.E.C.	5	6	5	5	7	–	–	–	1	3
Total trade	135	157	140	165	195	84	86	112	118	131

Source: O.E.C.D. Trade by commodities, *Analytical Abstracts* Jan–Dec 1969, Jan–Dec 1970; *Country summaries* Jan–Dec 1971.

Note: All figures rounded to nearest $1m.

Table 19: *Percentage composition of Turkey's trade by country, 1963–72*

	1963 E	1963 I	1964 E	1964 I	1965 E	1965 I	1966 E	1966 I	1967 E	1967 I	1968 E	1968 I	1969 E	1969 I	1970 E	1970 I	1971 E	1971 I	1972 E	1972 I
Total E.E.C.	38	29	36	29	34	29	35	33	34	35	33	37	40	35	40	34	39	39	39	42
W. Germany	17	15	15	15	16	15	16	16	16	20	17	20	21	18	20	19	19	18	21	19
Belgium-Luxembourg	3	1	4	2	5	1	5	2	3	2	3	2	3	2	4	2	3	2	3	2
France	4	5	6	4	4	4	5	6	6	4	4	4	5	3	7	3	7	6	6	7
Netherlands	2	2	2	2	2	2	3	2	2	2	3	3	3	2	2	2	4	3	3	3
Italy	12	5	7	6	7	6	7	8	7	7	5	9	8	9	7	8	6	10	6	11
U.K.	13	11	11	11	9	10	10	11	7	13	7	13	6	12	6	10	5	10	5	11
U.S.	20	31	18	29	18	28	16	24	18	18	15	16	11	17	12	19	10	15	12	12
Other[1]	29	29	35	31	39	33	39	32	41	34	45	34	43	36	42	37	46	36	44	35

Source: U.S.A.I.D. *Economic indicators – Turkey.*

Note: 1 None of the countries included in 'Other' have had a share exceeding 10%.

142

labour export does not yet seem to have affected her own export competitiveness, it may have had a slight impact on keeping down the prices of some of her imports from Germany.[1] But this is unlikely to have affected the prospects for any Turkish infant import substitute industries because of the strict import controls enforced. In other words, there is as yet no evidence at all that Turkish labour export has affected either her export or import substitute industries through its (in any case small) impact on host country prices.

However, two important qualifications need to be made about all this. The first is that so far, the exchange rate has been assumed to be fixed without taking into account the repercussions of undertaking a labour export policy. For if repatriated earnings come to constitute a major proportion of foreign exchange receipts then the country will have to maintain an exchange rate which is not so overvalued as to hold back remittances, and this will obviously influence Turkey's trading pattern.

The second factor which has as yet been ignored is Turkey's association with the E.E.C. (see above, p. 33). *Inter alia,* this entails the gradual dismantling of Turkey's import controls against E.E.C. countries and so of the system of protection of new import substitute industries. Turkey will virtually be committed to a more export orientated growth strategy, but may then find that any disinflationary effect of the use of migrant labour in the E.E.C. countries is a more serious problem for the development of export markets there and of import substitute industries at home, even though a unilateral withdrawal by Turkey from the system of labour export would have little effect.

4.2.8   *The proportion of migrants who settle permanently abroad*

As yet comparatively few migrant workers have returned permanently to Turkey. By the end of 1972, 654 467 officially recruited workers had been despatched. On the assumption that official departures amounted to four-fifths of all departures (§3.1.2) this means that total worker migration had been of the order of 820 000, of whom only 160 000 had returned by the end of 1972. And according to the S.P.O. survey, most of a group of workers who had supposedly returned permanently were planning to re-emigrate (§3.6.14).

There is no way of estimating the proportion who have settled permanently abroad, as whether or not those who aspire to do so are permitted to stay depends crucially on host country policy.

But whether or not a migrant worker eventually returns is of considerable importance to Turkey. If he settles abroad with his family, not only are the resources used in his upbringing and any skills learnt in Turkey or acquired while abroad permanently lost to his home country, but also the level of his repatriated earnings is likely to fall off substantially. And if the host country controls immigration by imposing an upper limit on the total stock of immigrant workers, then his presence as a permanent settler prevents the despatch of a new worker who will repatriate more foreign exchange. On the other hand, his permanent departure means one person less seeking employment in Turkey.

---

1   Such an effect is unlikely to have been very strong since German exporters had in any case to face world competition.

4.3 The impact of Turkish export of labour: a crude assessment

Unfortunately data are not available to assess the detailed impact of emigration on all the factors discussed in Chapter 2. However an attempt has been made to describe the impact in each case in the following table:

Labour force:
overall decrease but small increase in economically active women[1]

Age structure:
depletion of 20—40 age group[2]

Rate of population growth:
slight decrease (because migrants delay marriage to work abroad, married couples are often separated and the birth rate abroad is lower)[3]

Rate of urbanization:
small increase (because the proportion of ex-rural returned workers who settle in towns on return is higher than the proportion for the indigenous population)[4]

Agricultural output:
small increase (because some rural returnees introduce improved techniques)[5]

Agricultural incomes:
increase (money incomes increase because remittances more than offset any fall in income from farming; in any case government tries to keep up farm incomes by raising the support price for agricultural commodities though since the 1970 devaluation, such increases have not kept up with the rate of inflation)

Agricultural employment:
decrease (because not all workers who leave are replaced by ones who return; however, disguised unemployment will fall; also see §4.4)

Industrial output:
increase (because of additional demand from expenditure out of savings and remittances)

Industrial wages:
increase in money wages where skilled labour shortages have been difficult to fill and possibly where remittance expenditure has led to excess demand, but a smaller increase in real wages because of inflation[6] (see also §4.4)

---

1 For instance, the S.P.O. survey showed that housewives who worked abroad often continued in employment on return.

2 The proportion of the population between the ages of 15 and 64 has in any case been declining since 1950.

3 The German data show that the proportion of migrant Turks who are married is lower than for the corresponding age group in the indigenous Turkish population and the size of family is also smaller.

4 Tuna and S.P.O. surveys.

5 S.P.O. survey.

6 The index of real wages of insured persons in non-agricultural employment rose from 100 in 1963 to 137.6 in 1970 but fell to 133.8 in 1971.

Industrial employment:	probable increase: remittances provide the demand and resources for new ventures and so new jobs, but this is partly offset by the extent to which departing workers are not replaced[1]
Service sector output and incomes:	increase (because returned workers establish 'modern' service sector businesses)[2]
Service sector employment:	increase (because returned workers move into services and because of increased demand for service sector products)[3]
Unemployment:	reduction (because of temporary absence of many workers and permanent departure of some; but also necessary to take into account the effects described above by sector of employment).
Supply of skilled labour:	decrease (because skilled worker departures outnumber returns)
Production techniques:	some new machines brought back by returned workers; probably some shift to more capital intensive techniques to offset loss of skilled labour.
Aggregate demand:	increase (because of expenditure from savings and remittances)
Savings:	increase; also propensity to save out of savings and remittances higher than propensity to save out of domestic income[4]
Investment:	increase, though little of this channelled into producer goods[5]
Inflation:	small increase in general; probably greater impact on urban land market
Balance of payments:	very large improvement because of repatriated earnings
Transfer of social capital:	substantial because of high proportion of skilled workers among migrant workers

4.4   The impact of migration on the migrant and the home country population

The impact of migration on the migrants themselves has been described in Chapter 3. In material terms, most migrant workers were better off on return, but some were

1 Krahenbuhl's survey; employers' reports to the Turkish Employers' Confederation.

2 S.P.O. and Abadan 1971 surveys.

3 S.P.O. survey.

4 *Ibid.*

5 *Ibid.*

worse off (e.g. those who were employed before they left, but who came back with virtually no savings, having failed to settle in a job abroad, and then could not find employment on return). For most not only had higher incomes on return, but also some accumulated savings left to draw on, and better living accommodation. But despite this, three quarters of the S.P.O. sample felt that their living standard on return was not as high as that abroad, even though data on their budgets abroad show that most were living on the breadline there, and most studies show that they were living in very bad housing.In other words, although their actual standard of living had improved, rising expectations brought about by familiarity with European living standards meant that they were not satisfied with it. For many, a work period abroad had not solved their problems, but instead created a host of new ones. Only a minority (often rural migrants who had successfully set up farms) seemed to have settled down again in their native land and to have felt reasonably satisfied with their situation.

The detailed impact of migration on the distribution of the personal incomes of the home country population cannot be assessed because of the absence of data. Migrants leaving the agricultural sector will obviously tend to reduce the magnitude of disguised unemployment and, through their repatriated earnings, to raise incomes. However, since most have come from the ranks of the middle and upper peasantry, the landless proletariat have probably gained little. Returned workers who have bought land and agricultural machinery and set themselves up as farmers have probably helped to raise the incomes of other local farmers (by making available machinery for hire) but by so doing may have increased unemployment among the landless agricultural labourers. Those who have gone abroad through the agricultural co-operative scheme, actually kept up their dues and brought back farm machinery will have improved the incomes of other co-operative members. However, such migrants have been few in number (§3.6.11), and in any case, co-operatives have not been established in the poorest villages in Eastern Turkey where semi-feudal agriculture still survives.[1]

If emigration has affected the distribution of wages within industry, its only influence has been to prevent skill differentials from narrowing as much as they would otherwise have done. It is difficult to discover whether or not migration has had an adverse effect on the growth of industrial employment owing to introduction of more capital intensive techniques, because of all the other pressures (e.g. the interest rate structure) which have tended to bring this about in Turkey. However, isolated employers' reports suggest that there is some evidence for this effect, so that all migrants departing from the industrial sector are not replaced, and the extent of new job creation is less than it would otherwise have been.

The other distributional effects of migration are even more difficult to assess. Insofar as it contributed to the 1970 devaluation and subsequent inflation it has also contributed to the consequent deterioration in agriculture's terms of trade.[2] Also, because urban migrants have well outnumbered rural ones, urban areas have

1 In 1968 there were about 2000 co-operatives with just over one and a quarter million members.

2 Even though the government raised agricultural support prices by 15–20% in 1971, this has been more than overtaken by the rate of inflation.

obtained a larger share of repatriated earnings. Since a large part of the repatriated earnings of both urban and rural returnees have been spent on industrial output or land, this has tended to raise business and landowners' profits. And since emigration does not seem to have had much impact on raising wages, this means that it has tended to raise the share of profits in national income. Finally, it has led to no improvements – and possibly to a deterioration – in the regional distribution of income. This is because a majority of migrants have come from richer provinces, and a significant proportion of those from poorer ones have moved to richer ones on their return, taking their repatriated earnings with them.

4.5   Summary

It is now possible to identify where Turkey stands as compared with the extreme cases described in §2.3 above, and to summarize the effects of the migration system on Turkish income and its distribution. It has not just been the unskilled unemployed but also the skilled industrial workers who have migrated, and who have been more likely to settle permanently abroad. However, until 1972 no serious skilled labour shortages had emerged, so that it is unlikely that there were any consequent output losses. There is little evidence as to whether or not the loss of skilled workers has raised wages, discouraged training and encouraged utilization of more capital intensive techniques, though isolated reports suggest that these effects have occurred to a minor extent. Savings and remittances out of earnings abroad have been mainly utilized not for agricultural or industrial investment but for consumption expenditure (pp. 114–120). However, these repatriated earnings do not seem to have had much inflationary impact, and the proportion spent on imports after return has probably been low. But despite the government's hopes, there have, not surprisingly, been few examples of returned workers setting up their own productive enterprises to create new employment opportunities for themselves. Indeed insofar as ex-migrants have attempted to establish businesses, they have tended to be in the service sector, though rural migrants have tended to set themselves up as small farmers. Few returned workers have learnt new skills abroad (other than unskilled, or possibly semi-skilled work on the production line), and those who have done so have not tended to use them on return. However, there is little evidence to suggest that their employment abroad has had any adverse impact on the pattern of trade.

In other words, emigration has not provided substantial for capital formation and has tended to reduce the supply of trained manpower for new industrial projects. Although it has obviously alleviated the unemployment problem, it has also encouraged employers to reduce their dependence on workers who may leave to work abroad whenever an opportunity becomes available. On the other hand, it has had little inflationary impact and has proved to be a crucially important source of foreign exchange.

By no means all migrant workers have been able to improve their standard of living in Turkey as a result of work abroad. Some have actually become worse off; others have lost their savings in a badly chosen work venture and finished up no better off than they were before they left. Many have earned higher incomes on return, but of these few have been satisfied with their situation. And since the poorest among the Turkish population have not been recruited for work abroad, and have shared in little, if any, of the rewards from the operation of the migration system (possibly in some instances being made worse off), the adoption of a labour export strategy has probably not improved and may have actually worsened the distribution of income in Turkey.

But although the Turkish government could have avoided more of the unfavourable and have realized more of the potentially favourable effects of labour export, and could have adopted policies to make the income distributional effects more equitable (Chapter 5), there remains the question of whether this would nonetheless turn Turkey into a satellite of the industrial metropolis to which it exports its labour, or whether it would constrain Turkey's development strategy in other ways. The answer to the first question is yes, in the sense that Turkey has become dependent on the prosperity of the host countries for the employment of her nationals and so for the acquisition of foreign exchange from repatriated earnings. A severe Western European recession — or major policy change as that in 1973 — not only cuts such earnings but also presents Turkey with the prospect of a mass of repatriated workers whom it cannot absorb (see Ch. 5). On the other hand, labour export has provided Turkey with the opportunity of savings, foreign exchange and trained manpower for economic growth, and so with the opportunity of reducing and ultimately eliminating the need for mass labour export. In other words, the dependence arising from mass labour export need not be permanent. Whether or not this is so depends on the development policies pursued by the Turkish government.

Thus the argument advanced against this assessment amounts to saying that the Turkish government has not been realizing many of the potentially favourable effects of labour export and has not been utilizing those it has to pursue the sort of policies which will ultimately reduce dependence on it. Indeed it may be argued that receipt of repatriated earnings has had an adverse effect in that it has permitted the government to postpone essential reforms which are required to mobilize domestic resources for development, such as the introduction of fundamental tax reforms. Although this cannot be proven one way or the other, it does bring out the importance of the conduct of Turkey's general economic policy on the impact of sending workers abroad on a temporarily recruited basis. And it is only fair to say that Turkey's record so far is one of increasing dependence on labour export, with repatriated earnings amounting to 57% of the import bill and about 7% of G.N.P. in 1973, and with just over 5% of the economically active population working abroad. In view of the serious situation with which Turkey was presented at the end of 1973 because of such dependence on the economic situation in and policies pursued by the labour importing countries, it seems more appropriate to characterize Turkey's experience with the operation of a labour export policy as being closer to the adverse than to the favourable situation outlined in Chapter 2.

Has labour export imposed other constraints on Turkey's economic policies? Again the answer is complicated. For an important part of the impact of labour export is its influence on attitudes and expectations. Even the eastern Anatolian peasant will have heard about life in Germany and will probably have seen the goods brought back by an ex-migrant. He will become increasingly familiar with European modes and life-styles. On a national scale this is likely to increase the minimum acceptable increase in per capita income and, as new wants are created, the propensity to consume. This will tend to reduce the maximum feasible increase in

148

savings, and to affect the balance between investment in investment and in consumer goods industries. On the other hand, contact with the West may stimulate hard work to raise incomes and may have a particularly beneficial effect on the adoption of improved techniques, the situation of women and the acceptance of family planning, and so may assist rather than constrain government policies in these fields. The implications of labour export on foreign trade policy have been extensively discussed above, but in any case Turkey's decision to join the E.E.C. has ruled out any possibility of undertaking a policy of self-reliance.

It remains to touch on the political implications of labour export. From the political standpoint of the emigration country government, labour export is a high risk strategy with potentially large gains and losses. For whereas it provides for all the hope of being the fortunate migrant who returns with his nest egg, and so syphons off discontent and despair, it also presents the possibility of mass repatriation in the event of a severe European depression, an event which, in Turkey at least, would be politically dangerous for the governemnt,[1] Also it tends to increase criticism of government policy as conditions in Turkey are compared with those abroad, and demands made for their improvement. And in the long run, this may turn out to be the most important result of labour export.

1 Many left-wing Turks believe that such a mass repatriation would culminate in serious civil disturbance and possibly revolution; however, it may equally lead to the reimposition of military dictatorship.

5

Problems, policies and lessons[1]

5.1   Introduction

By the end of 1973 the labour export system described in the previous chapters
had been brought to an almost complete halt. With 50,000 foreign workers among
nearly half a million unemployed in W. Germany, the German Government began
to consider measures to encourage the re-export of their unemployment (see p. 23,
fn. 1 above) And despite German assurances that they hoped that the ban on non-
E.E.C. recruitment would be lifted when the economic situation improved,[2] there
is little doubt that social and political pressures will prevent the scale of labour import in the W. European host countries from ever again reaching that of its heyday
in the late 1960s and early 1970s.

For all the emigration countries, labour export had been a high risk strategy
whose termination could have serious consequences. But this was much more so in
the Turkish case where the *scale* of the existing unemployment problem was so much
greater. Furthermore, the situation was worsened because termination of labour export happened at a time when the increase in the price of oil meant a sharp rise in
subsequent import bills. Since the rapidly changing world economic environment
makes any attempt at detailed quantitative forecasts of the effects on the Turkish
economy liable to large errors, and since at the time of writing (January 1974) it is
too early to evaluate the effects so far, all that is attempted in this chapter is a sketch
of the main problems to which the temporary – or permanent – moratorium on
mass labour export has led, together with some brief preliminary comments on certain problems, policy considerations and policy conflicts for emigration countries as
suggested by the Turkish experience. For although the Western European host
countries seem to have abandoned further mass labour import, it is possible that a
similar system may be introduced in the future in some of the sparsely populated oil
producing countries[3]. Consequently the issue raised by Turkey's experience are not
purely of academic interest. Throughout the subsequent discussion, it is assumed that
the government of the emigration country is pursuing a capitalist development policy
which primarily involves trying to achieve sustained growth and capital accumulation.

---

1   This chapter does *NOT* summarize the previous chapters of the book as each contains its
    own summary at the end. For summaries of the main empirical results, the reader should
    turn to §3.7 and §4.5.

2   *The Guardian,* Jan. 11th, 1974.

3   Already in 1973, 30,000 Egyptian workers were employed in Libya.

5.2 Problems and policy considerations in the operation of a labour export system

5.2.1 *Selection of applicants*

When, as in the Turkish case, the emigration country government plays an important role in selecting migrant workers out of an excess supply of applicants, various policy considerations and important policy conflicts arise.

  (i) skilled migrant workers tend to repatriate more foreign exchange but their departures may create serious labour shortages and are more likely to be permanent.

 (ii) The poorest peasants and workers are not likely to get the opportunity to work abroad unless accorded special assistance and priority.

(iii) Introducing age limits to keep the queue of applicants down to manageable proportions is a very crude instrument which tends to encourage all those eligible to apply so they do not lose their chance, and to increase the possibility of corruption in the selection process.

(iv) Unaccompanied married workers tend to repatriate more foreign exchange, so that ruthless emigration country governments may be tempted to discourage family emigration.[1] Here there is a direct conflict of interest between the welfare of the migrants themselves and the policy of using labour export to obtain foreign exchange.

5.2.2 *Improving migrants' living and working conditions abroad*

By far the most striking problem created by operation of the labour export system has been the great misery and hardship caused to many of the workers and their families. The basic problem here is that virtually all substantial changes require co-operation of host country governments, or employers, or both. For instance, foreign employers are only likely to train workers who are prepared to stay permanently. On the other hand, host country governments might be persuaded to improve housing conditions since this would reduce social tension, as would other measures to improve the social conditions of immigrants.

5.2.3 *The repatriation of earnings and return of workers*

(i) In order to achieve sustained repatriation of earnings, it is necessary to provide the means and the incentive – which entail, *inter alia*, making the remittance procedure straightforward, and offering workers a sufficiently high rate of exchange. The latter may necessitate the operation of a dual or multiple exchange rate system, and so lead to serious black market problems or may necessitate devaluation of a unified rate (§ §2.2.7 and 4.2.7). In any case, migrants may well prefer to hold their savings abroad, where they earn interest in foreign currency. The emigration country government may try to influence this by offering contractual savings schemes, with

---

1 This may perhaps explain why certain emigration country governments have not put more pressure on host country governments to make family migration easier.

premia for regular in-payments over a specified period, and could also try to persuade migrants to purchase Turkish produced consumer durables on their return rather than foreign ones while abroad.[1] But all policies to persuade migrants to spend or save their money in Turkey involve giving additional monetary incentives to persons who by Turkish standards already constitute an élite.

(ii) Although a significant part of repatriated earnings may be spent on some work-related expenditure, policy measures are required if this is not to result in many unsuccessful small business ventures, or in proliferating service sector concerns under conditions of imperfect competition. The main requirement is savings schemes suitable for small savers plus (given the assumed commitment to both public and private sector development of industry) a more broadly based capital market suitable for workers who wish to invest a larger amount. It is also necessary to provide information and guidance about potential investment projects. It is ridiculous to expect returned migrant workers to be able to evaluate correctly market opportunities and successfully set up, produce and market the produce of anything except a very small enterprise without any technical or managerial experience.[2]

As long as the government maintains a strict import regime, it can control the extent to which repatriated earnings are spent on imported commodities on return, and distinguish between applications for the import of consumer and of producer goods. (However, as Turkish tariffs are progressively reduced according to the Treaty of Association with the E.E.C., this would become a more serious problem).

(iii) The emigration country needs to provide an employment exchange service in the host countries for workers planning to return. This would not just try to place workers, but would give general information about the employment situation, and preliminary guidance to those planning to become self-employed. It could also register and certify which job(s) a worker had held while abroad, and any training received. Even so, such an organization would not be able to do much for the unskilled, as if there were high urban unemployment, home country employers would probably just take their pick of those whom they could interview themselves.

(iv) The emigration country also needs to provide labour re-absorption services in the home country, concerned not just with employment but also with savings and investment (see (ii) above). However, to identify the services and policies most required, considerably more information is needed about the problems which migrants face on their return. This is discussed in §5.3.

5.2.4 Macroeconomic issues

The emigration country government faces two potential sources of inflation, firstly that arising from skilled labour shortages caused by migrant departures, and secondly

1 The latter would require the provision of Turkish durables at specially reduced prices for workers paying in foreign exchange. However, a Turkish government scheme to import consumer durables to sell at duty free prices at customs ports would lead only to a slight foreign exchange gain, i.e. the difference between the government's buying and selling prices.

2 In Turkey projects would to some extent be vetted if they were submitted to the Halk Bank for a small industry loan, or to the Ministry of Industry for an investment permit (required for larger projects such as industrial joint ventures). A self-financed project would go through no control procedures unless it were sufficiently large to be subject to Ministry of Industry control.

that caused by unexpected increases in spending out of repatriated earnings. The former requires short run action to stop the outflow, combined with measures to train a greater supply; the latter in theory requires short run control of aggregate demand[1] together with medium term creation of new capacity to produce the required supply. However since such fine tuning in the control of demand is virtually impossible for an L.D.C., direct controls may be necessary on a temporary basis — or possibly on a more long-term one if supply cannot be increased much, as is the case with urban land.

The exchange rate problem to which labour export may lead has already been mentioned in §5.2.3. As compared with this, the adverse trade balance effect (at any *given* exchange rate) to which labour export may lead is comparatively small. In theory, of course, any loss in export competitiveness could be offset by introducing an export subsidy. But this would require co-operation from trading partners. In Turkey's case, unsubsidized textile exports already face quotas in E.E.C. markets, and other commodities could be expected to face the same fate if they showed unduly favourable expansion prospects. Similarly, Turkey's association with the E.E.C. raises difficulties over the question of protection for new import substitute industries, the required degree of which may become higher as a result of labour export.

5.2.5 *The possibility of joint action by labour exporting countries*

The above discussion shows that many of the problems of labour export are completely dependent on host country policy. For as long as host countries can get labour as cheaply elsewhere, any attempt by one of the labour exporting countries to improve the situation of their nationals abroad can be countered by utilizing more labour from a less demanding neighbour. And as long as this is so, the tales of misery and exploitation will continue. The most obvious possibility is that of joint action between the labour exporting countries, particularly in matters where they have a common interest, such as improving the housing, social conditions and levels of training of workers abroad. This may ultimately reduce the total demand for temporarily recruited migrant labour, but this would be no loss if it meant a reduction in the numbers living in atrocious conditions.

It would be a mistake to overestimate the concessions which could be extracted by united action by labour exporters, for such action would only be a real threat during upswings in the cycle, when net recruitment was rising, and, in any case, the policy changes of 1973 have substantially reduced its potential effectiveness. Also, in the longer term, host countries could always turn to other sources of supply (for instance, South and South-East Asia) or to less labour intensive production techniques. Furthermore, there is no guarantee that concessions negotiated with host country governments would be implemented by employers. However, the emigration countries have little to lose from trying.

5.3. The statistical requirements for successful policy formulation in Turkey

Despite the fact that Turkish migration to Western Europe has been taking place for almost a decade and a half, remarkably little is known about what happens to those

1 Insofar as the goods are demanded from industries working at full capacity.

workers who return to their home country. Perhaps the most glaring lacuna is any reliable estimate of how many have returned permanently. One possibility would be to expand the information required on the anonymous departure and arrival cards which are currently used at frontier posts to include questions on (i) the number of times the worker has left (for departure cards) or re-entered Turkey (for arrival cards) during the last 5 years, and (ii) (for non-first-time departures) the duration of the most recent period spent in Turkey. These questions could be answered safely by unofficial as well as official migrants, and would permit much more accurate estimates of permanently returned workers to be made. Secondly, if the T.E.S. were to do a detailed follow-up survey on an annual basis of a small sample of the workers who on re-entry had stated that they had returned permanently, it would not only be possible to discover if and how long it was before they changed their minds, but also to obtain detailed information about all aspects of their fate on their return, and particularly about their employment, use of new skills, consumption patterns, use of repatriated earnings, and, in the case of farmers, their effect on incomes and employment in local agriculture. Such time series data on the characteristics and attitudes of returned workers are essential for the formulation of policies designed to facilitate successful reintegration into the domestic economy. But since the T.E.S. re-entry survey has so far been carried out anonymously, the sample would have to be selected on a random basis and the co-operation of participants sought over a period of time (which might require some form of material incentive).

But since it would be at least a year before the results of the first sample survey became available, and a number of years before time series could be constructed, other more immediate methods of acquiring such information are required. One possibility would be to carry out another survey along the lines of the one made by the S.P.O. in 1971, or to try to relocate and resurvey the S.P.O. returned migrants themselves. Secondly, small surveys could be carried out on specific groups, e.g. ex-migrants who have become farmers, small entrepreneurs, factory workers, etc. These would be fairly easy to do — a few towns or villages could be selected and trained investigators sent to interview all ex-migrants of a particular kind that they could find. The results would obviously not permit of generalization, but would be extremely useful in constructing policies to facilitate the reintegration of particular groups.

The other main field for investigation is migrant workers' life abroad. Detailed information about this is required if migrants are to be instructed how to avoid the problems and hardships they may run into, and how to make the most of their residence there. It is also required if pressure is to be put on host country governments to introduce improvements. One possibility would be to request permission to send investigating teams to supplement the work of the existing Turkish commissions in dealing with workers' complaints, by carrying out small sample surveys to enquire into aspects of workers' life abroad, and requirements associated with their return etc. For instance, in addition to gathering basic social data it would be useful to find out the magnitude of workers' savings held in foreign banks and invested in other ways abroad, as well as information about their attitudes to learning new skills if opportunities were provided, and about the way in which they decide how much of their earnings to send home for family maintenance purposes. Since the host countries have become much more concerned about the problems of their migrant workers, many of whom have virtually become permanent immigrants, they might well be willing to co-operate in obtaining information which might help to reduce sources of conflict, as well as improve the situation of the workers themselves.

5.4 The impact on the Turkish economy of the moratorium on mass labour export[1]

Even if the moratorium on mass labour export were temporary, it entails the prospect of future balance of payments problems and of increased unemployment. A simplified exposition of the effects on repatriated earnings is given in Chart E, on the assumption that each worker's time cycle of repatriated earnings is identical and positively skewed.[2] Even if no workers already abroad were sent home, repatriated earnings would ultimately fall as (i) no new workers would arrive to offset the decline in repatriated earnings as the existing stock abroad 'age'[3] (RD in diagram); and (ii) those abroad would repatriate less than they would otherwise have done because of unemployment, no overtime working, etc. in the short-run (QD). If 'normal' departures are allowed for, the path of remittances would be QE, and if recently arrived workers are repatriated in addition, the path would be QF. However, the level of remittances would be raised somewhat if repatriated workers returned with accumulated savings rather than using these to 'top up' unemployment benefit[4] in the hope of getting another job abroad, or if those who returned were paid a departure gratuity by the host country. But as the largest gratuity suggested so far in West Germany (£340) is somewhat lower than average annual repatriated earnings per capita in recent years, this would only delay the impact on the balance of payments, though it would leave time to try to negotiate contingency foreign loans.

But although the balance of payments effects may not be too severe in the short-run, the immediate impact on employment might well be more serious. Unemployment in Turkey rose annually despite the export of workers, and would obviously rise after this was stopped, though probably by less than the original emigration target, as by no means all departing migrants would be replaced (§ 4.3). In addition to this, all repatriated workers would be seeking jobs. On the other hand, they would return with savings accumulated abroad (and possibly with a departure bonus), and

1 The original draft of this section, which contained various suggestions about contingency arrangements which the Turkish government could negotiate so as to mitigate the potentially disastrous effects of the termination of labour export, was rapidly overtaken by events. However, if the West European economies reintroduce policies of mass labour import, the introduction of such policies should be an obvious priority for emigration country governments.

2 Empirically this seems plausible for workers who settle permanently abroad. Alternatively, repatriated earnings might drop sharply from the time when the worker obtains the right to and makes the decision to settle permanently (shown by the dotted line in the left-hand corner diagram of Chart E).

3 Long standing migrant workers with accumulated rights will be in much the same situation as indigenous workers during a recession; the burden of adjustment is placed mainly on those who have recently arrived (§ 3.3.2 above). While the former will probably suffer from reduced earnings, the latter may well be forced ultimately to return.

4 For instance, foreign workers in Germany are entitled to one year's unemployment benefit equal to 62.5% of their wage.

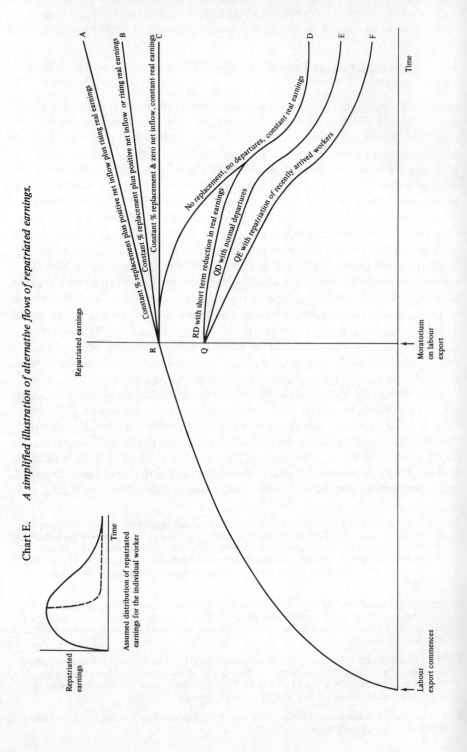

Chart E. *A simplified illustration of alternative flows of repatriated earnings.*

the expenditure from these would have positive multiplier effects which may help
to offset the negative ones arising from the influence of the W.European recession.
But even on the (unlikely) favourable assumption that industrial output grew
at the rate achieved during the second plan, this would mean additional unemployment equal to that part of the new entrants to the labour market who would have
been unemployed anyway, plus most of those who would have gone abroad, plus
most repatriated migrant workers (for some would return to family businesses or
family farms). Crude estimates of these figures for 1974 would be 70 000 unemployed
new entrants, plus 65 000 disappointed migrants (i.e. three-quarters of planned labour
export), plus 45 000 unemployed repatriated migrants (i.e. assuming that one
third of a *minimum* estimate for those whose contracts come up for renewal in
1974 are repatriated, together with an additional 20 000 longer stay migrants who
would have been planning to return anyway, and that 20% of this total are reabsorbed
into family concerns). Unemployment would rise by 180 000 during 1974, of which
9 000 would be directly attributable to the change in labour export policy. And if
the probability that the growth rate of non-agricultural output would fall is taken
into consideration, then it is necessary to add an additional 30 000 or so per annum
for each percentage reduction in the growth rate of output.[1] If, in addition, a less
conservative estimate were used for workers repatriated,[2] the total *increase* in
unemployment during 1974 would be over 250,000, most of which would be concentrated in urban areas. But the numbers actually repatriated may well be kept
down as host country employers can no longer replace them easily.

The only way to even begin to absorb numbers of the above magnitudes into productive employment would involve radical change in the agricultural sector, including
a complete transformation in rural institutions of a much more fundamental character
and on a much greater scale than has so far been envisaged in Turkey. And although
the introduction of a programme of radical rural change seems extremely unlikely
in view of Turkey's recent experience with very modest land reform proposals, the
dangers which the political parties would face if the unemployment situation sharply
deteriorated may just persuade them to consider new solutions — though they would
perhaps be more likely to lead to the reimposition of military dictatorship.

Whereas repatriated earnings might fall comparatively little in the short-run
because of lags and of the impact of repatriated workers' savings (and, possibly, of
their departure bonuses), the situation would become much more serious in the
medium term[3] when the magnitude of any additional return flows of foreign exchange
because of workers' repatriation would be small as compared with the induced
decline as those remaining abroad 'age'. The government could attempt to offset the
reduction in foreign exchange earnings by adjusting the exchange rate. This would

1 With the 7% overall growth rate and the 8% non-agricultural growth rate of the last 5 years
   the domestic economy has been able to absorb about half of the 400 000 or so who became
   of employable age each year.

2 Since it is usually easiest for host countries to repatriate workers who have arrived recently,
   and since in Germany such workers are likely to be Turkish as nearly one quarter of post
   1970 recruitment was from Turkey. It was predicted that half a million foreign workers
   would be repatriated from Germany during the first few months of 1974 (*The Economist*,
   Jan 26th, 1974); on this assumption one would expect at least 125 000 Turkish workers to be
   repatriated.

3 Unless it were possible to locate new mass labour importing countries.

probably involve a large general devaluation, together with little change in the rate for Turkey's important primary commodity exports (and with price controls to mitigate the sort of rapid inflation which followed the 1970 devaluation). But it is extremely unlikely that such adjustments would generate enough export earnings to cover the import bill, since these would have to cover not only the fall in repatriated earnings, but also the increased cost of oil,[1] and since the success of such an export drive would depend on the state of demand in Turkey's markets. The crucial rôle of repatriated earnings in the balance of payments before the energy crisis can be seen clearly in Table 20. With these reduced and the oil price increased, the Turkish government would be forced to seek additional foreign aid and reduce the import bill. Although for political reasons the Western aid-giving countries would probably consider Turkish requests sympathetically, they might be in no position to grant them, and indeed might be pursuing competitive devaluations themselves to try to improve their own economic situations. But if Turkey did obtain little additional foreign aid (and more so if expected allocations were cut), this would have a major effect on Turkish industry. Precisely how long this would take to appear would depend mainly on the particular form of the relationship between repatriated earnings and length of stay abroad and on the timing and magnitude of worker repatriation (see Chart E).[2] However, the foreign exchange shortfall would reduce both industrial production (because of shortages and delays in components and spares) and industrial investment, and so would reduce growth.[3]

Any such reduction in the medium term growth rate would worsen the employment situation. This would also depend on how vigorously employment creation and migrant reintegration policies had been pursued, and whether employers made any adjustments in techniques to be utilised, which they might have done if they believed that wages would be kept down and trained workers would be less likely to leave. But as in the short-run, most productive labour absorption would have to occur in the agricultural sector, and since the necessary reforms may not be carried. out, Turkey will instead be left with a virtually unmanageable unemployment problem.

Clearly a permanent end to mass labour export can be expected to have important effects on the Turkish economy. Of course, some of the effects discussed above are attributable to the impact of European recession rather than to the moratorium on labour export per se. However, the point is that the effects of the dependence of the Turkish economy on labour export made it more vulnerable to the impact of such a recession. But just as its introduction may have permitted the survival of a development strategy which might otherwise have been transformed, its termination may bring about much more fundamental changes to the Turkish policy, economy and society than would ever have occured otherwise.

1 In 1972 repatriated earnings amounted to 84% and in 1973, 89% of the value of exports, while petroleum imports amounted to about 20% in 1972 and 15% in 1973 of the value of exports. Turkey's oil bill for 1974 is estimated at about $560m (a 267% increase over 1973), and for 1980, at between $1200m and $1640m.

2 As a *very* rough estimate, if no new workers are recruited, and about 5% are repatriated in each of the first two years, three repatriated earnings would have fallen by about 30% by the end of the third year, and the situation would worsen continually after that.

3 And so might encourage the government to try to increase private foreign investment.

Table 20:   *Turkish balance of payments, 1972*   ($m)

I. Current account		
A. Foreign trade		
Exports f.o.b.		885
(Agricultural products)		(656) (75%)
(Manufactures)		(171) (19%)
(Minerals)		(58) (7%)
Imports c.i.f. of which		~~1562~~
(Mineral fuels)		(155)
(Iron & Steel and products)		(148)
(Machinery)		(394)
(Electrical machinery)		(122)
(Motor vehicles)		(112)
Foreign trade balance		−678
B. Invisible transactions		
Interest payments[2]		−62
Tourism and travel (net)		44
Workers remittances		740
Profit transfers		−35
Payments for services from project credits		−35
Other invisibles (net)		−12
Invisible transactions (net)		640
C. Infrastructure and offshore		30
Current account balance		−8
II. Capital account		
1. Debt repayment[2]		−230
2. T.L. grain imports		16
3. Private foreign capital		43
4. Project credits		222
5. Suppliers' credits		—
6. Imports with waiver		39
7. Consortium credits[3]		73
		163
Over-all balance		155
III. Reserve movements		−566
IV. Short-term capital movements		413
V. Special drawing rights		−18
VI. Net errors and omissions		16

Source: U.S.A.I.D., *Economic and social indicators, Turkey 1973*, Ankara 1973.

Notes: 1. Provisional figures
2. Excluding postponed payments
3. Also includes other foreign aid

5.5   Lessons

Since the system of temporarily recruited labour migration is continually evolving, any conclusions based on experience so far are of limited validity. Furthermore, the countries of emigration differ substantially, so that what has happened in one case cannot necessarily be presumed to apply to another.

Nonetheless, the Turkish case does provide some lessons of which governments of some of the other (particularly the most recent) countries of emigration might well take note. Since the impact of labour export on the Turkish economy has been summarized at the end of Chapter 4, only a few more general considerations will be

159

mentioned here. Firstly, participation in labour export is virtually enforced on an L.D.C. government once comparatively highly paid host country job vacancies have been publicized there — the question is rather one of whether or not to try to regulate recruitment and to assist emigrants and their families. Secondly, without vigorous policy measures, many potentially favourable effects of migration on the home country economy and on the migrants themselves, will not occur, while many adverse ones will. Thirdly, labour export will — unless deliberate active efforts to change the situation are made — do comparatively little to improve life for the poorer strata of society who will neither be offered the opportunity to work abroad nor to whom will accrue any of the rewards arising through the labour export policy. Fourthly, although labour export will tend to reduce unemployment and bring in foreign exchange, it will have many other important effects on the economy, and will, in particular, make it highly dependent on the host countries to which it sends its workers, and constrain the development policies open to it. Finally, the emigration country government may fail to appreciate the risk attached to a development strategy based on labour export, and may use the respite which it offers as an opportunity for postponing the basic mobilization of resources required to obtain sustained growth in the longer term, rather than for accelerating the transformation which would ultimately render labour export unnecessary. Now that the proposals mooted in Western Europe to stem additional inflows of workers have materialized, it will become much easier to identify in which of these ways Turkish governments during the last decade and a half have used the opportunities which labour export created. All one can say is that the moratorium is likely to have major consequences in both the short and longer run.

Appendix 1
Bibliography[1]

Part I   A guide to the source material on the economic aspects of Turkish migration to Europe

Introduction

In the autumn of 1972, observation of the vast amount of unco-ordinated work which had either taken place or was in progress on the subject of Turkish migration finally prompted me to make an attempt to compile some sort of annotated guide in the hope that it might be of use to others working in the field, and that it might perhaps prevent wasteful duplication of research. The response to the original version left no doubt about the need for such a guide, and so an updated version is included below, instead of just a list of the publications referred to in the text of this study.

I have necessarily had to be selective and so have excluded (a) general research on European migration unless the results are relevant to work on the economic aspects of Turkish migration (thus, for instance, most of the work on the sociological aspects of foreign migrants in Germany is not included), (b) the more minor secondary sources. However, exclusion of an item should not be taken to imply that it falls into one of these two groups. It may well be due to an error or omission on my part.

The guide is arranged as follows:
- A. Turkish sources: (i) official   (ii) newspapers
- B. Other official national sources.
- C. International organization and U.S.A.I.D. studies.
- D. Academic studies.
- E. Selected sources on the postwar utilization of migrant labour in Western Europe,[2] (i) books and articles, (ii) newspaper reports.
- F. Work in progress.

The capital letter following the publication date of references cited in the text indicates the part of the bibliography in which the work is described.

---

1 Particularly useful items which became available to me while this book was in press are listed on p. 176.

2 Whereas the references in the previous sections contain at least some detailed information on or statistics about *Turkish* migrant workers, those in this section do not. Since there is a very extensive literature on this subject, many important and useful articles have had to be excluded.

A. (i) *Official Turkish sources* (Official organizations are listed alphabetically)

Central Bank Statistics (T.C. Merkez Bankası (Aylık Bülteni)). This is the basic source for data on the foreign exchange brought back by migrants.

The Ministry of Labour (Çalışma Bakanlığı) has set up a special department to deal with migration abroad. Although it has not yet published any of its own research, it was responsible for presenting a paper prepared by the General Directorate of Workers Abroad at the CENTO Seminar on Industrial Relations (see Yaşer 1972C).

State Institute of Statistics(Devlet İstatistik Enstitüsü).
S.I.S. Tourism Statistics. The Turkish State Institute of Statistics publish annual tourism statistics (*Turizm İstatistikleri*). These give data on Turkish citizens departing from or returning to Turkey by country of visit, purpose of visit, province of residence in Turkey, occupation, means of transport, etc. All travellers have to complete a short form on crossing a Turkish frontier, and a special section is included to find out how many were employed as workers abroad and how many are planning to return to a workplace there; from this data, an estimate can be made of the number of returning workers. As from January 1972, the S.I.S. started to publish their data on a monthly basis as well in *Turizm İstatistikleri Aylık Bülteni*.
S.I.S. Monthly Foreign Trade Statistics. These give details of imports with waiver (*bedelsiz ithalat*), i.e. goods imported without going through the foreign exchange allocation system. The main constituent of *bedelsiz ithalat* are goods brought into Turkey by returning migrants.

The State Planning Organization (S.P.O.). Insofar as the S.P.O. is concerned with planning the economy, research to estimate the magnitude of future flows of labour and of remittances is normally in progress as an integral part of research on employment creation and on financing the imports required for planned development. Thus migration and remittance projections are included in the *2nd 5 Year Plan, 1968–72* and in the *3rd 5 Year Plan, 1973–8*.

However, the S.P.O. has also commissioned special studies on the socio-economic effects of the migration itself. The earliest of these was Abadan, N. *Batı Almanya' daki Türk işçileri ve sorunları*, Siyasal Bilgiler Fakültesi, Ankara University, for the State Planning Organization, Ankara 1964. (Turkish workers in Western Germany and their problems). This is a survey of 494 Turkish migrants to Germany which gives a very detailed and useful socio-economic picture of these vanguard migrants. It is basically concerned with the social characterisitcs of the migrants and the social problems which they face, but also includes data on occupation, skills, wages, etc., and some information on savings and remittances. The results of this study have also been published in German (Abadan 1966D).
The second main study commissioned by the S.P.O. was Tuna's *Yurda dönen işçilerin intibakı sorunları*, (An enquiry into the reintegration of workers who have returned from abroad), Social Planning Department, S.P.O., August 1967. This surveyed 280 migrants (of whom 31% were women) in the Marmara region (including İstanbul, Tekirdağ, Kırklareli, Edirne, Çanakkale, Balıkeşir, Bursa, Sakarya and Kocaeli). Although this was a fairly representative sample of early migrants most of whom came from Marmara, because this region is the richest and most industrialized in Turkey, the sample could not be considered as representative of later migrant flows. The study contains basic socio-economic data on the migrants included, but

162

more importantly, information about the fate of the worker on return as compared with his circumstances before departure and while abroad. It also contains estimates of savings and remittances. (Note: this study should be considered in conjunction with Tuna's larger study (1966D)).

In February 1971, the S.P.O. conducted the most comprehensive survey to date on returned migrants in Turkey. Initially it collected the names and addresses of about 4000 workers who had supposedly returned permanently by the autumn of 1970. It then attempted to select a representative collection of towns and villages, and took a 50% random sample from these. Unfortunately, owing to a bias introduced when the original list of names was compiled, the sample cannot be regarded as representative of the returned migrant population. (In particular, the unemployed, small scale industrial and service sector workers (on their return) together with women, are probably under-represented — see Appendix 3). The study is divided into three main sections: information about the migrants before their departure, while they are abroad, and on what had actually happened to them since their return. Nonetheless, since the sample necessarily included a high proportion of pioneer workers (because it surveyed migrants who had returned by 1970) it should not be regarded as representative of current returnees. The complete results are presented and described in Paine, 1972D.

T.E.S. Official data: The Turkish Employment Service (İş ve İşçi Bulma Kurumu) has published data on the vacancies for and despatch of migrants, together with data on their geographical origins, industry, occupation, co-operative membership, etc., ever since the agreement with Germany was signed in 1961. These data, which of course only cover officially assisted migrants, are published monthly in the *İş ve İşgücü Bülteni* (Work and Manpower Bulletin), and summarized annually in the *Calışma Raporu* (Employment Report).

T.E.S. surveys: In addition, the T.E.S. conducted four more detailed surveys in 1967, 1968, 1969 and 1971. (*Yurt dışındaki Türk işçileri ve dönüs eğilimleri.*) In 1967, 20 897 workers were covered, in 1968, 15 573, in 1969, 13 393 and in 1971, 27 730. They were interviewed at the frontier when re-entering Turkey and so (i) include both temporary and permanent returnees, and (ii) tend to be unrepresentative of the total migrant stock abroad (for instance, certain of the results differed significantly from those obtained from German sources). They do, however, provide basic socio-economic profiles of the migrants included, plus information about their intentions on their return.

Other T.E.S. publications. The T.E.S. also made two enquiries into migrant workers' problems abroad (*Avrupa memleketlerinde Türk işçileri ve problemleri*, 14 Nisan 1966 — 14 Mayis 1966, and *Avrupa memleketlerinde Türk işçileri ve sorunları*, ikinci kitap, 10 Haziran 1968 — 9 Temmuz 1968).

In 1970 the T.E.S. conducted a short study of the conditions of Turkish workers in France (*Fransâ'da çalişan Turk işçileri*, T.E.S. publication No. 79, Ankara, November 1970). *Inter alia*, this gives a short description of the living and working conditions of Turks in France, together with practical information on the social security system, occupational training centres, etc.

In 1970 the T.E.S. also published those bilateral agreements on the supply of Turkish migrants made with *W. Germany* (30th October, 1961), *Austria* (15th May,

163

1964), *Belgium* (16th July, 1964) *Holland* (19th August, 1964), *France* (8th April, 1965), *Switzerland* (10th March, 1967), and *Australia*, (5th October 1967).

Türk İş, the major trade union federation, summarizes the migration situation in its annual report, and also issues certain publications to assist the migrants themselves. See also the report of the Türk İş special conference, *Ortak Pazar işgücü hareketleri,* (Common Market manpower movements), January 1970.

The Union of Chambers of Commerce (Türkiye Ticaret Odaları, Sanayi Odaları ve Ticaret Borsaları Birliği, Ankara) also summarizes the situation in its annual report on the Turkish economy, and sometimes does research into specialized aspects (e.g. investment of workers' savings). From 1970–1972, it published a fortnightly economic newspaper, *Economic News Digest*, which often had items on migrant workers (see especially No. 18, July 1, 1971, and No. 25, October 15, 1971).

A.(ii)   *Other Turkish sources*
The Turkish press provides a considerable amount of useful material on the fortune of Turkish workers abroad and on their return.
Milliyet and *Cumhurriyet* have provided some particularly useful reports: see for instance the series of articles on the educational problems of Turkish children abroad (*Milliyet* March 9th–13th, 1973) and the detailed discussion of the whole Turkish migration problem ('Almanya, Türk işçileri ve işsizlik', *Milliyet* April 22nd, 1973).
Other articles referred to in the text include:
'Tarım dışında 810 000 işsiz var', February 23, 1973. Reports on April 10th, 1972, November 13th, 1972 and November 24th, 1972.

B.   *Other official national sources* (listed alphabetically by country).

Official Austrian Sources. As from July 1971, the number of Turkish workers in Austria has been published monthly in the statistical supplement to *Monatsbericht,* Österreichisches Institut für Wirtschaftsforschung, Statistiche Übersichten.

Official Belgian Sources. Data on migrant worker flows to and from Belgium are published in Royaume de Belgique, Ministère des Affaires Économiques, Institut National de Statistique, *Statistiques Demographiques*. The data are broken down by nationality, including Turkey.

Official Dutch Sources. Data on foreign workers in Holland are published in Centraal Bureau voor de Statistiek, ed., *Sociale Maandstatistiek*, 's-Gravenhage (The Hague).

Official French Sources. The French counterpart to the German Bundesanstält für Arbeit is l'Office National d'Immigration, which publishes *Statistiques de l'Immigration.* For other published information on foreign migrants in France, see the *Bulletin mensuel de statistiques sociales* published by the Ministry for Public Health and Social Security and the Ministry of Labour, Employment and Population, and certain issues of (and supplements to) *Statistiques du Travail,* published by the Ministry of Labour, Employment and Population, and also Institut National de la Statistique et des Etudes Economiques. *Annuaire Statistique de la France*. Since 1970, data on Turkish migrants to France has been published separately and not aggregated with other nationalities in a residual category.

Official W. German Sources. The basic W. German source is *Ausländische Arbeit-nehmer*, published annually by the Bundesanstält für Arbeit, Nürnberg. This gives fairly detailed information on the origins, family status, occupation, education, etc. of the new flows of migrants, and on the jobs which they take in Germany. It is particularly useful since it contains data on the actual and on the official migrant flows. It also contains some data on the total migrant stock, and on occasion (e.g. in the 1970 edition covering a survey in autumn 1968), more detailed surveys of the social and economic characteristics of the total migrant stock. The 1968 survey covered a random sample of 9100 foreign workers classified by nationality and sex, and was administered by the labour exchanges. A similar survey, but of males only, was carried out in 1966. Statistics of all Turks (i.e. both workers and their families) are published once a year in *Wirtschaft und Statistik*, Statistisches Bundesamt, Wiesbaden.

Official Swiss Sources. Data on foreign migrants in Switzerland is published in Le Départment Federal de l'Économie Publique, *La Vie Économique*, though in the monthly tables Turkey is not listed separately. Data on the stock of Turkish residents is given in Le Bureau Federal de Statistique, *Annuaire Statistique de la Suisse*.

C.   *International Organizations and U.S.A.I.D.* (Listed alphabetically by
          organization).

C.E.N.T.O.
Sengölge, Ö. 'Turkish workers in Europe', *C.E.N.T.O. Symposium on manpower planning and statistics*, Tehran, Iran, November 24 – Dec. 5, 1969. This summarizes the results of the early T.E.S. surveys.
Yaşer, Y. 'Industrial relations and social problems of Turkish workers abroad', *C.E.N.T.O. Seminar on Industrial Relations*, Tehran, February 12th–17th, 1972, pp. 141–158. This described the situation at the time of writing together with new policies being introduced by the Turkish government.

The Council of Europe.
An extremely comprehensive survey of international migration in Europe was pre-pared for the 2nd European Population Conference held by the Council of Europe by Livi-Bacci, M. and Hagmann, H.M. (*Report on the demographic and social pattern of migrants in Europe, especially with regard to international migrations* (1971)). This is particularly concerned with projection of the future demand for and supply of migrants, but also contains a wealth of socio-economic data about the migrants abroad. This study is summarized in Mclin (1972E).
As part of a special advisory committee on problems raised by the return of migrant workers to their home country, the Population and Vocational Training Division of the Council of Europe compiled a paper on *Turkish limited company for trade and industry*, mimeo, Strasbourg, 27th October, 1966, RS 99 (1966), which describes the legal position underlying the foundation of joint ventures.

E.E.C. Research on intra-European migration, particularly in connection with the implementation of free movement of labour between member states.
See especially: *La libre circulation de la main d'oeuvre et les marchés du travail dans*

la C.E.E., Brussels, February 1966, February 1967, February 1968, June 1969, June 1970.
See also: *Exposé annuel sur les activités des services de main-d'oeuvre des États membres de la Communauté* and *Les problèmes de main-d'oeuvre dans la Communauté* (annual).

The I.B.R.D. The population and Employment Studies Division of the World Bank has been engaged on estimation of workers' remittances from W. Europe, and has published a suggested estimation method as part of a general background summarizing the migrant worker situation within W. Europe (Hume, I.M. *Migrant workers in Western Europe*, Economics Staff Paper No. 102, October 1970). A shortened version of this paper has been published as 'Migrant workers in Europe', *Finance and Development*, Vol. 10, No. 1, March 1973 pp. 2–6.

The I.I.L.S. The International Institute for Labour Studies encouraged research on intra-European migration in the mid-1960s: see *Symposium on migration for employment in Europe*, October 1965, and especially Altüg, Y. *Turkish aspects of migration for employment to Europe*, I.I.L.S. SEM/II, October 1965: Danieli, L. & Brandt, S. *Employment of foreign workers in some Western European countries: a statistical picture* I.I.L.S. SEM/10, 1965;

N.E.S.A. Alpat, S. 'The effects of Turkish workers going abroad on labour force', *N.E.S.A. Employment Conference*, Katmandu, 1970. A short paper describing the situation at the time of writing.

O.E.C.D. Regular reports on the migration situation are made by the Manpower and Social Affairs Committee. In addition, certain special reports have been commissioned. These include:
Abadan, N. *La main-d'oeuvre turque en Allemagne Fédérale, problèmes relatifs aux retours conjoncturels,* mimeo, Paris, September 13th, 1971. This is the Turkey country report summarized in Kayser 1972C. It reports the results of a survey made in 1970 of 89 Turkish workers in nine German towns, but also draws heavily on the results of the Tuna (1967A) and Neuloh (1970D) studies, together with her own previous report (1964A). Note: this study is still regarded as confidential by O.E.C.D. However, its main results are summarized in Abadan 1972D.
Kaupen-Haas, M. *Reintegration problems among Turkish workers,* Technical Assistance Programme, Turkey, Project No. 42, mimeo, Paris 1967 MS/M/503/251. This report is based on interviews conducted in Germany and in Turkey from May–July 1967. It discusses the problems faced both in adapting to the German environment and in subsequently readapting to conditions in Turkey. This study is still classified as restricted by O.E.C.D.
Kayser, S. *Manpower movements and labour markets*, O.E.C.D., Paris 1971, contains a summary of the Krahenbuhl study (1969C) together with four similar country reports (on Italy, Spain, Greece and Portugal).
Kayser, S. *Cyclically-determined homeward flows of migrant workers and the effects of migration*, O.E.C.D., Paris, 1972. This is a summary report based on four country reports (Turkey, Greece, Yugoslavia and Portugal) which attempted to assess the fate of migrant workers (and their savings) when they returned to their native country – with special reference to the effects of the return flows generated

166

by the 1966–1967 German recession. A summary of Kayser's report was published in the *O.E.C.D. Observer*, June 1972.

Krahenbuhl, R.E. *Emigration and the labour market in Turkey*, Working Party on Migration, Enquiries on the Economic Aspect of Migration, mimeo, Paris 1969, MS/M/404/301. This is an extremely useful paper based mainly on research by the author in İzmir, Zonguldak and Kocaeli. *Inter alia*, it discusses what happened in the labour markets in these areas after migration from them had got under way. The study is still classified as restricted by O.E.C.D. but a summary was published in Kayser (1971C).

Neyzi, N.H. *Turkey country study on emigrant workers returning to their home country*, Report to International Management Seminar on emigrant workers returning to their home country, held in Athens in October 1966, Paris 1967.

Norwegian Joint Mission to Federal Republic of Germany and Switzerland, *The employment of foreign manpower*, S.A.D. Programme for Employers and Unions, National Missions 1966, Report No. 2, O.E.C.D., mimeo, Paris 1965. Contains some information on the housing of Turks in Cologne.

Rodié, R. *Workers abroad and their reintegration in the local economy under the Second 5 Year Development Plan (1968–72)*, Technical Assistance Programme, Turkey, Project No. 42, mimeo, Paris 1968 MS/M/503/273. This describes the procedure for the recruitment and despatch of migrants, and reports the results of the T.E.S. 1967 survey, making proposals for the reintegration of migrants on the basis of these. The study is still classified as restricted by O.E.C.D.

U.S.A.I.D. (Ankara) Although U.S.A.I.D. has done little in the way of original research on the migration question, it has produced a number of useful survey articles (see also p. 176):

Miller, D. *Emigrant Turkish workers: a socio-economic analysis*, 1971, published in Miller, D., ed. *Essays on labor force and employment in Turkey*, Ankara 1971. This suggests a simple model to explain the determinants of remittances.

Özşahin, S. *Turkish-European manpower movements*, mimeo, Ankara, May 1970.

Redding, D.A. *Turkish workers in Western Europe – a comparative study*, mimeo, Ankara, June 1967.

U.S.A.I.D., *Remittances from Turkish workers in W. Europe 1964–6*, mimeo, Ankara, March 1966.

D.   *Academic studies* (Noted alphabetically by author)

Abadan, N. *Studie über die Lage und die Probleme der türkischen Gastarbeiter in der Bundesrepublik Deutschland*, in Europäische Schriften des Bildungswerks Europäische Politik, *Arbeitsplatz Europa* Heft II, Cologne 1966. Contains the results of Abadan (1964A).

Abadan, N. 'Le non-retour à l'industrie, trait dominant de la chaine migratoire turque', *Sociologie du Travail* No. 3, 1972, pp. 278–293. Summarizes the results of Abadan (1971C). See also p. 176.

Aker, A. *İşçi göçü, Nisan 1970 ile Nisan 1971, arasinda Almanya'ya giden Türk işçileri üzerinde sosyo-ekonomik bir örnekleme arastirmasi*, Sander Yaymları, Istanbul 1972. (Migrant workers: a sample socio-economic study of Turkish workers going to Germany between April 1970 and April 1971). A total of 590 workers were interviewed and details of selected socio-economic characteristics and plans on return were collected. The information on the socio-economic characteristics of the migrants prior to departure is particularly detailed, but the nature of the survey precluded any questions about the *actual* fate of the migrants and their savings on return. The survey results include some interesting information on the migrants' social and political attitudes. Dr. Aker attempted to obtain a representative sample of departing migrants and for this reason his results are of particular value.

Bingemer, K. et al., *Leben als Gastarbeiter – geglückte und misglückte Integration* (Köln und Opladen) West Deutscher Verlag, 1970. The main results of this study are published in English in Böhning (1972aE). The study uses Hentschel's data (1968D).

Clark, J.R. (University of Michigan) *Residential patterns and social integration of Turks in Cologne*, paper presented to the M.E.S.A. conference, November 1972, based on a survey of 180 Turkish workers in Cologne in 1971. Eldridge, R.H. 'Emigration and the Turkish balance of payments', *Middle East Journal*, Vol. 20, 1966.

Gökmen, O. *Federal Almanya re Türk isçileri*, Ankara, 1972.

Grandjeat, P. *Les migrations de travailleurs en Europe*, Cahiers de L'Institut International d'Etudes Sociales, No. I, December 1966. This is more concerned with the countries of labour immigration, although there is a short chapter on countries of emigration, including Turkey. Grandjeat reports on the surveys of others, contributing no new data himself.

Hentschel, R. et al., *Die Integration der ausländischen Arbeitnehmer in Köln*, Tallenband, Köln, mimeo, 1968. Although the sample size in this survey was 1010, only 100 workers of each of the four nationalities covered were interviewed, and of these, all were males. Thus the sample was not representative of the total foreign population. Furthermore, on occasion (e.g. p. 99) the results were weighted to give the impression that the sample actually included 1010. As Böhning (1972aE) says, this does not inspire confidence in the results. Though it brings out certain special characteristics of Cologne's migrant situation and shows how they differ from the national figures for 1966–68, the study claims to be representative of migrants in Germany, which it is decidedly not. The survey was carried out in 1967.

Hume, I.M. *Some economic aspects of labour migration in Europe since World War II,* paper presented at the Conference of the International Economic Association on 'The economic aspects of population growth', in Velascure, France, September 1973.

Krahenbuhl, R.E. *The acculturation potential of labour migration between Turkey and Western Europe*, University of California, L.A., Ph.D. dissertation, date unknown.

Miller, D. 'Emigrant Turkish workers – a framework for analysis', *M.E.T.U. Studies in Development No. 3*, Fall 1971, pp. 529–541. This includes a model for estimating remittances (see Miller 1971C).

Miller, D. 'Racing toward the critical limit – problems and prospects of Turkish workers in the Federal Republic of Germany', *International Labour Journal*, November 1973. This paper describes the problems which led the W. German government actively to consider alternatives to importing labour on a temporarily recruited basis.

Miller, D. and Çetin, İ. *Migrant workers, wages and labour markets*, Istanbul

168

University Press, forthcoming, Spring 1974.

Miller, D. and Çetin, I. *The international demand for brawn-power and the wealth effect of migration: a Turkish case study*, paper presented to the M.E.S.A. conference, November 1972. This is a summary paper which covers Miller's early results and then goes on to reproduce some of the preliminary uncorrected results of Paine (1972D).

Monson, T.D. *Experience-generated learning and infant industries: a case study of Turkey*. Ph.D. dissertation, University of Michigan, 1972. This study attempts to estimate learning curves for Turkish workers employed in Turkey and in Germany in order to test whether, and to what extent, there are inter-country differences in learning behaviour. Unfortunately, the author encountered serious data problems (for instance, for the German firms he had to use wages as a proxy for labour productivity) so that his results must be treated with extreme caution. A summary of this was presented at the M.E.S.A. conference, November 1972: '*A comparison of industrial learning behaviour of Turkish labour at home and abroad'*.

Neuloh, O. (with Kramer, H.L.), *Industrialisierung und Gastarbeit als sozio-ökonomische Faktoren für die überwindung struktureller Arbeitslosigkeit in der Türkei*, Institut für Empirische Soziologie, Saarbrücken, 1970. Neuloh surveyed 939 workers, of whom 774 were questioned in Turkey and 163 in Germany. 50 women were included in the sample, and all the workers were over 20. Neuloh concentrated very much on the sociological aspects of migration — reasons for departure and return, work discipline in the German factory environment, relationships with employers, foremen and other workmen, reasons for satisfaction/dissatisfaction on return, attitudes to women's employment, religious beliefs, etc. Some information on earnings and savings is included.

Paine, S.H. *Report on the results of the Turkish State Planning Organization survey of returned migrant workers conducted in February 1971*, mimeo, Faculty of Economics, Cambridge University, July 1972, contains the complete results of this survey.

Selcen, I. *Berufliche Wertmuster des türkischen Gastarbeiter und die sich daraus ergebenden Anpassungsprobleme an die deutsche Industriearbeiterschaft*, unpublished sociological diploma thesis, Cologne 1965.

Sertel, A.K. '*Turkish women in Europe'*, paper delivered at the M.E.S.A. conference, Nov. 1973. The paper examines the changes in the status of Turkish women workers in W. Germany, and is based on the results of a small scale survey and of informal interviews. (Information about this study was received too late for incorporation into this occasional paper).

Tuna, O. and Ekin, N. *Türkiye'den F. Almanya'ya işgücü akımı ve meselerleri:*
1. Rapor: F. Almanya ve Türkiye'nin emek arz ve talebi bakımından tetkiki (Study on the demand and supply of labour in W. Germany and Turkey), Istanbul, 1966.
2. Rapor: F. Almanya'ya işgücü akımı ile ilgili organlar ve meseleleri (Study on matters concerned with labour in Germany); Istanbul 1966.
3. F. Almanya' da calisan Turk iscilerinin isledikleri tahlili (Analysis of the crimes committed by Turkish workers in Germany), Istanbul 1966.
The two volumes of interest to economists mainly survey the officially available data at that time. Volume 2 gives a lot of useful information on the organizations concerned in some way with Turkish migration abroad. The work also includes a useful,

though dated, bibliography which contains many Turkish items.

Volker, G.E. (Middle Eastern Technical University), *Turkish labor migration to Germany: impact on both economies*, paper presented to the M.E.S.A. conference, November 1972.

Yaşer, Y. (Director of the Turkish S.I.S.) published a study on Turkish population problems and migrant workers abroad (*Nüfüs problemleri ve yurtdişi işçi sorunlari*, mimeo, Ankara 1973).

Yilmaz, B. *Die volkwirtschaftlicher Auswirkungen der auswanderung türkischer Arbeitskräfte auf die wirtschaftliche Entwicklung in der Türkei.* (The economic effects of the emigration of Turkish workers to Europe on economic development in Turkey), Ph.D. dissertation, University of Bonn, 1973. The study is largely theoretically orientated, but also attempts to estimate the multiplier effect of repatriated earnings on the Turkish economy. However, the model used is such that the impact of repatriated earnings depends linearly on the amount repatriated. The study uses only the German Bundesanstalt für Arbeit and Turkish S.P.O. published data.

E. *Selected sources on the postwar utilization of migrant labour in Western Europe.* (Arranged alphabetically)

Note: a useful bibliography of work published before 1969 is given in O.E.C.D. *Bibliography: international migration of manpower*, Paris 1969.

(i) Books and articles (see also p. 176)

Bain, T. and Pauga, A. 'Foreign workers and intraindustry wage structure in West Germany', *Kyklos*, Vol. XXV, 1972. Fasc. 4, pp. 820–24. *Inter alia*, this found that an increase in the employment of foreign workers in an industry tended to retard wage increases in Germany.

Barentsz, J. 'Migration, labour and employers' in Van Houte and Melgert, 1972E.

Begtić, M. 'Yugoslav nationals temporarily working abroad'. *Yugoslav Survey*, Vol. 13, No. 1, Feb. 1972.

Bericht der Studienkommission für das Problem der ausländischen Arbeitskrafte, Bern Bundesamt für Industrie, Gewerbe und Arbeit, 1964.

Amongst the research which has been carried out into European semi-permanent (polyannual) migration, some of the work of Dr. Böhning is particularly useful; see Böhning (1970a), 'Foreign workers in post-war Germany', *The New Atlantis*, Vol. 2, No. 1, pp. 12–38.

Böhning, W.R. (1970b), 'The differential strength of demand and wage factors in intra-European labour mobility: with special reference to W. Germany 1957–1968', *International Migration*, Vol. VIII, No. 4, pp. 193–202.

Böhning, W.R. (1972a), *The social and occupational apprenticeship of Mediterranean migrant workers in W. Germany*, University of Kent, Centre for Research in the Social Sciences, 1970, published in M. Livi-Bacci, ed., *The demographic and social pattern of emigration from the Southern European countries*, Firenze, Dipartimento Statistico Matematica, 1972. This relies heavily on the Hentschel (1968D) and Bingemer (1970D) results.

Böhning, W.R. (1972b), *The migration of workers in the United Kingdom and the European Community*, Oxford University Press, 1972. Although this book is chiefly

170

concerned with analyzing the implications for the U.K. of the free movement of labour provisions of the E.E.C., it contains a useful summary of Böhning's previous publications on European migration.

Böhning, W.R. and Stephen, D. *The E.E.C. and the migration of workers: the E.E.C.'s system of free movement of labour and the implication of U.K. entry*, London, Runnymede Trust, 1971.

Botas, E. 'Some economic aspects of short-run Greek labour emigration to Germany', *Weltwirtschaftliches Archiv* Band 102, 1970.

Probably the single most useful publication on the utilization of migrant workers in Western Europe is Castles, S. & Kosack, G. *Immigrant workers and class structure in Western Europe*. This surveys the origin of and postwar growth in the use of migrant labour, the workers' social and political situation, and the attitude of trade unions toward them, and discusses the rationale of importing and exporting labour from the host and emigration countries' point of view. See also Castles, S. and Kosack, G. 'The function of labour immigration in Western European capitalism', *New Left Review 73*, May–June 1972.

A Marxist analysis of the use of immigrant labour is made by Cinanni, P. *Emigration und Imperialismus*, München 1970 (originally in Italian).

Danieli, L. 'Labour scarcities and labour redundancies in Europe by 1980', in M. Livi-Bacci 1971E, contains estimates of the supply and demand for migrant labour.

Danieli, L. 'Final report', in Livi-Bacci 1971E.

Delgado, J.M. *Anpassungsprobleme der spanischen Gastarbeiter in Deutschalnd: eine sozialpsychologische Untersuching*, dissertation, Cologne 1966.

Descloîtres, R. *Adaptation of foreign workers to industrial work and urban life*. MS/S/66.167, O.E.C.D. June 1966.

One of the main studies suggesting that use of immigrant labour has had adverse consequences is:

Föhl, C. 'Stabilisierung und Wachstum bei Einsatz von Gastarbeiten', *Kyklos*, Band XX 1967, pp. 119–146. A different view is held by Garbers, H. and Blankart, B. 'Lohnbildung und ausländische Arbeitskräfte', *Kyklos*, Band. XXVI, 1973, pp. 817–819, who found that increased immigration control was accompanied in Switzerland by much sharper wage increases, though this was questioned by Rossi and Schiltknecht 1972E.

Another Swiss study is

Gnehm, A. *Ausländische Arbeitskräfte – Vor und Nachteile für die Volkswirtschaft*, Bern 1966. This analyzes the impact of the employment of foreign labour on inflation in postwar Switzerland.

A more sociological approach to the immigration question is used in

Houte, H.V. & Melgert, W. *Foreigners in our community*, Report of the congress held in Amsterdam in August 1971, Keesing Publishers, Amsterdam & Antwerp. The congress was mainly concerned with the social problems of immigrants – their education, vocational training, housing and political rights, and the way in which they are discriminated against.

Hüfner, K. 'Problems of educational and vocational training of migrant workers and their children', in van Houte and Melgert, eds. (1972E).

I.L.O. 'Migration of workers as an element in employment policy', Ch. IV of *Some*

171

growing employment problems in Europe, Report II of the Second European Regional Conference, January 1974. This is a useful summary of the situation in mid-1973, and particularly of the problems to which labour migration has led. It contains a number of policy suggestions, and a brief discussion of migratory movements in E. Europe.

Kade, G. and Schiller, G. 'Foreign workers – development aid by LDCs?' *Intereconomics*, No. 1 1972. This argues that use of immigrant labour has had a stabilizing influence on Germany as well as adverse effects on the labour exporting countries. It also includes a useful bibliography on foreign workers in Germany.

The best known study arguing that the postwar use of migrant labour in Europe has benefitted host and supplying countries alike is

Kindleberger, C.P. *Europe's postwar growth and the role of labour supply*, Oxford 1967. The sections of particular relevance for the countries of emigration were published in

Kindleberger, C.P. 'Emigration and economic growth', *Banca Nationale del Lavoro* Quarterly Review, No. 75, September 1965.

La conférence demographique Européene, *Population*, Vol. 22, 1967.

Lahalle, D. 'Les travailleurs immigrés d'une grande entreprise', *Sociologie du Travail*, No. 3, July–September, 1972.

Another very important study is

Livi-Bacci, M., ed., *The demographic and social pattern of emigration from the southern European countries*, Serie Richerche Empiriche No. 7, Dipartimento Statistico Matematico dell'Universita di Firenze, Comitato Italiano per lo Studia dei problemi della popolazione, Firenze, 1971. This contains the paper given by Professor Livi-Bacci at the Second European Population Conference 1971C, together with a paper by Dr. Böhning on migrants in W. Germany (1971E), a very detailed paper by C. Corsini describing the results of a survey of Italian migrants and their remittances (*The CISP survey on the families of Italian emigrants abroad*), and a useful final report by Mrs. Danieli, who also provided detailed estimates on labour scarcities in Europe by 1980.

Mackie, M.L., *Some aspects of foreign workers in Europe with reference to Western Germany*, M.A. thesis, University of Liverpool, February 1972. This is a most useful summary of the situation since the war, concentrating on the situation in Germany.

Magnet Bundesrepublik, Informationstagung der Bundesvereinigung Deutscher Arbeitgeberverbände, Bonn, 1966.

Mclin, J. *International migrations and the European Community*, American Universities Field Staff Reports, W. Europe Series, Vol. 7, No. 1, 1972. Summarizes Livi-Bacci (1971C).

Minces, J. *Les travailleurs étrangers en France*, Seuil, Paris, 1973.

Mishan and Needleman have been leading advocates of the view that in the existing circumstances, immigration has been inflationary, at least in the British case – see

Mishan, E.J. and Needleman, L. 'Immigration, excess aggregate demand and the balance of payments', *Economica* May 1966.

Mishan, E.J. and Needleman, L. 'Immigration: some economic effects', *Lloyds Bank Review* No. 81, July 1966.

Nikolić, M. Some basic features of Yugoslav external migration, *Yugoslav Survey*,

Vol. 13, No. 1, February 1972.

Nikolić, M. Yugoslav skilled labour temporarily employed abroad. *Yugoslav Survey*, Vol. 13, No. 4, November 1972.

The work by Nikolinakos, M. (*Politische-Ökonomie der Gastarbeiterfrage*, Hamburg 1973), is the most comprehensive Marxist analysis of the situation. See also Nikolinakos, M. 'Zur Frage der Auswanderungseffekte in den Emigrationsländern', *Das Argument*, Vol. 13, No. 9/10, Dec. 1971.

O.E.C.D. (1973a): Böhning, W.R. *The economic effects of the employment of foreign workers: with special reference to the labour markets of Western Europe's post-industrial countries*, MS/M/404/415, mimeo, Paris 1973, (to be published). In this most valuable and comprehensive (though not completely uncontroversial) paper, Böhning uses his stage theory of migration to analyse and review the evidence on the effects of the use of migrant labour in W. Europe.

O.E.C.D. (1973b): Maillat, D.R. *The economic consequences of the employment of foreign workers: the case of Switzerland*, MS/M/404/426, mimeo, Paris 1973.

O.E.C.D. (1973c): *Research into the economic consequences of the employment of foreign workers*, MS/M/404/441, mimeo, Paris 1973. This contains a summary exposition and critical discussion of the Böhning and Maillat papers previously cited. A useful earlier study is Rose, A.M. *Migrants in Europe*, Minnesota 1968. This includes as an appendix T. Stark's valuable table on the laws governing foreign workers in the mid-1960s, Stark, T. 'Situation of migrant workers from countries of the E.E.C. as compared with that of workers from other countries', International Institute for Labour Studies, Symposium on Migration for Employment in Europe, mimeo, Geneva Oct. 1965.

Rossi, A. and Schiltknecht, K. 'Übernachfrage und Lohnentwicklung in der Schweiz — eine neue hypothesese', *Kyklos*, Vol. XXV, 1972, pp. 239–254.

Rüstow, H.J. 'Gastarbeiter — Gewinn oder Belastung für unsere Volkswirtschaft' in 'Probleme der ausländischen Arbeitskräfte in der Bundesrepublik', *Beihefte der Konjunkturpolitik*, Heft 13, Berlin 1966. This is a leading example of the view that the postwar utilization of migrant labour has had an inflationary impact.

Salowsky, H. *Gesamtwirtschaftliche Aspekte der Ausländerbeschäftigung* (General economic aspects of the employment of foreign labour), Beiträgt des Deutschen Industrie-Instituts (Contributions of the Institute of German Industry) No. 10/11, 1971. Dr. Salowsky has summarized part of his argument in his paper, 'Economic impact of foreign labour', *Intereconomics*, February 1973.

Schmid, G.C. 'Foreign workers and labour market flexibility', *Journal of Common Market Studies*, Vol. IX, 1970–1, pp. 246–253. This argues that part of Germany's better economic performance as compared with Britain can be attributed to the additional flexibility which it obtained through the use of migrant labour.

E(ii)   *Newspaper reports*[1]
Daily Telegraph
'Priest leads Renault migrant workers' strike', 24 April, 1973.
The Economist
'Jugoslavia: one of my armies is missing', 27 January, 1973.

1 Only those referred to in the text have been included.

'Europe's own Bantu labour force', 31 March, 1973.
'Guests who have outstayed their welcome', 5 May, 1973.
'The reserve labour army', 25 August, 1973.
'Germany – enough's enough', 1 December, 1973.
'Migrant workers – Germany follows Enoch', 8 December, 1973.
'West Germany – holiday at your peril', 26 January, 1974.
Financial Times
'Dutch consider curbing flow of foreign labour', 21 February, 1973.
'Germans looking for still more foreign workers', 6 April, 1973.
The Guardian
'Immigrants in France to get a better deal', 11 May, 1973.
'More W. Germans unemployed', 11 January, 1974.
Le Monde Diplomatique
'Le sort des travailleurs émigrés en Europe', Supplément *Turquie*, Oct. 1973.
Newsweek
'Yugoslavia: the guest workers', 9 April, 1973.
Sunday Times
'Yugoslavia's problem export – manpower', 22 April, 1973.
'The slave workers of Europe', 22 July, 1973.
The Times
'Many benefits for foreign workers but housing a serious problem',
Made in Holland, supplement. 1 November, 1972.
'Future conditional for immigrant workers', 30 July, 1973.
'Europe's migrant workers face a rising tide of hostility', 10 September, 1973.
'Bonn considers departure bonus for foreign labour', 11 January, 1974.
'Time for new policies toward immigrant workers', Times *Europa* supplement,
5 February, 1974.
The Times Literary Supplement
'*Migration, work and class*', Review of Castles and Kosack (1973E), 24 August, 1973.

F.   *Work in progress* (1973/4)
I.B.R.D. The World Bank has been working on Turkish emigrants and their remittances as part of their country report on Turkey (see Population and Human
Resources Division, Development Economics Department).
I.L.O.   The Employment Planning and Promotion Department of the I.L.O. are
working on two major studies, one on the short-term and on the long-term employment effects of labour migration in both receiving and sending countries, and one on
the likely future flows of migrant workers into European countries from both inside
and outside Europe.
ISOPLAN (Institut für Entwicklungsforschung und Sozialplanung GmbH) has been
working on a project (financed by the German Federal Ministry for Economic
Cooperation) on the Turkish companies available in Germany for the investments
of Turkish workers. It will form the basis for a larger project on the reintegration of
Turkish workers on their return.
Kolan, T. *Labour migration and economic development*, summary of research in
progress on a cost-benefit analysis of Turkish migration from the Turkish point of
view, for presentation at the M.E.S.A. conference, November 1972.

174

Turkey: Ministry of Labour, T.E.S. and S.P.O. All three organisations have work in
progress on various aspects of migration, and particularly on the reintegration of
migrant workers on return.

Part II Other references

Berg, E.J. 'The economics of the migrant labour system', in Kuper, H. Ed.,
Urbanisation and migration in West Africa, Berkeley 1965.
Bulutay, R., Timur, S., Ersel, H., *Türkiye'de gelir dağilinii 1968*. Ankara
Universitesi, Siyasal Bilgiler Fakultesi Yayınları No. 325, Ankara 1971.
Cripps, T.F. and Tarling, R.J. *Growth in advanced capitalist economies 1950–70*,
Cambridge University Department of Applied Economics, Occasional Paper No. 40,
1973.
Enos, J.L., 'Türkiye'de gelir ve vergi dağılısı' *Yön*, Vol. 2, No. 59, Ankara, Jan. 30th,
1963.
Foot, P. *Immigration and race in British politics*, Penguin, 1965.
Franck, P.A. *Turkey*, in Committee on the International Migration of Talent,
The international migration of high level manpower, Praeger, 1970.
Friedlander, S.L. *Labour migration and economic growth*, M.I.T., 1965.
Griffin, K.B. and Enos, J. *Planning development*, London, 1970.
Grubel, H.B. and Scott, A.D. 'The international flow of human capital', *American
Economic Review* 56, 2 May 1966, 268–274.
Hamurdan, Y. 'Surplus Labour in Turkish agriculture', in D. Miller, ed. *Essays on
labour force and employment in Turkey*. U.S.A.I.D. Ankara, 1971.
Hirsch, E. *Poverty and plenty on the Turkish farm*. Colombia University Press, 19
Jones, K. and Smith, A.D. *The economic impact of Commonwealth immigration*.
Cambridge University Press for National Institute of Economic and Social Research,
1970.
Kaldor, N. *The causes of the slow rate of economic growth of the United Kingdom*,
Inaugural lecture, Cambridge 1966.
Kennedy, C. 'The character of improvements and of technical progress', *Economic
Journal*, Vol. 72, December 1962.
Knight, J.B. 'Wages and employment in developed and underdeveloped economies',
Oxford Economic Papers, 23, 1 March 1971, 42–58.
Kryzaniak, M. and Özmucur, S. *The distribution of income and the short run
burden of taxes in Turkey, 1968*. Rice University Programme of Development
Studies, Paper No. 28, 1972.
Maddison, A. *Economic progress and policy in developing countries*, London 1970.
O.E.C.D. *Statistics of the occupational and educational structure of the labour
force in 53 countries*, Paris, 1969.
O.E.C.D. *Turkey – 1963*. Paris, 1963.
O.E.C.D. *Turkey – 1967*. Paris, 1967.
Paine, S.H. Wage differentials in the Japanese manufacturing sector. *Oxford
Economic Papers*, July 1971.
Paine, S.H. The Turkish first five year development plan, a different assessment.
Economic Journal, June 1972.
Şnurov, A. and Rozaliyev, Y. *Türkiye'de kapitalistleşme ve sınıf kargaları*.
A.N.T. Yayınları, 1972.

Tekeli, I. Regional planning in Turkey and regional policy in the first five year development plan. S. İlkin and E. İnanç eds., *Planning in Turkey*, Ankara, 1967.

Thomas, B. *Migration and economic growth*, Cambridge 1954.

Torun, O.N. 'The investment policies of state economic enterprises and their role in the realization of the Turkish development plan', in Economic and Social Studies Conference Board, *State Economic Enterprises*, Istanbul, 1969.

Turkey, State Institute of Statistics, *Annual Foreign Trade Statistics*.

Turkey, State Institute of Statistics, *Census of population, 1965*.

Turkey, State Institute of Statistics, *Census of population 1970, Sampling Results*, Ankara 1972.

Turkey, State Planning Organisation, *First five year development plan 1963–7*, Ankara 1962.

Turkey, State Planning Organisation, Sosyal Planlama Dairesi, *Kooperatifcilik sorunları araştirması*, Ankara, 1972.

Turkey, State Planning Organisation, *1973, Yılı Program*, Ankara 1973.

Turkish Employment Service (İş ve İşçi Bulma Kurumu, Genel Müdürlügü), *İşyerleri işçi ıhtiyacı arastirması*. Ankara, 1970, 1971 and 1972.

Wilson, F. *Labour in the South African gold mines 1911–1969*, Cambridge, 1972.

World Bank, 'The World Bank Atlas', *Finance and Development*. Vol. 9, No. 1, 1972.

World Bank, 'The World Bank Atlas: population, growth rate and G.N.P. changes', *Finance and Development*, Vol. 10, No. 1, March 1973.

Yalçintas, N. 'Manpower and employment objectives and the role of research and statistics', D.R. Miller, ed. *Essays on labour force and employment in Turkey*. U.S.A.I.D. Ankara, 1971.

Yaşer, B.S. *Economic aspects of the devaluation of the Turkish lira of August 10th 1970*, U.S.A.I.D. Discussion Paper No. 5. Ankara, April 1972.

Addenda (Publications which have become available since this book went to press.)

B.
Bundesanstalt für Arbeit, Institut für Arbeitsmarket – und Berufsforschuns: H. Werner, *Freizügigkeit der Arbeitskräfte und die Wanderungsbewegungen in den Ländern der Europäischen Gemeinschaften* (Free movement of labour and migration movements in E.E.C. countries), Nürmberg, 1973. This examines the extent to which successive introduction of the free movement of labour provisions affected the extent of migrations between the E.E.C. countries, and found that this was very low.

C
Çetin, I. *Emigrant workers in the Federal Republic of Germany – revisited*, U.S.A.I.D. Discussion Paper No. 18, Ankara, Feb 1974. This paper summarizes Miller and Çetin 1974D, and attempts to project the stock of Turkish workers in Germany and their repatriated earnings up to 1977.

D.
Abadan-Unat, N., ed. *Turkish migration*, Brill and Leiden, forthcoming.

E.
Marshall, A. *The import of Labour: the case of the Netherlands*, Rotterdam. This book provides the most thorough analysis yet available from a Marxian standpoint. It then discusses in detail the Netherlands' experience, and concludes with a chapter on the effects on the countries of emigration.

176

Appendix 2
Statistical data

Introductory note
As previously explained, the diverse sources of statistics about Turkish migrant workers vary considerably in their reliability (see particularly Table 4, and the additional details supplied in Appendices 1 and 3). On the whole, by far the most reliable data came from German official sources (notably the Bundesanstalt für Arbeit). However most of the main results of the S.P.O. survey have been included in this appendix for reference purposes, despite the important qualifications which must be made when interpreting them. Where the response was low, absolute figures have been presented. There are some discrepancies in percentage totals because of rounding, and also a number of multiple choice questions where percentage totals exceed 100. Also, in the S.P.O. survey the 'rural' and 'urban' subsamples refer to place of residence on return (see §3.4.3).

Table A1. *Foreigners and foreign workers in W. Germany. January 1st 1972, (1000s)*

	Foreigners		Foreigners (excluding Berlin)				Foreign workers		
	No.	%	Total	Women	%[a]	Children	Total	No.	%[b]
Country of origin									
Turkey	652.8	19	603.7	136.4	37	100.1	449.7	100.8	22
Yugoslavia	594.3	17	559.9	164.4	47	44.8	434.9	138.8	33
Greece	394.9	12	385.2	133.9	77	76.3	264.4	113.6	43
Spain	270.4	8	268.0	76.2	52	45.7	174.0	53.4	31
Italy	589.8	17	583.5	136.2	41	118.5	384.3	95.5	25
Portugal	75.2	2	74.9	20.5	46	99.9	57.2	17.0	30
Tunisia	12.4	0	11.6	1.0	10	0.5	10.1	0.9	9
Morocco	15.2	0	14.9	0.6	4	0.9	12.4	0.2	2
Other E.E.C. (France, Belgium, Neths, Benelux)	176.3	5					127.9		
Other European	390.6	11					161.6		
Other non-European	266.8	8					n.a.		
Total	3438.7	100					2076.5[c]		

Sources: Foreigners: Statistisches Bundesamt, Wiesbaden, *Wirtschaft und Statistik*, p. 446*
Workers: Bundesanstalt für Arbeit, Nürnberg.

[a] Women as % of *adults* by nationality.
[b] Women as % of *total workers* by nationality.
[c] Excluding other non-European workers.

Table A2. *Distribution of Turkish migrant workers according to channel through which migration took place – S.P.O. survey 1971*

	Total		Urban		Rural	
	No.	%	No.	%	No.	%
1st year						
T.E.S.	284	79	155	75	129	84
Tourist passport	41	11	19	9	22	14
Teacher	3	1	3	2	0	0
Through relatives	15	4	13	6	2	1
Through an intermediary	10	3	10	5	0	0
Other	8	2	7	3	1	1
2nd year (if different from 1st)						
T.E.S.	2		2		0	
Tourist passport	8		3		5	
Other	2		1		1	
Total	12		6		6	
3rd year (if different from 2nd)						
T.E.S.	1		1		0	
Teacher	1		1		0	
Total	2		2		0	

Table A3. *Ratio of officially recruited to total arrivals of foreign workers in Germany by country, 1961–71 (1000s)*

Year	Turkey Total	Turkey % Officially recruited	Yugoslavia Total	Yugoslavia % Officially recruited	Greece Total	Greece % Officially recruited	Spain Total	Spain % Officially recruited	Portugal Total	Portugal % Officially recruited	All 5 Countries % Officially recruited
1961	7.1	17	10.0	n.a.	36.6	57	51.2	53	0.9	n.a.	79[1]
1962	15.3	72	25.1	n.a.	47.6	67	55.0	66	1.0	n.a.	67[1]
1963	27.9	84	19.4	n.a.	58.0	70	51.7	68	1.5	n.a.	84[1]
1964	62.9	87	17.5	n.a.	65.1	62	65.9	68	3.9	46	71[2]
1965	59.8	76	31.0	n.a.	61.8	53	65.1	62	11.1	73	64[2]
1966	43.5	74	50.9	n.a.	39.7	67	38.6	68	9.2	79	71[2]
1967	14.8	48	15.4	n.a.	7.7	25	7.8	41	1.8	46	41[2]
1968	62.4	66	76.8	n.a.	37.2	65	3.2	72	6.7	69	67[2]
1969	121.5	80	192.2	35	65.1	78	50.1	83	13.2	86	61
1970	123.6	77	202.4	52	64.0	77	48.9	83	20.1	90	67
1971	112.1	56	113.3	64	42.0	72	37.5	78	17.9	86	65
1972											
1961–1971	651.0	73	507.9[3]	48[3]	524.9	67	503.7	69	84.0[4]	80[4]	

[1] Excluding Yugoslavia and Portugal.
[2] Excluding Yugoslavia.
[3] 1969–1971.
[4] 1964–1971.

Source: Bundesanstalt für Arbeit, *Ausländische Arbeitnehmer* 1971, Nürnberg, 1972. Table 14, p. 89.

Table A4.   Officially recruited departures and actual arrivals of Turkish migrant workers by host country, 1961–1971 (1000s)

	W. Germany		Belgium		France		Netherlands		% of official departures to actual arrivals in all 4 countries	% of official departures to actual arrivals in W. Germany
	Official	Actual	Official	Actual	Official	Actual	Official	Actual		
1961	1.5	7.1	—	—	—	n.a.	—	n.a.	n.a.	17
1962	11.0	15.3	—	0.1	—	n.a.	—	n.a.	n.a.	72
1963	23.4	27.9	5.6	5.0	0.1	n.a.	0.3	0.7	n.a.	84
1964	54.9	62.9	6.7	7.0	—	0.2	3.0	4.9	86	87
1965	45.6	59.8	1.7	4.1	—	0.4	2.2	4.3	72	76
1966	32.6	43.5	—	1.4	—	0.5[a]	1.2	6.9	65	75
1967	7.2	14.8	—	0.6	—	1.2[a]	—	1.4	40	49
1968	41.4	62.4	—	0.1	0.2	1.7[a]	0.9	3.7	62	66
1969	98.1	121.5	—	0.1	—	2.6[a]	3.4	5.8	78	81
1970	97.0	123.4	0.4	n.a.	9.0	8.8[a]	4.8	n.a.	n.a.	79
1971	65.7	112.1	n.a.	n.a.	7.9	5.7[a]	4.9	n.a.	n.a.	59

Note: a – Excluding seasonal workers.

Sources: Official departures of workers: Germany – Table 2. Actual arrivals of workers: Germany – Table A3; France – Office National d'Immigration; Belgium and Netherlands – E.E.C. *La libre circulation de la main d'oeuvre et les marchés du travail dans la C.E.E. 1966–70.*

Table A5. *Proportion of Turkish workers among new foreign worker entrants, by host country*

		1961	1962	1963	1964	1965	1966	1967	1968	1969	1970	1971
Belgium												
Total entrants (1000)		12.4[a]	22.5[a]	33.3[a]	40.7[a]	38.7[a]	19.5	14.2	8.8	2.5	n.a.	n.a.
% Turks		0	0	15[b]	17[b]	11[b]	7	4	1	5	n.a.	n.a.
Germany												
Total entrants (1000)		360.5	399.7	377.5	442.3	524.9	424.8	181.9	390.9	646.1	713.9	570.3
% Turks		2	4	7	14	11	10	10	16	19	17	20
France – Permanent workers [b]												
Total entrants (1000)					153.3	153.1	131.5	107.8	93.2	167.8	174.2	81.0
% Turks					0	0	0	1	2	2	5	7
Netherlands												
Total entrants (1000)				17.1[a]	30.9[a]	31.2[a]	35.8	17.6	19.9	28.5	n.a.	n.a.
% Turks				4	16	14	19	8	19	20	n.a.	n.a.
All E.E.C. permanent workers [d]	% Turks						9	6	13	15	n.a.	n.a.
	% Yugoslavs						10	9	16	24	n.a.	n.a.
	% Italians						32	26	27	17[c]	n.a.	n.a.
	% Portuguese						10	13	7	11	n.a.	n.a.
	% Spaniards						14	12	11	9	n.a.	n.a.
	% Greeks						7	3	7	8	n.a.	n.a.

Notes:
a Including seasonal workers.
b Turks account for an almost zero proportion of seasonal workers.
c Excluding Italians entering Belgium.
d In addition to the countries listed above, there has been a small amount of Turkish immigration into Italy, but this has never exceeded one per cent.

Sources: Germany – Bundesanstalt für Arbeit, *Ausländische Arbeitnehmer*; France – Office National d'Immigration; other countries – E.E.C., *La libre circulation de la main d'oeuvre et les marchés du travail dans la CEE*, Brussels 1968–70.

Table A6. *Turkish workers in W. Germany, 1960–73*

Year	1. Stock of Turkish workers	2. Turks as % of foreign worker stock	3. T.E.S. despatch to Germany	4. Actual Turkish arrivals in Germany	5. Turks as % of new foreign worker arrivals	6. Officially recruited Turkish worker arrivals in Germany	7. T.E.S. despatch as % of actual arrivals (3/4)	8. Actual arrivals less T.E.S. despatch (4−3)	9. Vacancies notified for Turkish workers	10. Shipments as % of vacancies (3/9)	11. Net outflow of Turkish workers (Jan.–Jan.)	12. Net outflow of Turkish workers (Sept.–Sept.)	13. Actual arrivals as % of vacancies	14. Net inflow of Turkish workers (Jan. to Jan.)
1960 Jul.	2495	1												
1961 Jun.	5193	1	1476	7116	2	1207	17	5909	4127	36			172	6330*
1962 Jan.	10130	3												
Jun.	15318		11025	15269	4	11024	72	4244	10716	103	3345	n.a.	143	11924
1963 Jan.	22054	4												
Jun.	27144		23436	27910	7	23436	84	4474	32855	76	5011	5581	85	22899
1964 Jan.	44953	8												
Jun.	69211		54902	62879	14	54918	87	8777	57917	93	12857	10093	109	30022
1965 Jan.	94975	11												
Jun.	121121		45572	59816	11	45553	76	14254	53081	86	21791	16482	113	38025
1966 Jan.	133000	12												
Jun.	157978		32580	43499	10	32516	75	10919	32606	100	40244	27353	113	3255
1967 Jan.	136255	13												
Jun.	137081		7199	14834	10	7233	49	7635	9290	78	27703	52104	160	12869
1968 Jan.	123386	14												
Jun.	139336		41409	62376	16	41450	66	20967	53457	78	14744	23888	117	47632
1969 Jan.	171018	16												
Jun.	212951		98142	121529	19	98142	81	23387	117194	75	20124	22367	104	101405
1970 Jan.	272423	18												
Jun.	327985		96936	123420	17	96936	79	23784	106827	91	22843	n.a.	116	100596
1971 Jan.	373019	21												
Jun.	424374		65684	112144	20	63777	59	46500	68322	96	5508*	n.a.	164	76657
1972 Jan.	449676	22												
Jun.	497000		65000*	90000*	n.a.	65000*	72*	25000*	n.a.	n.a.	n.a.	n.a.	n.a.	78524
1973 Jan.	528200	23	103800*											
Cumulative total			616322	650792		510083								

Notes: Col 11. Net outflow for year t is stock at Jan 1st year t plus actual arrivals in year t minus stock at Jan 1st year $t+1$

Col 12. Net outflow for year t is stock at Sept year $t-1$ plus actual arrivals Sept year t, minus stock at Sept year t

Col 14. Stock at Jan. year $t+1$ minus stock at Jan. year t equals net inflow year t.

* Estimate

Sources: Cols 1, 2, 4, 5, 6: Germany, Bundesanstalt für Arbeit, *Ausländische Arbeitnehmer*
Cols 3, 9, 12: Turkish Employment Service, *Annual Labour Reports*

Table A7. *Changes in the stocks and flows of foreign workers in and to West Germany, and in the flow of officially recruited departures from Turkey*

	% change in Turkish migrant worker stock from previous year	% change in foreign migrant worker stock from previous year	% change in official Turkish departures from previous year	% change in actual Turkish arrivals from previous year	% change in total foreign arrivals from previous year	% change in all officially recruited departures from Turkey to Europe	% change in monthly average of all unfilled vacancies in Germany
1961	+163	+125					+19
1962	+118	+ 33	+647	+115	+ 10	+658	+ 4
1963	+104	+ 14	+113	+ 83	− 5	+171	− 3
1964	+111	+ 25	+134	+125	+ 17	+118	+10
1965	+ 40	+ 18	− 17	− 5	+ 19	− 22	+ 7
1966	+ 3	− 5	− 29	− 27	− 19	− 33	−17
1967	− 10	− 15	− 78	− 66	− 64	− 75	−44
1968	+ 39	+ 26	+475	+321	+157	+406	+62
1969	+ 59	+ 39	+137	+ 95	+ 65	+139	+53
1970	+ 37	+ 25	− 1	+ 2	+ 11	+ 24	+ 6
1971	+ 21	+ 10	− 32	− 9	− 20	− 33	−19
1972	+ 16	+ 9					−16

Sources: Turkish Employment Services *Annual Labour Reports*
Germany, Bundesanstalt für Arbeit, *Ausländische Arbeitnehmer*, 1962–72.

Table A8. *Migrant workers returning to Turkey (1000s)*

	Total workers who returned to Turkey	Turkish workers who returned from Germany as % of total Turkish workers who returned	Workers who stated that their return to Turkey was permanent	Percentage of ex-German workers among those who returned permanently to Turkey	Net outflow of Turkish workers from Germany
1962	n.a.	n.a.	n.a.	n.a.	3.3
1963	n.a.	n.a.	n.a.	n.a.	5.0
1964	n.a.	n.a.	n.a.	n.a.	12.9
1965	n.a.	n.a.	n.a.	n.a.	21.8
1966	n.a.	n.a.	5.6	n.a.	40.2
1967	123.2	82	17.8	83	27.7
1968	102.7	80	3.5	73	14.7
1969	157.7	84	4.1	79	20.1
1970	292.7	88	4.8	79	22.8
1971	372.4	83	5.7	75	5.5
1972	589.3	91	4.6	78	n.a.

Sources: Turkey, State Institute of Statistics *Tourism Statistics*; Table A6 for column 5.

Table A9. *Vacancies for and despatch of Turkish migrant workers to W. Germany by skill and sex, 1965–71*

Type of vacancy	1965 a	1965 b	1966 a	1966 b	1967 a	1967 b	1968 a	1968 b	1969 a	1969 b	1970 a	1970 b	1971 a	1971 b
Men	39.3	88	24.1	95	5.3	71	40.0	75	96.0	81	84.9	90	23.3	93
Women	13.8	81	8.5	115	4.0	87	13.5	84	21.2	98	21.9	93	5.7	94
Skilled workers	25.0	76	7.9	102	3.4	62	15.6	74	37.0	63	36.8	73	9.3	109
Skilled men	21.5	77	6.9	102	3.0	61	13.8	73	34.4	60	34.8	71	8.6	112
Skilled women	3.5	71	0.9	101	0.4	71	1.8	79	2.6	109	2.0	103	0.7	76
Unskilled workers	28.1	94	24.7	99	5.9	87	37.9	79	80.2	93	70.1	100	19.7	86
Unskilled men	17.8	100	17.2	92	2.2	84	26.1	77	61.6	93	50.1	104	14.7	82
Unskilled women	10.3	85	9.6	116	3.7	88	11.7	85	18.6	96	19.9	92	5.0	96
Total for current year	53.1	86	32.6	100	9.3	78	53.5	78	117.2	84	106.8	91	28.9	94
Of which vacancies for named workers	12.6	48	13.6	81	1.6	62	21.0	65	39.3	79	29.0	77	9.2	93
Vacancies left from previous year	9.6		14.3		4.5		1.8		12.2		29.2		11.4	
Total	62.7		46.9		13.8		55.3		129.4		136.0		69.8	
% vacancies filled	73		70		52		75		76		71		79	
% vacancies for skilled workers	53		24		37		29		32		34		32	
% of despatched workers who are skilled	42		25		29		28		24		28		37	

Source: Data supplied by Turkish Employment Service.

Notes: a Vacancies (1000)
b Workers despatched as % of vacancies.

184

Table A10. *Applications by Turkish workers for work abroad, by skill and sex, 1969 and 1970*

	1969	1970
Total applications (nearest 100)	807 000	1 001 500
% applications from men	96	93
% applications from women	4	7
% applications from skilled workers	18	15
Of which % from women	1	5
% applications from unskilled workers	82	77
Of which % from women	5	8

Source: Data supplied by Turkish Employment Service.

Table A11. *The proportion of males among Turkish and other migrant workers*

	Turkish migrant workers							% of stock in Germany by nationality				
	% in total official departures	% in official departures to Germany	% in stock in Germany (June of each year)	% in Turkish population	% in Turkish e.a.p.	% in Turkish non. agr. e.a.p.	% in survey samples[1]	Yugoslavia	Greece	Portugal	Spain	Italy
1960	95	100	92					82	79	89	81	93
1961	95	92	92									
1962	92	92	89									
1963	94	88	90									
1964	78	76	87			92						
1965	72	70	84	51	62							
1966	61	52	82				69 Tuna					
1967	74	78	78				92 T.E.S.					
1968	80	79	78				94 T.E.S.					
1969	84	79	78				94 T.E.S.					
1970												
1971	84	76	79				95 S.P.O. 89 T.E.S.	71[2]	58	73	70	77
Annual average	83	80	84									

Sources: (1) Turkish Employment Service, *Annual Labour Reports.*
(2) Germany, Bundesanstalt für Arbeit, *Ausländische Arbeitnehmer*

Notes: 1 Note that the year refers to the year of the survey, and not (necessarily) to the year of departure. For survey details, see Appendix 1.
2 As compared with an estimate for the total migrant worker stock abroad of 68.6% in March 1971 (M. Begtić, 'Yugoslav nationals temporarily working abroad', *Yugoslav Survey*, Vol XIII No. 1, Feb. 1972, p. 20.)

Table A12a. *Percentage distribution of Turkish migrant workers by rural-urban residence*

	Tuna survey (1967)					T.E.S. surveys				Turkey		
	B	BD	R	B & R same	BD & R same	1967	1968	1969	1971	1960	1965	1970
Province centre	48	69	69	67	90	39	30	29	37	33	35	39
District centre	28	24	24	44	90	17	20	14	20			
Sub-district centre or village	24	8	8	41	83	44	56	58	43	67	65	61
No reply						1	0	0	0			
Total				54	8							

Note: B = Birthplace
BD = Before Departure
R = On Return

Sources: O. Tuna, *Yurda dönen işçilerin intibakı sorunları,* S.P.D., D.P.T., Ankara,
August 1967;
T.E.S. *Yurt dışındaki Türk işçileri ve dönüs eğilimleri,* Ankara 1967, 1968,
1969, 1971;
State Institute of Statistics, *Population Census,* 1960, 1965, 1970.

Table A12b. *Percentage distribution of Turkish migrant workers by rural urban residence,
S.P.O. survey, 1971*

	(i) Birth Place			(ii) Before Departure			(iii) On Return		
	Total	U	R	Total	U	R	Total	U	R
Province centre	11	–	–	27	45	3	46	81	–
District centre	24	42	1	24	41	1	11	18	–
Sub-district centre	8	8	9	7	5	9	5	1	11
Village	49	20	87	43	10	88	38	–	89
Abroad	8	12	3	–	–	–	–	–	–
Residence same as birth				66	49	90	50	27	81
Residence same as before departure	66	49	90				67	67	75

U = Urban
R = Rural

Note: Percentages may not add to 100 because of rounding.

187

Table A12c. *Percentage distribution of Turkish migrant workers by size of place of origin*

	Abadan 1963	S.P.O. 1971	Aker 1970/71 B	Aker 1970/71 BD
Istanbul	41			
Ankara	6			
Izmir	4			
over 100 000	6	57	27	48
50 000–100 000	7			
20 000–50 000	7			
10 000–20 000			20	15
5000–10 000	11			
2000–5000		43	52	37
under 2000	18			

Notes: I. Selcen found 42% had lived in a village at some time.
        B = Birthplace
        BD = Before Departure
        Figures may not add to 100 because of rounding

Sources: N. Abadan, *Batı Almanya'daki Türk işçileri ve sorunları*, D.P.T. Ankara, Kasım 1964
         D.P.T. (S.P.O.) Survey of returned migrant workers 1971
         A. Aker, *Işçi göçü,* Istanbul 1972
         I. Selcen, *Berufliche Wertmuster des türkischen Gastarbeiter und die sich daraus ergebenden Anpassungsprobleme an die deutsche Industriearbeiterschaft* (unpublished sociological diploma thesis), Cologne, 1965.

Table A13. *Percentage distribution of Turkish migrant workers by age*

	Turkey												Germany 1968				Turkey S.P.O. survey 1971		
	Turkey e.a.p. 1965			Aker	T.E.S. 1967			T.E.S. 1968	T.E.S. 1969			T.E.S. 1971	Turks		All Foreign				
	M	F	T	T	M	F	T	T	M	F	T	T	M	F	M	F	Total	Urban	Rural
0–14	–	–	–	–	–	–	–	–	–	–	–	–					–	–	1
15–19	14	16	15	3	1	2	1	–	1	3	1	–	7	32	16	32	–	–	–
20–24	13	14	13	16	1	19	3	22	1	19	2	8	29	23	21	23	2	3	1
25–29	12	14	13	28	28	24	28	24	20	23	20	25	31	18	21	15	7	9	4
30–34	13	13	13	34	32	22	32	30	29	23	29	36	18	17	17	12	28	30	25
35–39	12	11	11	15	24	19	23	27	31	21	30	21	11		12	9	31	28	35
40–44	8	8	8	3	11	10	11	12	14	8	14	7	11 }	11	13	9	24	22	27
45+	28	25	26	–	3	5	4	4	5	4	5	2	4			9	8	8	9
Unknown	0	0	0	2	0	0	0		0	0	0								
Mean age																	37	37	38

Sources:

Turkey   S.I.S. Census of Population 1965;
T.E.S. *Yurt dışındaki Türk işçileri ve dönüş eğilimleri, 1967, 1968, 1969 and 1971;*
A. Aker, *İşçi göçü* Istanbul 1972;
S.P.O. *Survey of returned migrant workers,* 1971.
Germany   Bundesanstalt für Arbeit, *Ausländische Arbeitnehmer,* 1968.

Figures may not add to 100 because of rounding

189

Table A14. *Percentage distribution of Turkish migrant workers by marital status*

	Turkish population over 15 1965	Abadan 1963			T.E.S.				S.P.O. survey 1971 Before departure			S.P.O. survey 1971 While abroad			S.P.O. survey 1971 On return			Aker 1970 /71	Turks[1] in Germany 1968		All[1] foreign workers in Germany 1968	
		M	F	T	1967 T	1968 T	1969 T	1971	T	Urban	Rural	T	Urban	Rural	T	Urban	Rural		M	F	M	F
Single	18	41	37	41	11	8	5	6	22	34	5	21	32	5	6	8	3	14	18	29	29	36
Married	73	57	45	56	87	91	93	93	78	65	96	79	67	95	94	91	97	84	82	71	71	64
Widowed	7	1	9	1	1	2	1	–	–	1	–	–	1	–	–	1	–	–	–	–	–	–
Divorced	1	1	9	2	1	–	1	–	–	–	–	–	–	–	–	–	–	2	–	–	–	–
Unknown	1	–	–	–	–	–	1	–	–	–	–	–	–	–	–	–	–	–	–	–	–	–

	T.E.S. surveys				Stocks of Turks in Germany 1968		All foreign workers in Germany 1968	
	1967	1968	1969	1971	M	F	M	F
All married migrant workers								
% with family in Turkey	88	87	86	76	66	27	58	82
% with family abroad	12	11	14	22	34	73		
No reply	1	1	1	2				
Married migrant workers in Germany								
% with family in Turkey	87	n.a.	85	n.a.				
% with family in Germany	12	n.a.	14	n.a.				
No reply	1	n.a.	1	n.a.				

Note: 1 Only the categories of single and married were used.

Sources:
Turkey, State Institute of Statistics, *Census of Population*, 1965.
N. Abadan, *Batı Almanya'daki Türk işçileri ve sorunları*, D.P.T., 1964.
T.E.S. *Yurt dışındaki Türk işçileri ve dönüş eğilimleri*, 1967, 1968, 1969, 1971.
S.P.O. *Survey of returned migrant workers* 1971.
A. Aker, *İşçi göçü*, Istanbul, 1972.
Federal Republic of Germany, Bundesanstalt für Arbeit, *Ausländische Arbeitnehmer*, 1969, Nürnberg 1970.

Figures may not add to 100 because of rounding.

Table A15a. *Percentage distribution of returned migrant workers by number of children, S.P.O. survey 1971*

	% Married migrant workers		
	Total	Urban	Rural
Children			
0	7	9	3
1	19	27	9
2	17	20	13
3	22	23	21
4	19	12	28
5	7	7	8
6 or more	9	3	17
Per married migrant	2.9	2.3	3.6
Per migrant	2.7	2.1	3.5

Table A15b. *Percentage distribution of employed migrant workers in Germany with children by nationality and by number of children*

in %	1 Child	2 Children	3 or 4 Children	5 or more children
Italian	46	32	19	–
Greek	57	33	10	–
Spanish	43	33	20	–
Turkish	52	30	17	–
Portuguese	59	–	–	–
Yugoslav	68	–	–	–
Other	48	30	19	–
Total	49	31	17	3

Source: Bundesanstalt für Arbeit, *Ausländische Arbeitnehmer,* 1969, Nürnberg 1970, p. 57. Percentages as given in the original.

Table A16. *Percentage distribution of returned migrant workers by number of dependants, S.P.O. survey, 1971*

Dependants	Total	Urban	Rural
0	5	6	3
1	4	6	1
2	8	12	3
3	10	12	7
4	18	23	11
5	19	18	21
6	25	15	38
7 or more	12	8	17
Mean no. of dependants	4.6	4.0	5.3

Table A17. *Percentage distribution of Turkish migrant workers by educational attainment*

	Turkish economically active population								Turkish migrant workers															
	All Turkey 1965			Urban Areas 1965			Urban Areas 1967	All Turkey 1970	Abadan 1964			Tuna 1967			TES 1967	TES 1968	TES 1969	TES 1971	Germany 1968			S.P.O. 1971		
	M	F	T	M	F	T			M	F	T	M	F	T					M	F	T	Total	Urban	Rural
Illiterate	34	81	53	18	33	19	28	47[a]	3	1	3	0	10	1	4	3	10	6	9	21	10	3	0	6
Literate	18	5	13	16	7	15	14	10	15	13	15	12	10	11	24	29	24	15	25	17	24	7	2	14
Primary	39	12	29	47	25	46	34	36	57	35	49	58	68	59	60	59	61	73	62	49	61	63	53	77
Secondary	3	1	3	8	9	8	8	3	12	16	13	8	–	7	5	3	3	3	2	8	3	14	23	3
Lycée	1	0	1	3	8	4	6	4	3	10	4	1	–	–	1	1	1	1	0	2	1	3	4	0
Vocational	2	1	2	4	10	4	4	4	14	24	15	21	13	21	1	2	1	3	1	3	1	8	13	1
Higher	1	0	1	4	8	4	4	4	1	1	1	–	–	–	2	–	–	0	0	0	0	3	5	0
Unknown	0	–	0	–	–	–	–	1	0	–	0	–	–	–	–	–	0	1	0	1	0	–	–	–

Sources: Republic of Turkey, State Institute of Statistics, *Census of Population*, 1965
Republic of Turkey, State Institute of Statistics, *Census of Population*, 1970, Sampling results.
N. Abadan, *Batı Almanya'daki Türk işçileri*, D.P.T. 1964.
O. Tuna, *Yurda dönen işçilerin intibaki sorunları*, D.P.T. 1967.
T.E.S. *Yurt dışındaki Türk işçileri ve dönüş eğilimleri*, 1967, 1968, 1969, 1971.
W. Germany, Bundesanstalt für Arbeit, *Ausländische Arbeitnehmer*, 1969, Nürnberg 1970.
S.P.O. *Survey of returned migrant workers*, 1971.

Note: a Urban areas: 32%; rural areas: 55%; Ankara: 21%; Istanbul: 18%; Izmir: 26%.

A zero indicates figure rounded down to zero.

Figures may not add to 100 because of rounding.

Table A18. *Vocational training levels of Turkish migrant workers, S.P.O. survey, 1971*

	Total (No.)	Urban (No.)	Rural (No.)
Workers with some vocational training	97[1](27% total sample)	64[1](31% urban sample)	33[1](23% rural sample)
Workers specifying level of their vocational training	88	59	29

Level of training

  In Turkey

1 *In Workplace*

Before Employment	18	17	1
Apprentice	13	8	5
Qualified Workman	5	3	2
Master Workman	10	3	7
Chief Master	3	3	0
Monitor	1	1	0
Language Course	2	2	0

2 *Outside Workplace*

Before Employment	15	8	7
Apprentice	2	1	1
Qualified Workman	3	2	1
Master Workman	2	2	0
Chief Master	2	1	1
Monitor	2	2	0
Language Course	3	3	0

  Abroad

1 *In Workplace*

Before Employment	17	10	7
Apprentice	1	1	0
Qualified Workman	0	0	0
Master Workman	4	4	0
Chief Master	0	0	0
Monitor	0	0	0
Language Course	0	0	0

2 *Outside Workplace*

Before Employment	5	4	1
Apprentice	3	3	0
Qualified Workman	0	0	0
Master Workman	0	0	0
Chief Master	0	0	0
Monitor	0	0	0
Language Course	6	6	0

Mean duration of courses reported			
Courses in Turkey	8.4 months		
Courses abroad	5.1 months		

Note: 1 Column totals exceed this figure as 29 workers (25 urban and 4 rural) reported two types of training, in addition to the 9 workers who did not report the level of their training.

193

Table A19. *Percentage distribution of Turkish migrant workers by skill level before departure and on return, S.P.O. survey 1971*

		Before departure			On return		
		Total	Urban	Rural	Total	Urban	Rural
a	Unskilled workers	47	27	73	29	17	44
b	Semiskilled workers	2	2	2	4	7	1
c	Skilled workers	7	10	3	x	x	x
d	Apprentices	1	1	1	0	0	1
e	Qualified workmen	4	7	0	2	3	0
f	Master workmen	24	29	16	23	33	8
g	Chief masters	2	3	0	4	6	1
h	Technicians	5	8	1	3	5	1
i	.Officials	5	8	2	8	12	2
	No reply	0	0	0	21	14	30
	Unemployed	4	5	2	7	3	12
	Employment in private sector	89	85	95	69	81	54
	Employment in public sector	11	15	5	3	3	3
	No reply	0	0	0	28	16	43

x   Category not included in questionnaire

Totals may not add to 100 because of rounding.

Table A20a. *Percentage distribution of Turkish migrant workers by sector of employment and by employment status prior to departure, S.P.O. survey, 1971*

		Total %	Urban %	Rural %
I *Unemployed*[1]				
Unclassified		0	1	0
Agriculture		1	1	2
Industry		1	2	0
Services		1	2	0
Total unemployed		4	5	2
II *Employee*				
IIa Wage earner	A	3	2	5
	I	27	42	6
	S	9	11	5
Total wage earners		39	55	16
IIb Family worker	A	0	0	1
	I	0	0	0
	S	0	0	0
Total family workers		0	0	1
IIc Partner/sharecropper	A	1	1	1
	I	0	0	0
	S	0	0	0
Total partners/sharecroppers		1	1	1
Total employees		40	56	18
III *Self-employed*				
	A	31	11	57
	I	17	17	17
	S	8	10	5
Total self-employed		56	38	79
IV *Employer*				
	A	0	0	1
	I	1	1	1
	S	0	0	0
Total employers		1	1	1

Notes: A = Agriculture
         I = Industry (including mining and construction)
         S = Services
         1. Unemployment refers to the time of application.

Discrepancies in totals may occur because of rounding.

Table A20b. *Work status of Turkish e.a.p., 1955–70*

	Turkey e.a.p. aged 15–64			
	1955	1960	1965	1970
Wage earner	13	19	23	23
Employer	0	1	1	28
Self-employed	27	28	27	
Unpaid family worker	55	48	48	48
Unknown	5	4	1	1

Source: Republic of Turkey, State Institute of Statistics, *Census of Population* 1955, 1960, 1965, 1970 (1% sample).

Table A21. *Percentage distribution of Turkish migrant workers by sector of employment and size of industrial workplace prior to departure, S.P.O. survey, 1971*

	Total %	Urban %	Rural %
Agriculture	37	15	66
Industry	45	62	23
(Industrial workplaces with more than 10 employees)	(17)	(22)	(11)
Services	18	23	10
Unclassified	0	1	–

Totals may not add to 100 because of rounding.

Table A22a. *Percentage distribution of Turkish migrant workers according to their occupation before departure, while abroad and on return, S.P.O. survey, 1971*

	Occ. before depart.[a]			Occ. while abroad[b]			Occ. on return[a]		
	Total	Urban	Rural	Total	Urban	Rural	Total	Urban	Rural
Unemployed	4	5	2	–	–	–	7	3	12
Official/white collar worker	3	4	2	1	1	–	6	8	2
Mechanic/engineer Technician }	3	5	–	3	4	1	3	9	1
Teacher	1	1	1	x	x	x	1	–	1
Driver	3	3	3	1	2	1	4	3	6
Radio operator	–	1	–	1	1	–	1	1	–
Lokantası/ Kahveci/cook	2	2	1	–	–	–	3	3	1
Grocer	3	2	3	x	x	x	4	3	5
Street hawker	1	1	1	x	x	x	1	–	1
Misc. services	x	x	x	x	x	x	2	3	–
Farmer	27	9	52	x	x	x	19	2	42
Horticulturalist	–	–	1	2	1	3	1	–	1
Agricultural Labourer } Misc. agriculture }	4	1	8	1	–	1	3	1	7
Miner	–	1	–	9	3	16	–	–	–
Textile worker	–	–	–	8	7	7	–	–	–
Weaver	11	12	10	–	–	2	9	11	7
Tailor	5	3	4	5	8	2	3	4	1
Shoemaker	1	1	1	1	2	1	–	–	–
Stonemason	–	–	–	1	2	1	x	x	x
Planer/turner	8	13	1	15	21	6	6	10	–
Caster/moulder	1	1	–	6	8	8	1	1	1
Blacksmith	1	2	1	2	2	3	1	1	–
Welder	4	6	1	5	8	1	3	5	–
Milling mach. operator	x	x	x	–	1	–	x	x	x
Metal worker	1	1	1	2	2	3	1	1	–
Pattern maker	–	–	–	x	x	x	–	–	–
Assembler	1	2	–	9	12	6	3	5	–
Motor mechanic	3	5	1	2	3	2	–	–	–
Electrician	2	3	1	3	3	4	4	5	1
Plumber	–	–	–	–	1	–	1	1	–
Builder	2	1	3	3	1	5	–	–	1
Construction worker	1	1	1	15	9	23	1	–	2
Plasterer	–	–	–	–	–	1	x	x	x
Joiner	2	2	3	2	2	4	2	2	2
Skilled indust. worker	x	x	x	17	13	21	4	7	–
Car factory worker	x	x	x	8	11	3	x	x	x
Craft worker	–	1	–	x	x	x	1	2	–
Unskilled labourer industry unknown	1	2	–	x	x	x	6	9	2
Unskilled self-employed	x	x	x	x	x	x	3	2	5
Miscellaneous	6	7	2	x	x	x	2	3	1

x Category not used.

a Percentages for occupations before departure and on return do not add to 100 because of rounding (certain columns have a large number of percentages rounded up to 1%).

b Percentages exceed 100 because some workers reported more than one occupation.

Table A22b. *Percentage distribution of Turkish migrant workers' occupations prior to departure, T.E.S. surveys*

	T.E.S. Surveys (%)			
	1967	1968	1969	1971
Unskilled				
Agriculture	30	39	39	44
Construction	5	3	3	3
Production	4	3	2	2
Other	1	1	1	1
Total	40	45	46	50
Skilled[1]				
Carpenter	7	9	8	5
Bricklayer	6	9	8	4
Chauffeur	4	2	2	2
Weaver	3	4	3	4
Retail trade	3	3	3	3
Miner	3	4	4	4
Tailor	2	2	3	2
Office worker	2	1	1	1
Planer/turner	2	1	1	2
Mechanic/repairer	2	1	1	1
Welder	2	1	1	1
Plasterer	2	1	1	1
Electrician	1	1	1	1
Shoemaker	1	1	1	1
Blacksmith	1	1	1	1
Total skilled + semi-skilled	60	55	54	50

1 Main skill categories only are listed

198

Table A23. *Percentage distribution of Turkish migrant workers by earnings prior to departure and on return, S.P.O. survey, 1971 (Yearly net amount)*

		Before departure						On return					
		Total		Urban		Rural		Total		Urban		Rural	
		No.	%	No.	%	No.	%	No.	%	No.	%	No.	%
TL													
3000 or	B	93	26	19	9	74	48	42	12	9	4	33	21
less	S	26		7		19		29		10		19	
3001–	B	84	23	42	20	42	27	51	14	19	9	32	21
5000	S	12		4		8		8		4		3	
5001–	B	59	16	45	22	14	9	43	12	19	9	24	16
7500	S	2		1		1		5		3		2	
7501–	B	42	12	31	15	11	7	49	14	31	15	18	12
10 000	S	–		–		–		2		–		2	
10 001–	B	24	7	22	11	2	1	48	13	35	17	13	8
12 500	S	1		1		–		8		3		5	
12 501–	B	17	5	14	7	3	2	22	6	19	9	3	2
15 000	S	–		–		–		3		3		–	
15 001–	B	7	2	6	3	1	1	18	5	15	7	3	2
17 500	S	–		–		–		–		–		–	
17 501–	B	4	1	4	2	–	–	18	5	16	8	2	1
20 000	S	1		1		–		–		–		–	
20 001 &	B	8	2	8	–	–	–	32	9	26	13	6	4
over	S	–		–		–		5		4		1	
Unclassified		9	3	5	2	4	3	13	4	12	6	1	1
Unemployed		14	4	11	5	3	2	25	7	6	3	19	12
Total		361		207		154		361		207		154	
No. earning side income		42		14		28		60		28		32	
Mean total income (T.L)		6608		8492		4146		11 279		13 678		7896	
Mean base income (T.L)		6226		8165		3692		10 089		12 514		6670	
Mean side income (T.L)		382		327		454		1190		1164		1226	

Notes: In calculation of means, only the replies of the employed were used. TL 1500 was used as mid-interval value for the lowest and TL 22 500 for the highest income groups. See § 3.4.15 and § 3.6.10 for discussion of inflation adjustment.
B = Basic income, i.e. income from main occupation.
S = Side income.

Percentages may not add to 100 because of rounding.

Table A24. *Percentage distribution of Turkish migrant workers by motives for departure to work abroad*

Motive	Neyzi[a]	Tuna[b] Province Centre	Tuna[b] District Centre	Tuna[b] Village	Neuloh[c]	Aker[d] Primary Motive	Aker[d] Secondary Motive	S.P.O.[e][1] Total No.	S.P.O.[e][1] Total %	S.P.O.[e][1] Urban No.	S.P.O.[e][1] Urban %	S.P.O.[e][1] Rural No.	S.P.O.[e][1] Rural %
	%	%	%	%	%	%	%	No.	%	No.	%	No.	%
To earn higher income	+	+	+	+	} 30	} 62	} 9	} 292	} 81	} 151	} 73	} 141	} 92
Financial difficulties	20	+	+	+									
Save up money	1	67	66	100	10	13	22	4	1	4	1	–	7
Debts	+	+	+	+	+	1	2	17	5	6	3	11	2
Lack of work	+	+	+	+	22	11	9	13	4	10	5	3	8
Job dissatisfaction	+	+	+	+	–	+	+	30	8	17	8	13	1
To find new occupation/training	+	14	22	–	7	+	+	13	3	12	6	1	21
Continue education/study	+	8	3	–	–	1	0	71	20	39	19	32	5
Encouraged by others	+	+	+	+	–	+	+	16	4	8	4	8	1
Work found by others	+	+	+	+	+	+	+	7	2	6	3	1	+
Desire to live abroad/travel	+	6	3	–	13	+	+	+	+	+	+	+	+
Learn language	+	+	+	+	6	+	+	+	+	+	+	+	+
Raise children	+	1	3	+	+	+	+	+	+	+	+	+	+
Buy car	15	+	+	+	+	+	+	+	+	+	+	+	+
Buy house	7	+	+	+	+	+	+	+	+	+	+	+	+
Buy equipment for job	5	+	+	+	+	+	+	+	+	+	+	+	+
Guarantee future	19	+	+	+	5	+	+	37	10	30	15	7	5
Other	} 33	} 3	} 5	–	} 7	6	9	–	–	–	–	7	5
Unknown						5	50	–	–	–	–	–	–

+ Category not included in the survey
1 Totals do *not* add up to 100% as some workers specified no motive while others specified more than one.
  Other columns may not add to 100 because of rounding.
a Neyzi 1967C
b Tuna 1967A
c Neuloh 1970D
d Aker 1972D
e S.P.O. 1971A

Table A25a. *Percentage distribution of Turkish migrant workers by duration of stay abroad,*
S.P.O. survey, 1971

	Total %	Urban %	Rural %
6 months	9	11	6
6 – 11 months	14	13	16
1 yr – 1 yr 11 ms	27	24	32
2 yrs – 2 yrs 11 ms	22	17	27
3 yrs – 3 yrs 11 ms	15	14	16
4 yrs – 4 yrs 11 ms	7	11	2
5 yrs – 5 yrs 11 ms	4	5	1
6 yrs – 6 yrs 11 ms	2	2	1
7 years	1	2	0
Mean length of stay	2 yrs 4 ms	2 yrs 7 ms	2 yrs 1 m

Totals may not add to 100 because of rounding.

Table A25b. *Distribution of Turkish migrant workers by skill level and duration of stay abroad,*
S.P.O. survey, 1971

Skill level in last work year abroad	No. of workers	Mean duration of work abroad (years)
Unskilled	163	2.2
Semi-skilled	49	2.6
Skilled	70	2.8
Apprentice	1	2.0
Qualified	3	2.0
Master	58	2.9
Chief master	3	4.0
Technician	2	1.5
Monitor	6	3.3
Official	6	4.5

Table A26. *Percentage distribution of Turkish migrant workers in Germany by sector of employment and year*

		1963	1964	1965	1966 M	1966 F	1966 T	1967 M	1967 F	1967 T	1968 M	1968 F	1968 T	1969 M	1969 F	1969 T	1970 M	1970 F	1970 T	1971 M	1971 F	1971 T
Agriculture, fishing & forestry	%	1	1	1	1	0	1	1	0	1	1	0	1	1	0	1	1	1	1	1	1	1
Mining, energy & public utilities	%	13	15	12	12	0	10	10	0	8	8	0	7	8	0	6	9	0	7	9	0	7
Iron & metal industries	%	43	40	41	41	31	40	39	30	37	42	37	41	44	41	43	45	42	45	43	35	41
Manufacturing (excl. metal inds.)	%	16	15	19	18	52	24	19	49	25	21	47	27	20	45	26	19	43	24	19	45	25
Construction	%	18	22	19	21	0	18	21	0	17	20	2	16	20	2	16	19	0	15	20	0	16
Financial services	%	2	2	2	2	2	2	2	3	3	2	3	2	2	2	2	2	2	2	2	4	3
Performance of services	%	1	1	1	1	6	2	1	8	2	1	5	2	1	5	2	1	6	2	1	8	2
Transport and communications	%	2	3	3	3	0	3	3	1	3	3	0	2	3	1	2	3	0	2	3	1	2
Other services	%	5	3	3	2	8	3	3	10	5	3	7	4	2	5	3	2	5	3	2	7	3

Total Turks employed:

```
1963 – 32 962,      1964 – 85 172,     1965 – 132 777,
1966 – M 133 735,   F 27 215,          T 160 950
1967 – M 105 829,   F 25 480,          T 131 309
1968 – M 118 648,   F 34 257,          T 152 905
1969 – M 190 762,   F 53 573,          T 244 335
1970 – M 276 493,   F 77 405,          T 353 898
1971 – M 355 787,   F 97 358,          T 453 145
```

Source: Federal Republic of Germany, Bundesanstalt für Arbeit, *Ausländische Arbeitnehmer, 1963–1971,* Nürnberg 1964–72.

Totals may not add to 100 because of rounding.

Table A27. *Percentage distribution of Turkish migrant workers by number of jobs held while abroad, S.P.O. survey, 1971*

	Total %	Urban %	Rural %
One	69	71	66
Two	22	20	25
Three	8	8	8
Four or more	1	1	1
Jobs/migrant	1.39	1.38	1.43

Table A28. *Percentage distribution of Turkish migrant workers' occupations abroad, T.E.S. surveys*

	1967	1968	1969	1971
Unskilled				
Agriculture	2	1	1	1
Mining	5	3	2	4
Construction	19	22	21	14
Production	32	25	26	14
Other	1	3	3	14
Total[1]	59	54	52	46
Skilled[2]				
Carpenter	6	6	8	6
Bricklayer	5	6	7	5
Welder	3	3	3	3
Planer	3	2	2	3
Assembly worker	2	2	2	4
Weaver	2	3	3	5
Caster	2	3	3	4
Mechanical repairer	2	1	1	1
Tailor	2	1	2	2
Chauffer	1	1	1	1
Miner	–	2	2	2
Total skilled plus semi-skilled abroad	41	46	48	54
Total skilled plus semi-skilled in Turkey prior to departure	60	55	54	50

1 Discrepancies in totals may occur because of rounding.
2 Only the main skill categories are listed.

Note: The year denotes the time at which the survey was carried out at the point of re-entry into Turkey.

Table A29a. *Percentage distribution of Turkish migrant workers by skill level abroad, S.P.O. survey, 1971*

	1st year			2nd year			3rd year			4th year			5th year		
	Total	Urban	Rural	Total	Urban	Rural	Total	Urban	Rural	Total	Urban	Rural	Total	Urban	Rural
Unskilled	54	44	68	48	36	61	35	24	52	29	21	52	16	14	33
Semi-skilled	13	11	16	13	11	16	14	11	21	15	6	37	14	8	50
Skilled	15	19	8	19	25	12	24	30	14	28	37	7	30	32	17
Apprentice	1	1	1	1	1	1	1	1	1	1	2	0	2	3	0
Qualified	1	2	1	1	1	1	1	1	0	0	0	0	0	0	0
Master	14	19	7	15	20	9	20	24	13	16	22	4	26	30	0
Chief Master	0	1	0	0	1	0	1	2	0	1	2	0	0	0	0
Technician	1	1	0	0	1	0	0	2	0	0	2	0	0	0	0
Monitor	1	2	0	2	3	0	2	4	0	4	6	0	2	3	0
Official	1	2	0	1	3	0	2	4	0	4	6	0	9	11	0
Total no. of workers	361	207	154	279	158	121	167 (180)	104 (108)	63 (72)	95	68	27	43 (49)	37 (43)	6 (6)

Note: Figure in brackets is total from Table A26a if this differs from frequencies in this table.

Totals may not add to 100 because of rounding.

Table A29b. *Workers who were promoted or demoted abroad, S.P.O. survey, 1971*

	Total	Urban	Rural
Promotions			
Unskilled to semi-skilled	13	9	4
Unskilled to skilled	12	7	5
Unskilled to apprentice	1	–	1
Unskilled to master workman	6	3	3
Unskilled to official	2	2	–
Semi-skilled to skilled	9	6	3
Semi-skilled to master workman	2	2	–
Skilled to master workman	3	2	1
Master workman to chief master	1	1	–
Master workman to official	3	3	–
Demotions	6	3	3

Table A30a. *Percentage distribution of Turkish migrant workers by linguistic skills, S.P.O. survey, 1971*

Type of linguistic ability	Total %	Urban %	Rural %
Reading	21	32	6
Writing	20	29	8
Comprehension	60	59	62
At least 1	62	61	63
All 3	16	26	3

Note: Percentages add to over 100 as many workers reported more than one skill.

Table A30b. *Percentage distribution of Turkish migrant workers by the way in which foreign language was learnt, S.P.O. survey, 1971*

	Total %	Urban %	Rural %
School in Turkey	3	5	–
Language course in Turkey	4	6	1
Self-taught abroad[1]	67	54	83
Language course abroad	26	34	17

Note: 1 41 workers who had replied negatively or not answered in Table A31a replied positively here as self-taught abroad.

Table A31. *Results of the Neuloh survey on working conditions of Turkish workers in Germany*

%	Overall work situation	Work discipline	Work time	Work conditions (dirt, noise)
Content	46	49	42	46
Not content	10	14	13	31
Neutral	44	37	45	23

Source: Neuloh 1970D.

Table A32. *Percentage distribution of Turkish migrant workers by membership of a trade union or employees' organization before departure, while abroad and on return, S.P.O. survey, 1971*

	Before Departure			While Abroad			On Return		
	Total	Urban	Rural	Total	Urban	Rural	Total	Urban	Rural
Yes: unspecified which	1	1	0	0	0	0	0	1	0
Trade union	17	25	3	47	44	51	28	48	1
Other employees' organization	16	22	8	18	16	19	21	24	18
At least one	24	27	10	53	50	57	42	60	18
None/no reply	76	73	90	47	50	43	58	40	82

Table A33. *Percentage distribution of Turkish migrant workers by average monthly net earnings abroad, S.P.O. survey, 1971*

TL per month	Total %	Urban %	Rural %
200–300	0	–	1
301–550	0	–	1
551–600	–	–	–
601–700	3	2	3
701–1000	3	2	3
1001–1500	17	13	23
1501–1750	11	9	14
1751–2000	21	22	20
2001* and over	45	53	37
Mean earnings (TL)	2165	2303	1988

* TL 3000 was used as the mid-interval value for calculating the mean for males as this was the average for those cases where the precise amount was stated. TL 2500 was used for females.

Percentage may not add to 100 because of rounding.

Table A34. *Percentage distribution of Turkish migrant workers by average monthly expenditure while abroad (including housing, food and necessary expenses), S.P.O. survey, 1971*

T.L per month	Total %	Urban %	Rural %
150–250	3	2	5
251–350	4	1	9
351–450	8	5	13
451–650	20	14	29
651–850	21	22	19
851–1000	18	20	16
1.001* and over	25	36	10
Mean expenditure (T.L)	932	990	854

* TL 1500 was used as the mid-interval value for calculating the mean for males as this was the average for those cases where the precise amount was stated. TL 1200 was used for females.

Percentages may not add to 100 because of rounding.

Table A35. *Percentages of Turkish migrant workers earning more than T.L 2000, and of those spending more than T.L 1000, while abroad, by year, S.P.O. survey, 1971*

	Earning more than T.L 2000			Spending more than T.L 1000		
	Total%	Urban%	Rural%	Total%	Urban%	Rural%
1960	—	—	—	10	10	—
1961	50	50	—	42	36	75
1962	35	37	20	31	40	0
1963	43	49	16	28	33	10
1964	45	57	30	20	33	7
1965	52	63	37	23	34	7
1966	58	68	45	23	34	10
1967	57	74	40	29	43	11
1968	60	65	54	29	44	13
1969	71	78	62	44	62	22
1970	80	100	67	50	50	50

Table A36a. *Percentage distribution of Turkish migrant savers by place where savings kept while abroad, S.P.O. survey, 1971*

	Total %	Urban %	Rural %
Bank	79	72	87
Yourself	25	32	16

Note: Percentages add to over 100 because some workers replied positively in both cases.

Table A36b. *Percentage distribution of Turkish migrant savers by form in which savings were brought back to Turkey, S.P.O. survey, 1971*

	Total %	Urban %	Rural %
Money	42	35	52
Goods	4	4	4
Money and goods	54	61	44

Table A36c. *Percentage distribution of Turkish migrant savers by method by which savings transferred to Turkey, S.P.O. survey, 1971*

	Total %	Urban %	Rural %
Bank	22	20	25
P.T.T.	45	46	44
By yourself	55	53	57
By secret means	10	8	7

Note: Percentages add to over 100 because some workers used more than one method.

207

Table A37a. *Percentage distribution of Turkish migrants by the reasons given for their return to Turkey, S.P.O. survey, 1971*

		Total %	Urban %	Rural %
(i)	Family reasons	44	51	37
(ii)	Enough savings to set up work at home	18	17	18
(iii)	Find a better job at home	7	6	8
(iv)	Lack of adaptability to work surroundings	11	10	12
(v)	Invest savings to produce income	1	1	1
(vi)	Advance career	2	2	2
(vii)	Unemployed	3	3	3
(viii)	Chance to own house	1	1	3
(ix)	Other	21	21	21
	Military service	1	2	–
	Passport difficulties	3	2	3
	Illness/Unhappy	6	2	12

Percentages add to over 100 as some respondents gave two reasons.

Table A37b. *Reasons for change in place of residence by those workers living in different place since return, S.P.O. survey, 1971*

		Total No.	Urban No.	Rural No.
a	Forced to move with family	16	12	4
b	Children's education	4	4	–
c	Illness of family or self	–	–	–
d	Work situation	34	34	–
e	Dissatisfaction with place of residence prior to departure	4	4	–
f	Other	11	9	2
	No. of replies	55	49	6

Note: 14 workers (all urban) gave more than one reason.

208

Table A38. *Percentage distribution of returned Turkish migrant workers by their desired and actual employment status on return, S.P.O. survey, 1971*

	Desired Status			Actual Status			Before
	Total %	Urban %	Rural %	Total %	Urban %	Rural %	Departure %
Unemployed	x	x	x	7	3	12	4
Employee (unspecified)	13	20	3	1	1	0	–
Wage earner	x	x	x	41	65	8	39
Family worker	x	x	x	0	0	1	0
Partner/Sharecropper	x	x	x	1	1	3	1
Official/White collar	4	6	1	x	x	x	x
Self-employed	x	x	x	47	27	73	56
Employer	50	51	49	2	2	3	1
Other	31	21	44	x	x	x	x
No reply	3	3	3	1	2	0	0

Note: x Means that the category was not included as an option in the survey questionnaire.

Totals may not add to 100 because of rounding.

Table A39a. *Percentage distribution of returned Turkish migrant workers by length of time before finding a job and before starting work on return, S.P.O. survey, 1971*

	Finding a job			Starting work		
	Total %	Urban %	Rural %	Total %	Urban %	Rural %
Less than 1 month	32	24	42	39	43	33
1–3 months	9	10	8	8	12	3
4–6 months	6	5	6	4	6	2
More than 6 months	15	13	18	13	14	11
No reply (including unemployed)	39	48	26	36	26	51

Totals may not add to 100 because of rounding.

Table A39b. *Percentage distribution of Turkish migrant workers by agency through which work was obtained on return, S.P.O. survey, 1971*

	Total %	Urban %	Rural %
T.E.S.	1	2	1
Membership of cooperative	–	–	–
Own effort	41	49	31
Through relatives	14	20	5
No reply	44	29	64

Totals may not add to 100 because of rounding.

Table A40. *Usefulness of foreign language in finding work on return and in carrying out work now, S.P.O. survey, 1971*

	Finding work on return						Carrying out work now					
	Total		Urban		Rural		Total		Urban		Rural	
	No.	%	No.	%	No.	%	No.	%	No.	%	No.	%
Yes	25	7	23	11	2	1	36	10	32	15	4	3
No	227		125		102		212		115		97	
No (Adjusted)	(199)		(104)		(95)		(188)		(95)		(93)	
No reply	109		59		50		113		60		53	

Line 3 = Line 2 minus those who indicated that they had no linguistic ability.

Table A41a. *Percentage distribution of returned Turkish migrant workers by actual and intended membership of joint stock company or cooperative, S.P.O. survey, 1971*

	Planned membership			Actual membership		
	Total %	Urban %	Rural %	Total %	Urban %	Rural %
Joint stock company only	7	9	5	3	4	1
Cooperative only	4	2	5	6	5	8
Not specified which	21	19	24	2	3	1
(At least one)	(32)	(30)	(34)	(11)	(12)	(10)
No reply/None	68	70	66	89	88	90

Table A41b. *Reasons for not joining stock company or cooperative, S.P.O. survey, 1971*

		Total	Urban	Rural
Lack of trust	co.	68	40	28
	coop	62	35	27
Lack of knowledge	co.	64	33	31
	coop	51	26	25
Disinclination 'to be in vanguard	co.	26	13	13
partnership with the state'	coop	24	10	14
Influence of surroundings	co.	14	5	9
	coop	12	4	8
Other	co.	119	67	52
	coop	105	53	52
Total replies	co.	225	124	101
	coop	200	105	95

Table A42a. *Percentage distribution of returned Turkish migrant workers by whether they have a higher income on return, S.P.O. survey, 1971*

	Total %	Urban %	Rural %
Yes	28	32	23
No	69	64	75
No reply	3	4	3

Percentages may not add to 100 because of rounding.

Table A42b. *Percentage distribution of returned Turkish migrant workers by the aspects in which their living standard now is below that enjoyed abroad, S.P.O. survey, 1971*

		Total %	Urban %	Rural %
	None	25	28	21
	At least one	75	72	79
a	Housing	21	15	30
b	Clothing	57	50	66
c	Food	51	41	65
d	Amusement	60	57	64

Percentages for a to d add to over 100 as workers often stated more than one.

Table A43a. *Percentage distribution of returned Turkish migrant workers by whether or not they plan to go abroad again, S.P.O. survey, 1971*

	Total %	Urban %	Rural %
Yes	73	65	82
No	24	32	14
Don't know	3	2	4

Percentages may not add to 100 because of rounding.

Table A43b. *Percentage distribution of returned Turkish migrant workers planning to go abroad again by their reason given, S.P.O. survey, 1971*

		Total %	Urban %	Rural %
1.	Unable to find work	13	4	21
2.	Insufficient income	89	83	95
3.	Dissatisfied with work	20	20	21
4.	Dissatisfied with social life	21	27	15
5.	Offer from employer abroad	1	2	1
6.	Job found by relative abroad	1	2	–
7.	Other	13	16	10

Note: Percentages add to over 100 as some workers gave more than one reason.

211

Table A44. *Changes in land prices in the Ankara area*

Area	Year of original price	Price (T.L.)	Year of subsequent price	Price (T.L.)	Year of subsequent price	Price (T.L.)	Average annual % increase
Çankaya	1963	45 000	1972	975 600			230
	1967	24 000	1972	240 000			180
	1963	10 095	1972	40 000			33
	1967	6 000	1972	61 460			185
	1952	17 000	1959	50 000	1970	250 000	28
							36
Balgat	1962	6 000	1972	45 000			65
Altındağ	1953	2 000	1972	250 000			653
	1951	1 000	1953	1 474	1968	60 000	24
	1960	10 000	1970	100 000			265
	1966	15 000	1972	150 000			90
	1963	7 000	1972	75 000			150
							108

Source: Data supplied by Social Planning Department, State Planning Organization.

212

Appendix 3
The S.P.O. survey of migrant workers who had returned to Turkey, February 1971

In February 1971 the S.P.O.[1] conducted the most informative survey to date of Turkish migrant workers. Firstly, an attempt was made to locate as many returned migrants as possible by requesting their names and addresses from local chambers of commerce, employers and work organizations, district governors, village headmen, state and private enterprises. Approximately 4000 returned migrants were located in this way. The list of these 4000 workers constituted the sampling frame.

Secondly, what was considered to be a representative collection of towns and villages was chosen from those which had reported ex-migrants,[2] and then a 50% random sample was made of the workers located in these areas. Six qualified investigators carried out the interviews. The provinces in which the towns and villages selected are located are listed in Table A45. Six out of the nine geographical regions defined by the T.E.S.[3] were represented: the south-eastern, east-central, and Mediterranean regions were excluded owing to the poor response at the first stage of worker location. The S.P.O. did not think that this was a serious defect in the survey, firstly because the proportion of migrants who had originated from these regions has been relatively small, and secondly because the characteristics of the excluded regions were taken into account when selecting the survey centres in the other regions: thus Artvin was felt to represent both the north and the east.

Nonetheless, since the geographical distribution of the S.P.O. sample differed markedly both from that obtained by taking an annual average of official migrant departures 1963–9 and from that of the early years of migration (see Table A45), the S.P.O. sample cannot be regarded as geographically representative of the migrant population. This qualification is only important insofar as regional differences have a significant impact on migrants' economic characteristics and behaviour. But this sample was based on place of residence *on return*, so that one would not expect regional differences on that definition to have much explanatory power.[4] In any

---

1 State Planning Organisation (Devlet Planlâma Teşkilâtı).

2 For instance, in Tekirdağ province, migrants were selected from the villages of Kaşikçi, Gözsüz, Ahievren, Çukuryurt, and Beyazköy as well as from the town of Tekirdağ itself. In Artvin province, from the villages of Bereket, Ovacik, İncili, Ulaş and Başköy as well as from Artvin itself. (Altogether, there are 280 villages in Tekirdağ province and 292 in Artvin province (T.C. İçişleri Bakanlığı, İller İdaresi Genel Müdürlüğü: *Türkiye mülkî idare bölümleri ve bunlara bağ,* Ankara 1971.))

3 Turkish Employment Service (İş ve İşçi Bulma Kurumu).

4 Only about half of the sample were resident in their place of birth at the time of the survey (though the other half were not necessarily resident in a different region) (Table A12b).

Table A45: *Percentage distribution of returned Turkish migrant workers in the S.P.O. survey by province as compared with that of the total population and that of officially recruited migrant workers*

Province	Province population						Migrants in S.P.O. sample		T.E.S. region (1)	S.P.O.	Regional distribution of migrant workers		
	1965	% Turkish total population	% Population in these 10 towns	1970	% Turkish total population	% Population in these 10 towns	No.	%			T.E.S. 1965	T.E.S. 1969	T.E.S. 1963–9
Ankara	1 644 434	5	18	2 023 031	6	18	45*	10*	I	12*	13	16	17
Denizli	463 366	2	5	511 804	1	5	76	17	II }	28	18	19	15
İzmir	1 234 667	4	13	1 430 368	4	13	54	12	II				
Bursa	756 664	2	8	847 605	2	8	14	3	III }	29	35	16	31
İstanbul	2 295 359	7	25	2 995 191	8	27	93	21	III				
Tekerdağ	287 698	1	3	296 898	1	3	25	6	III				
Artvin	210 065	1	2	225 751	1	2	18	4	V	4	3	3	4
Trabzon	595 782	2	7	662 412	2	6	42*	9*	VII	9*	12	23	14
Kayseri	536 666	2	6	610 287	2	6	47	10	IX }	18	7	10	8
Konya	1 125 257	4	12	1 289 500	4	12	36	8	IX				
									IV	–	1	1	1
									VI	–	6	6	5
									VIII	–	5	5	4

* The precise breakdown between Trabzon and Ankara has been estimated; totals are correct.

(1) The regional divisions used by the Turkish Employment Service are:

I North Central	IV S.E. Anatolia	VII Black Sea
II Aegean	V N.E. Anatolia	VIII East Central
III Thrace & Marmara	VI Mediterranean	IX South Central.

Percentages have been rounded.

case, the differences in economic activities, income levels, employment, urban-rural balance, etc., which together constitute 'regional differences' are examined separately in the survey.

Unfortunately, the sample's geographical bias has been compounded in the results reported here because of the loss of the Ankara and Trabzon questionnaire replies[1] (during an administrative re-organization before this author obtained access to them). Although this loss is to be regretted, it is in fact not very serious because the complete sample could not have been treated as unbiased.

This is because the method of locating migrants favoured certain types of workers: for instance, migrants who returned to work in enterprises sufficiently large to be covered by employees' or employers' work organizations were more likely to be included. For whereas a special attempt was made to locate agricultural workers by surveying villages, no special measures were taken either to test for or to compensate for the probable under-representation of unemployed and small scale industrial and service sector workers in urban areas. Certainly the proportion of unemployed (on return) is lower, and that of wage employees higher than would be expected on the basis of previous surveys.[2] Furthermore, the proportion of women (5.5%) in the sample (Table A46a) is substantially below the annual average of 17.6% for the decade 1961–70 – a situation which is probably to be explained by withdrawal of some women from the labour force on return, or their employment in small or family concerns, which in either case rendered their inclusion in the sample relatively unlikely.

This 'sampling' bias[3] directly affected key features such as the occupational distribution of the migrants and proportion of women among them. Because of this, extreme care has to be taken with the interpretation of the results.

The sample was also slightly biased in favour of countries of destination other than Germany: 78% of the migrants in the sample had originally worked in Germany (Table A47) as compared with 85% of official migrant departures over the period 1960–August 1972. Fortunately this will have had little effect on the results as it is known from the T.E.S. surveys that migrants' experience varies little between the main countries, though it should be noted that German wage rates are usually higher.

A further difficulty concerns whether or not to treat the sample as permanently returned workers. The aim of the S.P.O. was to identify migrant workers who had settled down again in Turkey after employment abroad. Because of the fairly lengthy time lapse between commencing and completing the sampling procedure (during which time the workers must have been in Turkey), those included in the sample can reasonably be treated as having returned semi-permanently at least (workers who

---

1 As well as one from Bursa and one from Istanbul: thus the results reported below are all based on the 361 surviving questionnaire replies.

2 For instance, 23% of the men and 45% of the women in Tuna's Marmara sample were unemployed on return.

3 It would, however, have been quite difficult for the S.P.O. to avoid this. It arose because it was decided (1) to interview ex-migrants in their current place of residence (so that returned workers of some years standing were included, which would have been impossible had interviews been conducted at the frontier) and (2) to construct the sample without prior personal visits to the localities selected. This meant that the population from which the sample was eventually selected was compiled by local work organisations, authorities, etc.

Table A46a: *Percentage distribution of Turkish migrant workers in the S.P.O. survey by rural or urban residence and sex*

Sex	Absolute figures			Percentages of total		
	Urban	Rural	Total	Urban	Rural	Total
Male	189	152	341	52.4	42.1	94.5
Female	18	2	20	4.9	0.6	5.5
Total	207	154	361	57.3	42.7	100.0

Table A46b: *Percentage distribution of Turkish migrant workers in the S.P.O. urban and rural sub-samples by sex*

	Urban	Rural
% Male	91.3	98.7
% Female	8.7	1.3
Total	100.0	100.0

Table A46c: *Percentage distribution of Turkish migrant workers in the S.P.O. male and female sub-samples by rural or urban residence*

	Urban %	Rural %	Total
Male	55.4	44.6	100.0
Female	90.0	10.0	100.0

Note: 'Urban' and 'Rural' refer to places with more than 10 000 and less than 10 000 inhabitants respectively.

Table A47: *Percentage distribution of Turkish migrant workers in the S.P.O. survey by country of initial destination, and by proportion subsequently visiting other countries*

	Total	Urban	Rural
W. Germany	79	84	71
Austria	5	3	8
Holland	4	3	5
Belgium	8	3	14
France	1	1	1
Switzerland	2	3	1
Other European	1	1	0
Other Overseas	1	2	0
Subsequent visit to another country (or countries)			
Yes	7	7	8
No	93	93	92

return temporarily only remain for about one month). On the other hand, 73% (Table A43a) reported that they were thinking of going abroad again. This would suggest that for the majority of migrants, employment abroad is regarded not so much as a temporary interruption to life in Turkey but rather as a new way of life in

Table A48: *Percentage distribution of Turkish migrant workers in the S.P.O. survey by year of initial departure*

	Total %	Male %	Female %	Urban %	Rural %	Rural as percentage of total	
						By Year	5 year moving average
1957 or earlier	0	0	0	1	0	0	
1958	0	0	5	1	0	0	
1959	1	1	0	2	0	0	
1960	1	1	0	2	0	0	
1961	6	6	5	10	1	5	
1962	7	7	10	10	3	19	
1963	13	14	10	15	11	35	
1964	27	28	15	18	39	61	
1965	21	21	15	23	18	37	31
1966	12	12	10	10	15	54	41
1967	3	3	5	2	5	67	51
1968	3	2	10	2	3	50	54
1969	4	4	10	4	4	43	50
1970	1	1	5	2	1	40	51

Percentages may not add to 100 because of rounding.

itself. This issue has been discussed more fully above (§3.6.14). But for the purpose of analyzing the survey results, it would seem more appropriate to treat the sample as semi-permanent migrant workers, who had been sufficiently intent on return as to have left their jobs abroad.

Furthermore, it is important to emphasize just how rapidly the scale of Turkish migration has been changing. 99% of this sample first went to work abroad before 1970 (Table A48). Yet more Turkish migrants have left since then.[1] Indeed, since 77% of the total sample and 80% of the urban sub-group (Chart F) first worked abroad before 1966,[2] allowance must be made for the known differences between the pioneer migrant of the early 1960s and the migrant of today, when using the results of the survey for policy purposes.

In contrast to all the problems attached to interpreting the survey results, the replies themselves seem to have been reasonably accurate, and there is no reason to suspect that workers gave deliberately misleading information. However, the non-response rate to a few of the questions was high.

1 The cumulative total of official departures from 1961–9 inclusive is 351 221 as compared with 439 075 from 1970 up to December 1973.

2 Not surprisingly, the proportion of urban migrants in the sample exceeded that of rural migrants in the early 1960s. An average of 31% of the migrants during the years 1961–5 came from the rural sample as compared with 51% from 1966–70 (Table A48 and Chart F). Also, the sample does not bring out the rising migration of women: female departures are spread fairly evenly through the decade. But the two rural women did not leave until 1969 and 1970 respectively.

217

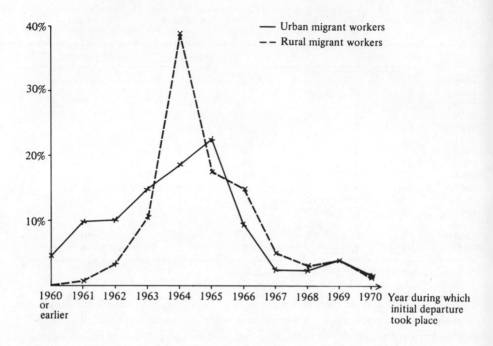

Chart F. *Percentage distribution of the urban and rural sub-samples in the S.P.O. survey by year of initial departure*

All the results were classified into urban male, urban female, rural male and rural female sub-samples.[1] But because of the low proportion of women in the sample, the results have normally been presented for the urban and rural sub-groups only.

---

1 Where 'urban' and 'rural' refer to places with more or less than 10 000 inhabitants.

Author Index

Subject Index

as a result of moratorium on mass labour export 157–158

devletçilik 29
D.I.S.K. 113
distribution of income, impact of labour export on, *see* l.e.
  impact of labour import on, *see* l.i.
  in Turkey, *see* Turkey
dual economy model 12
duration of stay abroad of T.m.w., *see* T.m.w.

earnings of T.m.w. before departure, while abroad and on return, *see* T.m.w.
economies of scale in h.c., impact of labour import on realisation of, *see* l.i.
educational attainment of T.m.w., *see* T.m.w.
Egypt, migrant workers from 150
emigration countries,
  changing composition of 27
  impact of labour export in, *see* l.e.
  investment in by h.c. 9, 11, 23
  labour shortages in 22
employers' attitudes towards Turkish ex-migrants 112, 132
employment, impact of labour export on, *see* l.e.
  in Turkey, *see* Turkey, labour market in, and unemployment in
  employment status of T.m.w. before departure, while abroad and on return, *see* T.m.w.
energy crisis 1, 22, 36, 158
ethnic composition of migrant workers in W. Germany, *see* Germany, W.
Europe. W., economic growth of 1, 17–23
  manufacturing employment in 18–19
European Economic Community, free movement of labour provisions of 7, 69
  Turkish association with 33, 69, 143, 152
exchange rate, impact of labour export on, *see* l.e.
expenditure abroad and on return of T.m.w., *see* T.m.w.
export-led growth in h.c., *see* h.c.
exports from h.c., *see* h.c.

factory life abroad of T.m.w., *see* T.m.w.
family migration, *see* migration
family status of T.m.w., *see* T.m.w.
financial motivation of T.m.w., *see* T.m.w.
finding a job on return, *see* T.m.w.
Finland, immigration from 7, 27
flows of T.m.w. to W. Europe, *see* T.m.w.
fluctuations in supply of T.m.w., *see* T.m.w.
Ford strike at Cologne 10, 99
foreign exchange allowance of T.m.w., *see* T.m.w.
foreign exchange earnings from T.m.w., *see* T.m.w.

France, migrant workers in 1, 6–8, 10, 26, 56–59, 82, 99
  migration regulations in 1, 7, 20
  National Immigration Office in 7
friends abroad of T.m.w., *see* T.m.w.

gastarbeiter, *see* migrant labour
Germany, E., immigration from 5
Germany, W.,
  arrivals of T.m.w. in, see T.m.w.
  ban on non-E.E.C. immigration into, 14, 27, 36, 150
  demand (gross and net) for T.m.w. by, *see* T.m.w.
  departure bonus for workers repatriated from 23, 155
  ethnic composition of migrant workers in 59, 60
  impact of labour import on inflation in 13
  investment costs of labour import in 17, see also h.c., inflation in
  migration regulations in 1, 6, 20, 69–71
  output changes in 63
  production techniques in 10
  recruitment costs of importing labour in 22, 70
  social infrastructural costs of migration in 17, see also h.c.
  use of temporarily recruited labour in 1, 12–23, 36, 150
Greece, migrant workers from 6, 22, 26–27, 28, 59, 60, 64, 65, 70, 72, 77, 83, 98, 122
  use of N. African migrant labour in 22
growth in host countries, impact of labour import on, *see* l.i.
  in W. Europe, *see* Europe, W.
guild system in Turkey 130

Halk Bank loan scheme 115
high level manpower, migration of from Turkey 56, 80
host countries,
  age structure of population in 9
  demographic factors in 9
  export-led growth in 12, 17
  exports from 15
  impact of labour import on, *see* l.i.
  investment in countries of emigration 9, 11, 23
  labour shortages in 8
  policies toward labour shortages in 9–11,
  rationale for importing labour 8, 9–11
  social infrastructural costs of migration in 14–17
  thresholds for immigrant workers in 20
house purchase on return of T.m.w., *see* T.m.w.
housing construction and costs in Turkey, *see* Turkey
housing, immigrants' in h.c. 108
Hungary, immigration from 5

222

illegal migration, *see* migration
Immigration Act, U.K., 1962, 7
immigration from
    the Commonwealth 7, 14
    E. Germany 5
    Finland 7, 27
    Hungary 5
    Indonesia 5
    Ireland 7
importing labour, impact of, *see* l.i.
imports to Turkey, *see* Turkey
imports with waiver of T.m.w., *see* T.m.w.
incomes of T.m.w., *see* T.m.w., earnings of
Indonesia, immigration from 5
industrial development in Turkey 30–33,
    116, 144–145
industrial partnerships of T.m.w., *see* T.m.w.
industrial sector, impact of labour export on,
    see l.e.
inflation, impact of labour export on, *see* l.e.
    impact of labour import on, *see* l.i.
    in Turkey 31–33, 137–138, 146, 147
investment costs of labour import in
    W. Germany, *see* Germany, W.
investment, impact of labour export on, *see*
    l.e.
    impact of labour import on, *see* l.i.
    in Turkey 30–32, 135–136, 147
    in work ventures of T.m.w., *see* T.m.w.
Ireland, immigration from 7, 27
İşbir 115–116
Italy, migrant labour from 2, 7, 26–27, 28,
    59, 60, 64, 65, 69, 77, 98, 121

Japanese large firms 8
joint ventures on return by T.m.w., *see*
    T.m.w.

Kartaş 115

labour export, determinants of the impact of
    47–50, 126–143
labour export, impact of in emigration
    country on
    aggregate demand 42–43
    agriculture sector 40, 51–52
    balance of payments 43–46
    distribution of income 40, 50–52
    employment 40, 41, 42
    exchange rate 41, 45
    industrial sector 41, 51–52
    inflation 40, 42–43
    investment 42–43
    labour force 39
    population 39
    production techniques 41, 42
    savings 42–43
    service sector 41
    supply of skilled labour 42
    transfer of social capital 46–47
labour export, impact of in Turkey on
    aggregate demand 145

agricultural sector 129, 144, 147
balance of payments 140–143, 145,
    155–160
distribution of income 145–149
employment 144–147, 155–158
exchange rate 31, 105, 130, 137, 143,
    157–158
exports 140–143
foreign exchange earnings 44, 101–106,
    131–136, 140, 147–148, 151, 155–
    158
imports 140–143, 158–159
industrial sector 129, 144, 145, 147
inflation 137–138, 146, 147
investment 129, 135–136, 147, 149
labour force 39, 144, 149
political situation 149
population 144, 149
production techniques 129, 145–146
savings 133–136, 145, 148–149
service sector 130, 145, 147
supply of skilled labour 126–133, 145,
    147, 151
trade with host countries 140–143, 147,
    149
transfer of social capital 145
labour exporting countries, *see* emigration
    countries
labour force, impact of labour export on,
    see l.e.
labour hoarding in h.c., impact of labour
    import on, *see* l.i.
labour import, impact in host country on
    capital accumulation 14, 19–21
    cyclical changes 13, 16, 21
    distribution of income 19, 22
    growth in output 12, 17–23
    growth in productivity and employment
    13, 21
    inflation 12–23, 140–143
    labour hoarding 13
    production techniques 16, 20–21
    profitability 12–13, 19–20
    realisation of economics of scale 18
    social infrastructure investment in 15–17,
    21
labour shortages, in emigration countries,
    see e.c.
    in host countries, *see* h.c.
land prices, changes in Ankara area 138
land reform bill in Turkey 31
learning abroad of T.m.w., *see* T.m.w.
legal situation of T.m.w. while abroad, and
    in Germany, *see* T.m.w.
Libya, migrant workers in 150
life abroad and on return of T.m.w., *see*
    T.m.w.
linguistic skills of T.m.w., and use on return,
    see T.m.w.
literacy of T.m.w., *see* T.m.w.
living standard of T.m.w. while abroad and
    on return, *see* T.m.w.

223

macro-economic policy considerations about labour export 152–153
male–female income differential of T.m.w., see T.m.w.
manufacturing employment in W. Europe, see Europe, W.
marital status of T.m.w., see T.m.w.
'maturity' of migrant labour flow 8
medical check on T.m.w., see T.m.w.
migrant labour
  counter-inflationary impact of on h.c., definition of 25
  from Algeria 7, 10, 27, 88
    Arab N. Africa 10, 22, 59
    Black Africa 22
    Finland 7, 27
    Greece 6, 22, 26–27, 28, 59, 60, 64, 65, 70, 72, 77, 83, 98, 122
    Ireland 7, 27
    Italy 2, 7, 22, 26–27, 28, 59, 60, 64, 65, 69, 77, 98, 121
    Morocco 27
    Portugal 2, 6, 7, 26–27, 59, 60, 70, 77, 79
    Spain 2, 6, 7, 22, 26–27, 59, 60, 64, 65, 70, 90, 98
    Tunisia 27
    Turkey 2, 6, 22, 26–27, Chapters 3–5 passim
    Yugoslavia 2, 22, 26–27, 59, 60, 70, 75, 77, 78, 79, 80, 82, 83, 122
  impact on h.c., see labour import, impact on h.c.
  in Austria 1, 26, 56–59, 81, 99
  in Belgium 1, 26, 56–59, 91, 99
  in France 1, 6–8, 10, 26, 56–59, 82, 99
  in Germany, W. 1, 6–7, 25, 26
  in the Netherlands 1, 26, 56–59, 61, 81, 99
  in Sweden 1, 7, 26, 57
  in Switzerland 1, 26, 56–59, 99
  in the U.K. 1, 7, 14
  magnitude of flows of 25–27
  measurement of use of 25
  use of in post-war Europe 1–3, 5–27
migration, family 6–7, 8, 70
  illegal 6–7, 28, 59
  phases of 8
  polyannual 6
  regulations in W. Germany, see Germany, W.
  semi-permanent 5, 65, 215–217
  system of
    permanently recruited 6,
    recruited seasonal 6, 37
    spontaneous permanent 6, 37
    spontaneous seasonal 6, 37
    spontaneous temporary 6
    temporarily recruited 1, 5–8, 37–38, 70–71, 148
    unofficial 6–7, 28, 59

moratorium on non-E.E.C. immigration into Germany and the Netherlands 1, 4, 27, 59, 150
  impact of on the Turkish economy 155–159
nenkō joretsu system 8,
Netherlands, anti-Turkish riots in 20, 109
  bar on non-E.E.C. immigration into 1, 4, 27
  cost of employing a foreign worker in 14
  departure bonus for workers repatriated from 23
  migrant workers in 1, 26, 56–59, 69, 81, 99
  migration regulations in 1, 6, 20
'new slaves', see migrant labour in France.
number of jobs abroad held by T.m.w., see T.m.w.
occupation of T.m.w. before departure, while abroad and on return, see T.m.w.
official departures of T.m.w., see T.m.w.
Paris, May Day parades in 7
permanently recruited migration, see migration, systems of
  phases of migration, see migration
Philippine workers in the U.K. 25
place of residence before departure and on return of T.m.w., see T.m.w.
planning in Turkey 29–33
policy problems in the operation of a labour export system 151–155
polyannual migration, see migration
population in emigration country, impact of labour export on, see l.e.
  Turkish 145–149
Portugal, migrant workers from 2, 6, 7, 26–27, 28, 59, 60, 70, 77, 79
prices, see s h.c., inflation in; Turkey, inflation in
production techniques, impact of labour export on, see l.e.
  impact of labour import on, see l.i.
profitability in h.c., impact of labour import on, see l.i.
promotions of T.m.w. while abroad, see T.m.w.
propensity to consume of T.m.w. abroad and on return, see T.m.w.
purchases on return of T.m.w., see T.m.w.
queue of Turkish applicants for work abroad 67–69, 122
radio broadcasts for T.m.w., see T.m.w.
reasons for departure and return of T.m.w., see T.m.w.
recruited seasonal migration, see migration systems of
recruitment costs of importing labour

224